INTERNATIONAL STUDIES OF THE

COMMITTEE ON INTERNATIONAL RELATIONS

UNIVERSITY OF NOTRE DAME

Understanding

World Politics

Understanding
World Politics

KENNETH W. THOMPSON

UNIVERSITY OF NOTRE DAME PRESS
NOTRE DAME--LONDON

Copyright © 1975 by
University of Notre Dame Press
Notre Dame, Indiana 46556

Library of Congress Cataloging in Publication Data

Thompson, Kenneth W   1921-
  Understanding world politics.

  (International studies of the Committee on Inter-
national Relations, University of Notre Dame)
  Includes bibliographical references and index.
  1. International relations. I. Title. II. Series:
Notre Dame, Ind. University. Committee on International
Relations. International studies.
JX1395.T53   327   74-12569
ISBN 0-268-00564-8

Manufactured in the United States of America

SOURCES

Earlier versions of some sections of this book were published as follows:

PART ONE

Chapter 1

"The Internationalist's Dilemma: Relevance and Rigor," *International Studies Quarterly* 12, no. 2 (June 1968).

Chapter 2

"National Interest and International Order" in Z. K. Matthews, ed., *Responsible Government in a Revolutionary Age* (New York: World Council of Churches—Association Press, 1966), pp. 84-100.

"Individualism, Nationalism, and International Morality" in *A World of Change,* Proceedings of the Dedication Program, Von Kleinsmid Center for International and Public Affairs (Los Angeles: University of Southern California, 1968), pp. 17-27.

"On Replacing Lost Gods," *Vista* 8, no. 4 (February 1973), pp. 12-15.

Chapter 3

"America: Promised Land or Wasteland," *The Review of Politics* 35, no. 3 (July 1973).

"War and the Absolutists," *Worldview* 3, no. 10 (October 1960), pp. 3-6.

PART TWO

Chapter 4

"The Explosion of Knowledge" in *The Challenge of Change,* Symposium Lectures (Decorah, Iowa: Luther College Press, 1964), pp. 15-27.

Chapter 5

"Education for What?" *Worldview* 13, nos. 7-8 (July-August 1970).

Chapter 6

"Education and Change," *Christianity and Crisis* 30, June 22, 1970, pp. 130-131.

Chapter 7

"Theology and International Relations," adapted from *Theology and Church in Times of Change,* edited by Edward LeRoy Long, Jr., & Robert T. Handy. Copyright © MCMLXX The Westminster Press. Used by permission.

Chapter 8

"Rhetoric and Reality," *Christianity and Crisis* 29, no. 23 (January 5, 1970), pp. 338-339.

"Liberalism and Conservatism in American Statecraft," *Orbis* 2, no. 4 (Winter 1959), pp. 457-477.

"Dogmas and International Realities" in Jeffrey Rose and Michael Ignatieff, eds., *Religion and International Affairs* (Toronto: The International Forum Foundation and House of Anasi Press, 1968), pp. 2-12.

PART THREE

Chapter 9

"Beyond National Interest: A Critical Evaluation of Reinhold Niebuhr's Theory of International Politics" in Fitzsimons, McAvoy, and O'Malley, eds., *The Image of Man: A Review of Politics Reader* (Notre Dame: University of Notre Dame Press, 1959), pp. 434-451.

"The Realism of Moral Purpose in Foreign Policy," *Cross Currents* 10, no. 3 (Summer 1960), pp. 201-209.

Chapter 10

"The Origins, Uses and Problems of Theory in International Relations" in Horace V. Harrison, ed., *The Role of Theory in International Relations* © 1964, courtesy D. Van Nostrand Reinhold Company.

"Theory and International Studies in the Cold War" in Abdul A. Said, ed., *Theory of International Relations: The Crisis of Relevance* © 1968. By permission of Prentice-Hall, Inc., Englewood Cliffs, New Jersey.

"The Social-Psychological Approach: Overview or Single View?" in Norman D. Palmer, ed., *A Design for International Relations Research: Scope, Theory, Methods, and Relevance,* Monograph No. 10 in a series sponsored by The American Academy of Political and Social Science, October 1970.

Chapter 11

"Norms and Realities in International Relations" in M. S. Rajan, ed., *Studies in Politics: National and International* (New Delhi: Vikas Publications, 1971), pp. 83-93.

"Moral Doubts About Present Political Diagnoses," *The Review of Politics* 33, no. 2 (April 1971).

To the memory of

REINHOLD NIEBUHR

*He maketh his sun to rise on the evil and the good,
and sendeth rain on the just and the unjust.*

Matt. 5:45

CONTENTS

ACKNOWLEDGMENTS

I wish to thank Professor Stephen Kertesz, Chairman of the Center for International Affairs at the University of Notre Dame, who for more than twenty years has encouraged my work and helped me to believe I might contribute something of value to scholarly fields. Without his encouragement I would not have written some of the papers in this book. Over the years he has combined the qualities of warm friend and stern taskmaster so often that I owe him more than I can ever acknowledge. The same is true of M.A. Fitzsimons, former editor of the *Review of Politics,* who suggested the present framework of the book. No one who has been "edited" by Professor Fitzsimons can doubt his high standards, his devotion to truth, and his unending struggle for clarity in what he and others write. I also benefited immensely from the careful and critical reading of the manuscript by Professors George Brinkley, Peter Moody, Claude Pomerleau, and Michael Francis, all of the University of Notre Dame, each bringing their separate viewpoints and differing professional competences to invaluable critiques and reviews.

The main burden of editorial work, however, has fallen to my extraordinarily able administrative assistant, Helen Danner. Without her help the organizing and writing of the book would neither have been begun nor completed. A strong person in her own right, she has spurred me on at every stage in the process while sparing herself even less than she has me. No one could be more fortunate in a secretary and administrative assistant. Her energy and skills, high intelligence and writing ability assure a bright future in editorial work. Shirley Johns and Catherine Kapoor also assisted with imagination and understanding in various stages of my work, as did Emily Shipley, Catherine Tolles, and Grace Welch in earlier years. I am indebted to all of them, and to my three sons Kenneth, Paul, and James for their forebearance, confidence, and support.

It goes without saying that I alone bear full responsibility for the character and content, main emphasis, and all too apparent weaknesses of the book.

Kenneth W. Thompson

INTRODUCTION

The paradox of the 1970s is that never in history has the average American, from morning to night, been exposed to so rich and varied an international diet. Through the mass media, he is present on the battlefield and at the council table, is taken inside the Pentagon and the State Department, arrives with the President in foreign capitals, and simulates flights to the moon. Two decades ago, a television network chronicled great events under the caption "You Are There." Today the daily fare of world newscasting has made this kind of coverage supplementary and even superfluous. The world is with us early and late, crowding our every conscious moment, and the risk is now one of surfeit and overexposure, not impoverishment of the news.

Yet somehow for the man in the street and even for the trained observer, the bewildering pace of events and the fragmented portrayal of the world make more often for confusion and bafflement than for clarity and comprehension. We grope our way and are, paradoxically, more uncertain than our ancestors, who knew much less but were persuaded that what they knew was a matter of certitude. It is instructive to review the key events of the recent past, asking ourselves how many could have been anticipated by any one of us. Who saw clearly in the 1940s that the United Nations, which for most of us heralded a brave new world, was to become a battleground of contending ideologies and power blocs in the world, of East against West, North against South, and Arabs against Jews? Who in the 1950s would have guessed that successive American Presidents would commit us to a struggle that would lead to half a million Americans fighting a grueling land war on Asian soil at the cost of forty-six thousand American lives? And who in the 1960s predicted that a rather conservative American President, who had once been the arch-symbol of anticommunism, would fly to Peking to meet the leaders of Communist China?

The thesis of this applied philosophical inquiry is that with respect to our sources of understanding and knowledge we are a land of abundance in every respect but one. We have data and statistics beyond any age of mankind. We have better figures on birth rates and death rates and more thorough and wide-ranging information about every facet of human behavior. We have

1

shaken loose from those constraints and taboos that we are told made for ignorance, deprivation, and frustration. What we lack are viable theories and frames of reference to fit together in patterns of meaning the avalanche of isolated, episodic news stories that confound and overwhelm us yet, according to rationalist assumptions, should give us unlimited knowledge and uninterrupted progress.

We are also bereft of the intellectual and moral resources that can guide us through a lifetime of triumph and tragedy. Secular and sacred worldviews have invoked the law of love and fraternity and made it appear a simple, practical possibility for the home, the nation, and the world. Peace, love, and friendship are goals that the high priests of personal and international relations have preached to young and old alike. In the family, this creed had a part, at least, in the 1960s in spawning a generation gap that knows few historical parallels. It helped to create the state of "twentyhood" wherein so many sixteen- to thirty-year-olds felt malaise and alienation toward all those institutions that once were seen as indispensable to self-realization but had not produced peace, love, and friendship. Therefore, the church, family, occupations, and government, for those in "twentyhood," had lost their central purpose, and in such a society youth saw itself as unwanted and unnecessary.

It could be that having rejected the existing structures, the young will create new ones, as the doctrine of Consciousness III suggests. Whether they succeed in this will depend on their ability to live with ambiguity and with the harsh realities of collective life. There is deep irony in the fact that at the very time we were hearing more about loving our neighbor and helping the poor, the disadvantaged, and the nation's youth, violence and hatred reached a crescendo that few anticipated in the 1940s and 1950s. The 1960s were years of hostility, bitterness, and rancor between white and black, young and old, rich and poor, and ethnic groups. Love bred hate, and men practiced violence and killing in the name of virtue with an intensity that has had few precedents in history. In fact, the "holy wars" of the Crusaders, the religious wars between Protestants and Catholics, the Civil War, and the wars of national self-righteousness in the twentieth century are among a handful of analogies that come readily to mind.

Yet if a goal such as love is insufficient as a guide to action or as a standard against which all human conduct can be judged, its opposite is still more destructive. If moralism has misled us, cynicism and nihilism would destroy us. Today, as throughout history, society becomes paralyzed at the moment it writes off those who question or reject present social and cultural structures. With Burke, we need to declare that we are unable to condemn a whole people, whether it be a social class or a particular ethnic or age group. No one is virtuous or wise enough to dismiss out of hand values that diverge from his own. It may assuage our consciences and confirm our virtue—but at the price of learning, however slowly and painfully, to live together, and of destroying the cohesion and cement that holds people together. Moreover, those who foster conflict and hatred for the sake of conflict and of wreaking the destruction of others are no less nihilists whether they labor in the highest or lowliest places.

The lesson that emerges is that we need to rediscover or construct anew a social philosophy that will help us cope with present realities in the home, the village, and the more intimate local communities in which we live. There is too much love and hate inseparably joined in each of us to make love a simple possibility. The recurrence of expressions of force, coercion, and authority is too universal to imagine it can be dismissed through moral or legislative writ. Every virtuous deed is grounded in both conviction and pride, goodness and self-interest, and compassion and ambition. Understanding this in our personal lives, we more readily accept it within the community—including the community of the family.

On the international level, the need for new frames of reference to unravel the complexities and contradictions that surround us is if anything greater. What could be more bewildering than the transformation into allies and friends of those who were yesterday's enemies? How are we to react to the possible abandonment of Nationalist China, a major recipient of postwar American assistance, as the price of recognizing the place of mainland China, whom we have seen as our major enemy in Asia? Why were Japan and India, the cornerstones of our Asian policy for more than twenty years, pushed aside as we opened up relations with China? Why did we fight in Vietnam but not in Hungary? How do we reconcile this with the principle of international law, *pacta sunt servanda* (treaties must be observed)? And where does another classical rule fit in: Nations have no permanent friends, only permanent interests?

Issues like these lie at the heart of the discussion which follows, which is a search for meaning where meaning has escaped us. The first requirement for understanding the world is to seek a framework that makes sense of what otherwise appears as "sound and fury, signifying nothing."

Part One:

The World and the Nation:

Problems and Prospects

SOME FIRST THOUGHTS
ON PROBLEMS AND PERCEPTIONS

And why man is a political animal . . . is clear. For
nature does nothing without purpose, and man alone
of the animals possesses speech.

Aristotle

Walter Lippmann, in his classic work *Public Opinion* (1922), tells the story of an island in 1914, on which lived a small group of Englishmen, Frenchmen, and Germans. Mail reached them only once every sixty days, and news of World War I came six weeks after the outbreak of hostilities. For six weeks they had lived as if they were friends when in fact the Germans had become the sworn and bitter enemies of the French and English. But this was on the European continent. Over the rest of the world, as late as August 1914, men went on producing peacetime goods they would not ship, planning enterprises that would not be carried out, and dreaming dreams that the war's outbreak made unrealizable. They trusted "the pictures in their heads" only to find that their images were far removed from reality.

Lippmann described perception as a triangular relationship between reality or man's action environment, his picture of this reality which Lippmann called a "pseudo-environment," and his response to the picture in his mind. The environment for any man is too big, too complex, and too fleeting for any direct acquaintance. Few men are equipped to deal with so much subtlety and variety. To manage it they reconstruct it on a simpler model, but this invariably expresses particular experiences, biases, and assumptions. To traverse the world, men need maps, and without help each draws the map to fit his stored-up images and preconceptions. Or he calls on the mass media to supply him with the map.

Lippmann concludes that this is a task that neither the press nor the isolated individual citizen can perform. Man, in Lippmann's phrase, can be no Aristotelean god contemplating all existence at a single glance. Instead he can just about span enough of reality to assure his survival and snatch a few moments of insight and happiness. Journalists, for their part, necessarily reflect or magnify trends and forces in the society for which they are paid to speak. The press, therefore, is incapable of clarifying opinion and perceptions. Not they but someone else must be the formulator of concepts and perceptions in advance of decision-making. Lippmann calls on political science to rise to this high calling, leaving to others apology or criticism after a decision has been made.

The discussion which follows, limited and defective though it may be, is in turn a response to Lippmann's challenge, for the need is as great as when he wrote more than five decades ago.

1: THREE PERSPECTIVES
ON UNDERSTANDING THE WORLD

THE NEED TO UNDERSTAND THE WORLD

It is better to understand a little than to misunderstand a lot.

Anatole France

We are entering a new era unlike the quarter-decade through which we have just passed. It is difficult enough to describe and characterize the era that is coming to an end, let alone speak with any confidence and authority about that which lies ahead. The best we can do is to speak of certain dominant trends, some disappearing, that for those of us over forty make up the only international experience we know.

The period since World War II has seen the end of many beliefs and illusions that have dominated thinking and shaped foreign policy, however much they were questioned by a handful of intellectuals and policy-makers. In the first place, the years from 1945 to 1970 witnessed the beginning of the end of the illusion of omnipotence. The United States had been catapulted into a position of world leadership which it neither sought nor fully comprehended. As this little chapter in the long historical process unfolded, it would be difficult to prove that any of our leaders believed that the United States should rule the world. Only a small group of influential publicists and unreconstructed policy-makers spoke openly and consistently of an American century or of our ability to police the world. Empires, however, may be born "in a fit of absentmindedness," and it was the objective world situation which invited the illusion of omnipotence. We were, after all, one of two great powers to emerge after World War II. The United States saw itself not only as a world power but also as the trustee of a political creed that had been a magnet and lodestar for nations everywhere. To see this, one has only to reflect on the number of constitutions slavishly patterned after the American constitution, some before World War II. Yet we and others were to discover that the social and political circumstances that gave birth to our system were

9

lacking in other societies—witness the Weimar Republic and the Latin American states.

Our sense of omnipotence had other roots. Postwar America was an island of plenty in a sea of great poverty. Given the Puritan ethic and the deeply ingrained view that outward success was a reflection of inner virtue, it was natural to conclude that American power stemmed from American virtue. Otherwise, how could one explain why a nation that had eschewed entangling alliances and denied itself the trappings of power could have become the world's greatest empire, capable of influencing nations anywhere in the world?

Another "grand illusion" was the belief that new institutions would transform, overnight, the nature of international politics. Many saw the United Nations as essentially the United States writ large. The preamble of its Charter and Articles 1 and 2 expressed for the world a faith in due process, the consent of the governed, and the rights of man derived from the founding constitutional documents and the Declaration of Independence of the American republic. Secretary of State Cordell Hull, on his return from the Moscow Conference, announced to the world that the United Nations would put an end to power politics and war among nation states. But early in its history the United Nations found, as our friends in Britain had prophesied, that it must play a more limited and modest role in harmonizing the differences among contending nation states. Its power to make laws and bring about peaceful change was far less than that of a national legislature.

Another illusion had roots in a too-simple view of the nature of the conflict. Given the postwar struggle for power between the Soviet Union and the United States, it is not surprising that Americans viewed the conflict as quite simply a struggle between their political ideologies and systems, or communism and freedom. Forgotten was the fact that the United States and the Soviet Union had coexisted for decades, not because communism had changed its spots but because in the years more immediately before World War II, communism was less explicitly and actively linked with historic Russian imperialism. Moreover, by the end of the war its position at home was more secure and its leaders could turn their attention to external problems. Yet following World War II, the dynamics of world communism and the tendency of the Soviet Union to fill power vacuums wherever they existed lent credence to the dogma of anticommunism as a basis of policy formulation, for the USSR occupied the heart of Europe, dominated its East European satellites, held sway over Communist parties in France and Italy, and incorporated substantial territories. More specifically, the Truman Doctrine, set forth as the keystone of American foreign policy, was passed on the proposition that the underlying purpose of American policy was resistance to the spread of communism everywhere in the world. Slowly and almost imperceptibly in the cold war, thinking changed, and influential policy-makers came to recognize that Russian imperialism and expansionism were the threat, not communism alone.

The final illusion was the belief that peoples everywhere, if given a chance, would choose freedom and the structure of parliamentary democracy. This ignored the residual impact of traditional values and the persistent influence of deep-seated cultural factors on the shape of political systems. A neutralist "third world" opposed both East and West, preferring to pattern itself after indigenous models rather than imported ones. Furthermore, the hesitation, ambivalence, and uncertainty of the United States in coming to their aid led the third-world nations to think more about self-help and self-defense and less about insoluble links with one or the other of the great powers.

It is essential, in seeking to understand the world, to recognize that most of these illusions are dead. The Nixon Doctrine made explicit what previous administrations had begun to see. No nation is powerful enough to resist communism everywhere. The main burden has to fall on local governments. Moreover, experience taught that it is possible to do business to mutual advantage with some communist states at some times, especially when they take the initiative. Yugoslavia and Russia are the oldest cases in point, but Rumania and now China may mark a new trend for the future. There has been a loosening up of the bi-polar system and a rise of new centers of influence and power.

Another factor is the far-reaching influence on world affairs of the relaxation of tension in the cold war. The debate continues to rage as to whether or not we are experiencing a genuine thaw in the cold war. Surely the open conflicts are fewer in number; and when they have occurred, they have occurred indirectly in certain developing areas. Many European states are convinced that the immediate prospect of Soviet expansion has passed and that the cold war has come to an end. The great powers themselves speak with a new vocabulary and rigid distinctions of ideology and power are sounded less often, if at all. However, as the late Ambassador Charles Bohlen observes in *Witness to History, 1929-1969,* Soviet leaders acknowledge that cooperation in certain specific areas in no way means the end of the ideological struggle.

Thus in understanding the world the greatest need is to be concrete about international and national problems and the resources that may be open to us to understand them.

THE INTERNATIONALIST'S DILEMMA:
RELEVANCE AND RIGOR

With all thy getting get understanding.

Proverbs

The quest for understanding of the world in which we live requires the working out of a disciplined and orderly approach to world problems. For some, this suggests the need for and possibility of a science of international relations; in the same way that medical and agricultural problems are worked out in laboratories or experiment stations, the goal ought to be a science of international politics. The reasoning seems to be that because it is necessary such a science is therefore possible. One problem that confronts such an approach is the difficulty of establishing laboratory conditions for the study of problems in human relations. Curiously enough Soviet theorists in the 1920s suggested that Russia was a huge laboratory with men at work producing a new society—but if it was such a laboratory it has proved to be one in which non-Communist scientists to this day are not welcome. The other difficulty is that problems which can be studied with rigor may not be those of greatest urgency and relevance.

For most of us, then, the primary criterion in selecting subjects for inquiry is either their relevance to the great central issues of the day or the rigor of methods and techniques that can be employed in their investigation. We often make the point, with a sophistication that at first seems persuasive, that our scholarly enterprise is intended to serve both purposes. Sometimes, as in the case of one particularly articulate political scientist of whom it was said that he did not know what he thought until he heard himself speak, we persuade ourselves this is true. Yet stripped of all verbiage, most of us opt for relevance or for rigor, and we had better learn to live in terms of this dilemma. It is not peculiar to the realm of international studies, but fundamental to the social sciences and to a certain extent to the physical and natural sciences as well. If we fail to perceive the permanent and inescapable quality of the dilemma, we open the door to unremitting warfare between two worthy and respected traditions, since scholars, being human, are all too prone to preempt the sum total of significant study for themselves.

At an annual meeting of the American Political Science Association in the late 1960s, Professor Hans J. Morgenthau, in a significant intervention, noted that there was not a single panel devoted to the problem of Vietnam. He further observed that he doubted whether there had been an issue since the founding of the United Nations on which individuals in greater numbers had taken a position. Apparently, therefore, Vietnam has been a relevant issue for study and reflection, but not for systematic scholarly review by full-time political scientists. Professor John Fairbank, in a similar vein, has lamented that this nation can boast only a handful of scholars for whom Vietnam is a serious specialization. One is tempted to ask whether Vietnam has declaratory but not analytical relevance for present-day internationalists.

It may be, of course, that Vietnam is a special case surrounded by heavy emotional and moral commitments. To raise it may raise other issues not germane to the subject. However, another omission in the discussions of the same annual meeting is at least as significant: the food and population problem. Population control, in the end, is a social and political question, but when it comes to study and action, with a few notable exceptions, those who know the broader socio-political order have been absent from the field. The case for urgency and relevance in this area is compelling, for by the year 2000 the world's population is likely to be more than six billion people. This problem of galloping growth calls for a comprehensive study of social attitudes, governmental policies, and public administration, yet society is apt to seek for solutions primarily from the demographers, biologists, and the activists championing a new technology. It is as if those who represent a broader social science approach had left social welfare, the national budget, or national security problems to social workers, a few government economists, or the Pentagon, respectively. There are limitations of qualification and interest, of course, and students of international relations cannot dabble everywhere. It can also be argued that some of the urgent problems we face must be explored in a national context and therefore are none of the internationalists' business. Yet even if this is true as a general proposition, it hardly applies to food and population, for if ever there was a problem with worldwide focus, it is the food-population equation. Its urgency derives from its heavy impact on the future of the poorer, developing countries and its increasing pressure on developed countries. Its relevance stems from the fact that it lies at the heart of the North-South problem. If the world is the internationalist's oyster, food and population must be part of his fare.

Father Theodore M. Hesburgh, President of the University of Notre Dame, makes a more general case for the internationalists in his challenging statement entitled "The Social Sciences in an Age of Social Revolution."[1] He discusses the late arrival of the social sciences, their relation to the physical sciences, and the need that both establish their relevance. There follows a questioning and an indictment of the social sciences that Father Hesburgh admits is not black and white but which, as "a dilemma of monumental proportions," must "be faced in all frankness." As parvenus among the sciences, the social sciences have sought in a too-unequivocal sense to establish respectability and status as sciences. He speaks particularly of

> many other understandable developments: the amassing of data for the sake of data, the attempt to quantify the unquantifiable, the cult of mathematical verification in an effort to establish theories ultimately beyond mathematics, the worship of objectivity to an extent that often sterilized what might have been very fruitful research, the confusion between counting heads and establishing what are essentially philosophical norms, the blurring of what is average and what is truly significant, the development of so-called scientific terminology and occult nomenclature that allowed an esoteric statement of obvious fact to masquerade as

scientific wisdom when it was in fact not only not worth stating, but was stated in murky and turgid rhetoric. Regarding this latter point, may I say that the inability to communicate signals the end of usefulness for any element in a culture, be it religion, art, or science.

In Father Hesburgh's view, the social sciences

need desperately to find their own identities, to elaborate their proper fields of inquiry and their proper methods, and, I will add, all the social sciences need desperately to develop fruitful relationships with other human knowledges and other methods of knowing, without ceasing to be their own valid, honest, useful, and respectable selves.

Father Hesburgh concludes his powerful challenge:

To say then that the social scientist is not interested in values is, to me at least, nonsense. Without values there is no science, no discernment, no judgment, no relevance, and certainly no meaningful relationship between social science and the age of social revolution in which we live . . . the dispassion of most social scientists for many years in the face of the Civil Rights problem did them no honor. . . . The hypothesis of the social scientist should be relevant to the real, critical, and urgent human problems of our day.

In reflecting on Father Hesburgh's assessment, it is increasingly apparent, on the one hand, that civil rights became and remains the internationalist's problem. As an American, one heard little else in the 1950s and 1960s when he visited abroad. On the other hand, the phenomenon occurs in numerous analogous forms of group rivalries, tribalism, caste systems, minority questions, human rights, and fundamental freedoms. In broader terms, therefore, it will not do to leave this area to international civil servants or petitioners before the United Nations, for this too is a world problem of relevance and urgency.

It should be noted that the 1968 program of the American Political Science Association, for the first time in years, set aside time for a section of panels on American foreign policy. Dean Don Price of the Littauer School at Harvard, commenting on this decision, noted that it seemed to reflect a return to old-fashioned political science. Whether excluding American foreign policy represents the new or the old political science, this choice has coincided with the rise of a host of problems that cry for responsible analysis: the power of the executive in foreign relations; congressional-executive relations; foreign aid; the processes of diplomacy and peace; the shape of United States' interests, capacities, and alternatives; foreign policy formulation; conflict anticipation; and conflict resolution.

If this were all, the issue of relevance would be crucial enough, but there are also questions of youth and generational differences on foreign relations, civil disobedience and national security, doctrines of war and peace, the anatomy of worldwide reactions to United States' leadership, the relationship between private and public activities in foreign assistance, foreign policy and the fourth estate, the world energy problem, the influence of nonnuclear powers in the negotiating of a nuclear proliferation treaty, the linkage of disarmament and security issues, and dozens of other questions with the gravest consequences for the future of mankind. The question we need to ask one another is whether these issues commend themselves to the internationalist and, if not, why are they excluded from his purview. I suspect one reason may be the preference of many for ordering research and study according to criteria other than those of relevance and urgent need.

The objection might justly be made that up to this point emphasis has been placed on one horn of the dilemma. I have not yet discussed the importance of rigor. As the evaluation of international studies makes abundantly clear, the demand for an organizing focus and for a dependable methodology are central to the field. Rigorous empiricism and rigorous theory-building are vital to international studies. The application of rigorous methods is traceable in half a dozen areas in the history of international studies.

The search for empirical reality is basic to the development of any intellectual or scholarly discipline. This is as true for the social sciences as it is for the physical sciences. Science was born when men began to analyze, count, and quantify phenomena instead of merely speculating about them. For example, at some point someone with a generous measure of intellectual curiosity decided to count the number of teeth in a horse's mouth, instead of accepting the assumptions set by custom and tradition that this fact was either unimportant or "irrelevant" or was already known. From the earliest stages, empiricism had an important role as the companion of formal knowledge. Analysis and comparison, classification and definition followed it, forming the foundations of a more exact science. Science gained its strength and validity when rigorous methods and empirical systems were established.

A vigorous empiricism dominated the early years of the social sciences as well. As sociology emerged after World War I in the United States as an independent discipline, its leading scholars were men who responded to an underlying surge of interest in the careful gathering and classification of data. They believed that theories advanced in the past had been grounded in neither observable facts nor concrete statistics. They attempted, therefore, to study the real facts, sending their students into deprived areas, factories, cities, and suburbs with checklists and questionnaires. Their sociological laboratory became the world around them.

Empiricism also played an important role in the development of political science, particularly at the University of Chicago under Professor Charles Merriam during the 1920s. It sought to discover how government functioned at every level (federal, state, and local), and a complex of efforts were linked together involving university scholars and those at the Public Administration Clearing House across the Midway.

Equally, at the beginning stages of the development of international studies, a rigorous empiricism was stressed. Historians held the center of the stage, and the principles of the historical sciences were reflected in their work. The general field of history recognized and respected diplomatic history as an established branch of historical studies, with its own time-honored methodology, complemented by the history of international law, going back to Samuel Pufendorf who held the first chair of the Law of Nature and Nations at Heidelberg in 1661.

Another approach, somewhat less rigorous but nonetheless continuous in the documentation of the facts of international relations, has been the use of the steady flow of reporting and commentary by newspapers and periodicals. This method sought to draw on the resources of the best newspapers and to introduce current materials into the classroom as the basis of a more lively and informed approach to the subject.

Alongside those who emphasized history and current events, there was yet another group of scholars who felt a need for research and instruction in public policy. Students were encouraged to think within a framework of policy alternatives, to view the world as it appeared through the eyes of the President or the Secretary of State. Textbooks and readings gave students a sound historical and strategic context for their study of such problems.

The problem inherent in the study of decision-making, however, is that to the outside observer of government the question "What are the real facts?" must remain unanswerable, no matter how thoroughgoing his empiricism.

Somewhat later during the period between the two world wars, the trend toward theoretical approaches to the study of international relations also began to develop, and demonstrated that international studies could benefit from the organizing concepts of other sciences. The impulse for theory-building was strengthened by an increasing realization in many circles that international relations did not have an adequate set of organizing principles.

This brief sketch of empirical and theoretical trends and the subsequent discussion in Chapter 10 point up, if this were necessary, the importance of rigor in international studies. The lessons that derive from the history of the social sciences underscore what is beginning to be visible in international studies. The takeoff point for any scholarly discipline is the formulation of central concepts through which the great masses of otherwise unrelated data can be organized and analyzed. Analysis in turn awaits rigorous methods of inquiry applicable to the defined subject matter. The many-sided and constantly changing character of international problems throws doubt on whether we can evolve a single set of methods deriving from fundamental disciplines but applied to particular international problems. This is not the place to discuss whether international studies is a discipline, a collection of disciplines, an interdisciplinary endeavor, or a common-sense synthesis of related and unrelated bodies of knowledge—but clearly this bears on the problem. What can be affirmed is that rigor has as much a claim to respect and is as appropriate in determining the direction of international studies as relevance. On this, surely, there can be consensus among scholars and observers of divergent views.

The real issue that divides us concerns what we are to say and do when the two principles are in conflict. A former colleague, the late Norman S. Buchanan, was wont to say that there are many urgent problems in the world on which knowledge is urgently needed but for only a few does the state of social science give us the required tools of analysis. He urged that social scientists concentrate on problems with some prospect of analytical payoff. An opposing view is that advanced quite recently by an antiestablishment group of sociologists attracted, we are told, by less researchable but more urgent problems such as peace, war, and interracial tensions. The *New York Times* reports of this group: "By and large they have great respect for a man like Professor Parsons, but think that his theoretical contributions in classifying and analysis have a built-in conservative cast that is out of tune with the times." I suspect a division somewhat comparable to this can be found in the other major disciplines and will continue into the future. The urgencies of national and international life are such that part of our scholarly competence must be addressed to them.

Perhaps a more troublesome and important split for international studies is that between practitioners or men of affairs, and scholars and theorists. It is a division that to the casual observer seems less evident between, say, economic theorists and economic policy-makers, where theory has become operationally relevant and where movement back and forth appears commonplace. However, it seems less likely that diplomats and foreign policy decision-makers would spring to the defense of the scholarly activities of internationalists. Henry Wriston, an advisor to successive administrations, wrote in a personal letter to the author: "I am concerned that the political scientists have isolated—and alienated—themselves to a large degree, and I think intentionally. They do not write as Plato, Aristotle, Thomas Jefferson, Ben Franklin, or James Madison, but have retreated into an artificial language, using esoteric terms and supplying pseudomathematical and scientific methods and jargon. I was a member of the Association for thirty-five years or so, but I resigned because the Journal seemed to me unreadable."

I have no solution to the sharp divisions reflected in this comment nor are there any obvious and easy ways of healing the breach. The intellectual interests of first-class minds range themselves on both sides of the great divide; in the realm of international studies there are many mansions. Fortunately for us all, not every analyst or observer must choose to follow his neighbor's preference. There will always be serious minds who by instinct, style, temperament, or conviction give first priority to the study of urgent problems—guided by criteria of relevance. In the same way, others will prefer to test to the limit the usefulness of rigorous methodologies. Each trades off one priority for the other. Associations, journals, and academic departments should strive to give free and full play to the best efforts of both orientations. It may even be that with luck they can succeed in encouraging genuine dialogue. The future of international studies will be best served if some, at least, maintain a certain reserve and humility claiming for their approach what the evidence warrants but containing where possible their skepticism and scorn for other worthy efforts. Cromwell's advice would seem germane: "Believe by the bowels of Christ you may be wrong." Editors of journals and promoters of international inquiries might take this as their watchword. The internationalist's dilemma between relevance and rigor can be, occasionally, mitigated, if not resolved, within a single extraordinary mind, but more often through exponents of parallel but differing intellectual trends that together contribute to the sum total of wisdom and knowledge.

THE NECESSITY AND IMPOSSIBILITY
OF PREDICTING THE FUTURE

No man can tell what the future may bring forth.
                                                    Demosthenes

No task in political science or diplomatic analysis is more baffling and uncertain than that of political prediction. Prediction is essential for leaders, but history is strewn with the record of failures to read the future. To say that we are at a watershed in the unfolding of contemporary international relations is to postulate the existence of deep-running social and political forces so powerful that they will carry international society into a new era. That important forces affecting international politics exist is beyond dispute; that these aspects of the present world are capable of transforming the relations among men and nations is far less susceptible of proof. The "impossibility" of forecasting the future is not a deterrent to looking ahead, but social scientists in particular should be humble about their claims and the self-righteousness with which they proclaim new methodologies for penetrating tomorrow's unknown.

It is sobering to look back to the dominant views concerning international society which were prevalent two decades ago. First, many saw in the establishment of the United Nations the possibility of removing power politics and rivalries among states from the international scene. It was widely hoped and believed that the new organization, dedicated to the maintenance of security and peace, would usher in a reign of international law and order. The main debate centered on whether the powers of this institution, which many considered an advance over the League of Nations, should not have been hammered out in the mold of a genuine world government. Forgotten or overlooked was the persistent character of national ambition, the recurrent quest for national security, and the deep ideological gulf between the two major powers. The struggle for peace and order still took place in a nation-centered world. Moreover, nations, like individuals, tended for the most part to put their own interests or conceptions of their interests first, thus moving along a fateful collision course with others proceeding on the same tack.

Since 1945 there have been, if anything, a larger number of well-publicized conflicts involving ambitious and insecure nations than there had been in an earlier era. Far from being a shrine for memorializing international peace, the United Nations has become the cockpit of worldwide conflict and strife. Those who saw in the United Nations the means of transforming the world have, with each passing year, grown more skeptical if not cynical about its role. Had the political predictions concerning the United Nations emphasized its capacity to provide new avenues for limiting and controlling inevitable conflict, some of this pessimism might have been avoided.

Another prediction, which has been largely realized but with consequences few could foresee, has been the emergence of a large number of small new states, some with few if any attributes of national sovereignty and power. One of the most recent members of the United Nations, Grenada, has a total population of 94,800 and a national budget of $17.8 million (1972 estimate), .00735 that of New York City. Observers have coined the word "mini-state" to describe the characteristics of these latest members. The United Nations, which numbered 51 states at its birth, now has increased to 138, with no end in sight. The preoccupation of these new states is often local and not worldwide, and their contributions to international society are difficult to evaluate at this point. The hope that they would be free of the parochial and selfish patterns their European forebears had displayed has scarcely been borne out in practice. Ideally, they can play the role Lloyd George assigned when, in a speech in September 1914, he declared: "God has chosen little nations as the vessels by which He carried His choicest wines to the lips of humanity to rejoice their hearts, to exact their vision, to strength-en their faith." But new states have not ushered in a new world. Instead, they have helped to complicate and extend the problems of the old world, making more intricate and demanding both the problems and the opportunities which international society confronts.

Third, it was widely believed that the United States, which for decades had slumbered in isolation, would prove capable of evolving new concepts, if not a totally new doctrine of foreign policy, to guide it in the choices it must make. Was it not evident that in World War II and in its championing of the United Nations the United States had committed itself unequivocally to a course of building an international order? We no longer stood aloof from the struggle; we undertook to provide strong world leadership. Our inheritance had been passed down from British, French, and other centers of European experience and power.

While accepting the challenge, we eschewed the working principles that had guided those going before us. The view tended to persist in high quarters, and still does, that both in policy and in exposition of policy, American leaders should not settle for following a morally prudent and politically pragmatic and empirical course. Instead, our policy-makers told us that the new world required devotion to the principles of the Charter of the United Nations, which were simple and straightforward. The irony of these propositions is that those who espoused them have been the architects of policies which set the United States at odds with the majority of the organization whose Charter had been quoted with such fervor.

The major challenge we face in the coming decades is, I believe, the development of a philosophy to help us differentiate among types of international and domestic conflicts and establish rational American responses to each. That conflicts will exist, particularly given the sweeping surge of self-determination and development around the globe, seems indisputable. That we need intervene or that the United Nations need intervene whenever or wherever the peace is threatened seems a more doubtful question. Former Secretary of Defense Robert S. McNamara, in his much-quoted Montreal speech in May of 1966, pointed out that over the previous eight years there had been 164 outbreaks of violence within nations around the world. Most of these were civil conflicts; 82 different governments were directly involved. In only 15 of the 164 instances of violence were there military conflicts involving two or more states. According to Istvan Kende, there were ninety-seven international wars from 1945 to 1969.[2] Yet in not a single one of these conflicts was there a formal declaration of war. Indeed, since World War II there has not been a single instance of a formal declaration of war anywhere in the world.

It seems clear that, far from having become a safer world in which to live, this planet, over which the threat of nuclear warfare continually hovers, is a world of growing rather than diminishing conflict. In the 1950s an average of fewer than twenty-five prolonged insurgencies were taking place throughout the world, while in the 1960s the average increased to more than forty. Outbreaks of warfare and violence, as distinct from insurgencies, also increased from about thirty in the 1950s to almost sixty by the mid-sixties.

Kende establishes criteria including the activities of regular armed forces both military and police on one or both sides, the degree of organization on both sides, and a strategical-tactical and organizational coherence between individual actions.

The form and character of violence and insurgency in the world pose a double challenge for the United States. We must develop some consistent and rational view of what role the United States and the United Nations can and should play in the face of these essentially domestic conflicts. It must be evident that not every conflict has the same configurations. Conflict anywhere is not necessarily a threat to world peace. Peaceful processes, if they are to be effective, must often be local and long-term. The United Nations Charter itself pays tribute to this principle by stating that members should seek to resolve disputes and differences before bringing an issue to the United Nations. The history of the years since World War II highlights the tendency of nations everywhere to throw their burdens on an already overburdened United Nations or to call upon the United States to assist them even while many of those sending up the call express ambivalence about American involvement.

We have been the recipients of an outpouring of serious thought and worthwhile discussion about the role of the United Nations in maintaining international peace and security. Most, if not all, of this writing has assumed that the task of any international organization would be to preserve the peace in the face of conflicts between two or more nations. However, most of the serious conflicts which either have engaged the United Nations or have generated discussion of its future role originated, at least, as conflicts within the same state. Korea, Berlin, Zaïre (the Congo), Cyprus, and Vietnam illustrate the emerging pattern.

The United Nations, whose architects imagined that most international disputes would involve the clash of sovereign states, as had been the case in the eighteenth, nineteenth, and early twentieth centuries, has instead been faced with internal conflicts. The involvement of other states has taken the form of participation by sponsors of the status quo or of revolutionary change who, like their forerunners engaged in supporting participants in the Spanish Civil War, have tried to shift the balance of power to one side or the other. The United Nations has faced the problem of being prevented, by Article II, Paragraph 7, from intervention in domestic affairs. While it has, at times, found ways to transcend this limitation, no one has drawn clear and definite lines distinguishing permissible from impermissible intervention.

However, if the problem confronting the United Nations in the elaboration of a doctrine is severe, that of the United States is even more sobering and perplexing. For almost a decade, we spent immense sums (over $30 billion per year at the end) in attempts to maintain stability within one small

Southeast Asian state. Other changes in far more vital and important areas of the world, such as the land mass of China, did not engage American resources. We accepted the maintenance of communist systems within East European states, and stood aside, except for two abortive and half-hearted interventions, while far-reaching social and political changes took place in Cuba, a few miles from our shores. The best we were able to do was to utter platitudes concerning the Monroe Doctrine, the Inter-American System, and the self-determination of peoples. We seem to be captives of onrushing events which force a course of action that at best can be rationalized and at worst is at odds with efforts to formulate a workable doctrine of foreign policy. What we do is often sensible and successful after the event, but the grounds on which our choices are made are seldom spelled out or clarified. It is apparently morally questionable for the policy-maker to pose the question: What are American objectives in country X or Y?

The great need, then, is for a working theory of foreign policy that would formulate and at least seek to clarify the central questions in advance: When should our national blood and treasure be committed and when should it be withheld? When should we turn to other national, regional, or worldwide bodies and when must we, in the national interest, carry the burdens ourselves? Is the ancient and historic tradition surrounding the ideas of national security and the national interest still relevant as a guideline to action, or does its only value arise in rationalizing or justifying action taken in accord with other purposes? How are we to define our national objectives if, having framed them in passive and narrow terms throughout the first three decades of the twentieth century, we now define them as the preservation of peace and order everywhere in the world? What are the strategic and political differences between the insurgencies which affect our national security and those that do not? What distinguishes the fifteen cases of outright international military conflict in one hundred sixty-four instances of national violence, and how are the seven instances in which American power and military capacity were engaged to be differentiated from the rest? Where can we find elements of a strategic doctrine which would help us to determine, before the fact, what policies we should follow in the face of violence and conflict close to our shores or at far-flung outposts? Perhaps the number of variables is too numerous, if not unlimited, for formulating a viable theory, but the task is so urgent that its difficulty cannot justify failure to try.

The other aspect of the problem concerns the relationship between the poor nations and conflict. At one extreme, it would be a grievous error to equate lack of economic development or burgeoning population growth with the inevitability of war. Proponents of this view could overnight become the new non-Marxian economic determinists of the 1970s. It would also discredit man's nobler instincts to maintain that something must be done for the poor so they won't become violent. Nevertheless, most of the conflicts which have arisen in the postwar era appear to have involved the poorer nations. Robert McNamara pointed out that in 1966 there were twenty-seven nations which had had per capita incomes of $750 or more a year since 1958, and that only one of these twenty-seven nations had suffered a major internal upheaval within its boundaries. However, among the thirty-eight very poor nations with per capita incomes of less than $100 a year, thirty-two had been victims of significant conflicts. Indeed, nations in this group had had on the average two major outbreaks of violence per country in the eight-year period. Between 1958 and 1966, eighty-seven percent of the very poor nations, sixty-nine percent of the poor nations, and forty-eight percent of the middle-income nations had been plagued by internal strife and violence. Mr. McNamara concluded that "there can . . . be no question but that there is an irrefutable relationship between violence and economic backwardness. And the trend of such violence is up, not down." It would be possible to draw similar conclusions eight years later.

Some effort is being made to reduce the number of economically backward nations, and yet every responsible study has indicated that the economic gap between rich and poor is widening rather than growing smaller. In the 1970s over half of the world's population lives in what are commonly known as LDC's (less-developed countries). These people command less than one-sixth of the world's total goods and services. By 1975, dependent children under fifteen years of age in the underdeveloped countries will equal the entire population of the developed nations of the world. By the end of this century, at present rates of growth, the most that the eighty underdeveloped nations which are members of the World Bank can hope for is a per capita income of $170 per year. In this same period, the United States' per capita income will have risen to considerably more than $6,000, its present level. Is it any wonder that mounting concern is being expressed about the consequences of the division of the world into rich and poor nations?

The second great challenge facing the United States therefore is to develop working concepts on how to assist in conquering or at least ameliorating the world-wide poverty and economic deprivation which is growing and deepening rather than diminishing. That the United States has only begun to face the problem is evident in the annual congressional contest and spectacle over foreign aid. (The most penetrating if highly critical review of foreign aid is Hans J. Morgenthau's celebrated article in the *American Political Science Review*.)[3] There is little if any foreign aid constituency among the wider American public, and no clear-cut or accepted view on how the United States should proceed. Programs which have gone forward with some success, in the public or the private sectors, are little known beyond the circles of those who have participated. It is fashionable in many influential circles to speak with contempt of most efforts in foreign aid. Perhaps extravagant talk about the first "development decade," which has drawn to its melancholy close, has helped to spawn such cynicism. But so has an almost total lack of awareness of the profound implications for the future of growing alienation and conflict between rich and poor.

Yet it should not be beyond the wit of men to think through, on some more organized and systematic basis, what can and cannot be done to assist developing nations. There are accomplishments and experiences in the field of agriculture overseas which bear on the problem.[4] Some efforts in population stabilization have been more successful than others. Efforts at education for development such as the Universidad del Valle in Cali, Colombia deserve note. It will not do to dismiss these simply as accidents of geography or history; we need to know more about successes and failures that have taken place in technical assistance experiments. The Marshall Plan, AID's efforts in India and Pakistan, and certain United Nations programs point up hopeful avenues for the future. Also, the other "donor" nations, including Great Britain and France, have had their conspicuous successes. Some of the smaller, privately financed programs may have especially useful lessons here. A beginning has been made in this area (e.g. the whole area of education, particularly experiences with university development programs abroad, is the subject of a major review sponsored by twelve donor agencies in the public and private sectors)[5] but much more remains to be done. Fresh thinking and new approaches must be called up by drawing on the past, without being limited by it.

The problem of working out clearer concepts and working principles for programs of national and international security and economic development around the world is the challenge of the future. With all the perplexities and uncertainties of forecasting the future, the possibilities of success are greatest when planning and thinking are directed to more or less well-defined needs and urgent problems.

NOTES

1. Address given at the dedication banquet of the Institute for Social Research, the University of Michigan, Ann Arbor, Michigan, March 30, 1966.

2. Istvan Kende, "Twenty-five Years of Local Wars," *Journal of Peace Research* 1 (Oslo, 1971), 5-22.

3. Hans J. Morgenthau, "A Political Theory of Foreign Aid," *American Political Science Review* 56 (June 1962), 301-309.

4. I would commend on this problem the book *Strategy Toward the Conquest of Hunger* by J. George Harrar (New York: The Rockefeller Foundation, 1963). My *Foreign Assistance: A View from the Private Sector* (Notre Dame: University of Notre Dame Press, 1972) might also be mentioned.

5. Higher Education for Development, a program of the International Council for Educational Development.

2: CHANGING PATTERNS
OF THE POSTWAR WORLD

It is sufficiently clear that all things are changed, and
nothing really perishes, and that the sum of matter
remains absolutely the same.

Francis Bacon

A first step in building a more coherent structure of thought is to grasp the context of contemporary international politics and in particular the changing patterns of the postwar world. America's role in all this has been crucial and we have lived through a series of dramatic changes in world order culminating in the struggles we refer to as the *cold war.*

MIDPASSAGE IN THE COLD WAR:
NATIONAL INTEREST AND INTERNATIONAL ORDER

American thinking on foreign policy has undergone at least four major and far-reaching changes since World War I. For most Americans, that war was a struggle to safeguard Western civilization and "to make the world safe for democracy." At the war's end, President Woodrow Wilson captured the imagination of a broad segment of mankind by his proclamation of a new international order. However, discovering the conditions of a lasting peace proved more difficult than defining the principles of a just war. In consequence, the Wilsonian "grand design" was rejected at home and abroad. This reaction stemmed in part from a rather general lethargy and yearning for normalcy, and in part from the gap that separated Wilson's idealism from the fact of a stubbornly recalcitrant world. Indeed, the collapse of the European system after Versailles was probably more fundamental than the reaction against Wilson. Nevertheless, a small but powerful body of American senators spearheaded the defeat of United States membership in the League of Nations and the triumph of American isolationism.

But responsible Americans were unwilling to turn their backs on the rest of the world. Intellectuals and policy-makers launched a campaign to revive the spirit of American internationalism and to draw a blueprint for a more durable world order. The churches and universities constituted a rallying ground for discussions that were to lead to proposals for a new international organization. For such groups, the shadows of World War II were at the same time the death knell of the League of Nations and a clarion call to support a new enterprise in international cooperation. It is no exaggeration to say that the birth of the United Nations was made possible by the labor and love of these new champions of international responsibility.

Their efforts and the life of the United Nations itself evoked a third response: a realistic critique rooted in a reaction against the utopianism that surrounded the ideological justification of that organization. A worthy institution that provided the framework for international cooperation had come to be viewed as an end in itself. Those who announced that it spelled the elimination of rivalry among states soon discovered that it was actually a new arena in which great and small powers vied for influence and power, and that all the novel techniques of "parliamentary diplomacy" could not supplant peace-keeping through strength and the balancing of power. Nor had "open diplomacy" removed the need for what Dag Hammarskjöld described as "quiet diplomacy."

More broadly, the demands of a world in change called for a marriage of realism and idealism, for peace with justice. The newly emerging states were pressing their claims for a place in the sun. It was not sufficient for the United States to keep the peace with friends and allies. Because of the moral principles for which it stood—self-determination, individual rights, social advancement, and economic progress—it had to be responsive to the winds of change. It took as its guide, therefore, both the constraints of national self-interest and the compulsions of being a friendly neighbor to those who were struggling for independence and self-government.

All those who have matured in the United States in the past twenty-five years have been influenced by the interplay of these several trends of thought. It would be folly to claim immunity from the tensions and conflicts between them. There are inevitably contradictions between putting national self-interest first and showing a decent, if not compassionate, regard for the interests of others. The "great debate" between the Morgenthau-Kennan school of thought and the "idealistic" approach illustrates this problem. Thinking about the international realm is, of necessity, uncertain and ambiguous. Problems of judgment intrude, and the facts are never fully at hand. Citizens of a nation that enjoys, if only for one fleeting moment in history, supremacy in world power, see the world differently than do those who speak for the smaller powers. They often overlook the legitimate claims of others and the changing needs of rising peoples; they become a target for dissatisfaction, resentment, suspicion, and fear. The most they can hope for is respect, since appreciation and affection are seldom a part of international relationships. They must strive unceasingly to be just, in the consciousness that their justice will never be complete. While helping others, they must satisfy their own people that they are being well served. While coming to the aid of friends in the new states, they cannot neglect their ties with friends in older states. In explaining their purposes, they must speak to varied audiences at home and abroad. And, as they debate on the course to follow, in free and democratic elections, they must know that their words may seem harsh, selfish, and vainglorious, and may offend those whom their chosen government would serve.

Between War and Peace

Throughout history, nationalism, industrialism and, more recently, modernization have shaped international relations. The nation-state has remained the primary unit of political organization, even though some of its functions may be obsolete. In fact, in the newly emergent and reawakening states of Latin America, Asia, Africa, and the Middle East, new forms of nationalism, embodying rudiments of the old, comprise a dynamic new factor that will, for better or worse, affect every plan of international cooperation.

Industrialism is another force that helped to transform the face of western Europe in the eighteenth and nineteenth centuries. It has spread its influence irresistibly through Russia, Latin America, and Asia. Its effects are evident today both in capitalist and communist states: it has led to greater concentrations of population, to specialization and division of labor, and to the need for community programs on behalf of less privileged groups. Marxism predicated that industrial, capitalist socities carry the seeds of their own destruction, that the rich would become richer and the poor poorer, and that eventually the more numerous poor would arise and throw off their chains.

Marx's prediction has been largely refuted—at least within the more developed societies, which despite abuses and social injustices, continue to find ways of regenerating themselves. They have succeeded in removing substantial areas of injustice through social legislation and reform. Now, Lenin's version of Marx—that rich nations would become richer and poor nations poorer, until the poor would be driven to revolt—is on trial on a worldwide scale. Can international society succeed in repudiating the Marxist prediction as national societies have done before them? In the absence of a worldwide sovereign legislature, the United Nations and multilateral agencies give the sanction of representative international bodies to this great task. The social costs of industrialization are being met on the national scene; men of goodwill are now striving to meet them at the international level. There is reason to believe that the complexities of the world situation cannot be explained through the assumption of obsolete Marxist theories any more than those theories fit the context of national societies at an earlier stage.

Modernization is a worldwide social phenomenon that knows no national or ideological boundaries. In developed and developing countries alike, it sets the framework for change and influences the patterns of national life. It accounts for many of the circumstances that influence competition and cooperation, and, because it encompasses the most basic factors of change, it contributes to shaping international and domestic conflicts.

Competition and cooperation are present in every human situation. Man is a social animal and discovers his true nature in cooperation with others. The necessity of living together in a shrinking world prompts men and nations to link their aims and policies; it leads to the building of new institutions. Yet rivalries are no less inevitable in every social grouping. Preachments and injunctions urging men to seek common purposes are fragile and often futile, unless joined with firm programs and controlling incentives. Cooperation must pay. The benefits and necessities of cooperation must be as visible as those of competition.

In the second half of the twentieth century, change has added a new dimension to competition and a new urgency to cooperation. Communism and democracy are the political creeds, not of the citizens of two countries, but of men and women around the globe. In the past, rival nations fought for territory and prestige; today's struggle is for "the minds of men." Communism parades as a revolutionary faith whose loyal adherents are pledged to the overthrow of the status quo. Democracy holds to beliefs that are both old and new. It is the product of more than two thousand years of experience and reflection on the political consequences of the nature of man. Yet its belief in the inalienable right of men and nations to govern themselves is ever new and revolutionary. In this focus on the living as against the written creed, democracy comes into view as a fundamentally political philosophy of change. An open society in which channels of public opinion and contests for authority are untrammeled is attuned to the forces of change. Contending men and principles compete in the free marketplace of politics and ideas. Communism, which controls men and subordinates individual rights to the single goal of social and economic justice, devolves into structures of power organized and managed by the few in the name of the masses.

The contest between two ways of life and two contending political orders is not trivial and imaginary: it goes to the heart of man's striving to build a better life. The outcome will decide whether generations to come will live in freedom or under tyranny. Freedom and order are gained and preserved, not once and for all, but through eternal vigilance within each nation-state—it has been said that "freedom is the one thing you cannot have unless you give it to others." When national determination flags, the cause of freedom is in jeopardy.

On a worldwide front, the early resolution of the contest between democracy and communism is foreclosed by the concentration of power in two great world systems. Despite strident statements in our country about victories in the cold war, successive administrations have learned to live with the facts of power. Moreover, changes take place even within monolithic structures. The Russia of Stalin gave way to the greater liberalism of Khrushchev and to the conciliatory if tough-minded pragmatism of Brezhnev. Russia and China, despite their common aim of winning the world for communism, found themselves drifting apart and finally in open conflict. The lesson that this teaches is not that communism will "change its spots," but rather that no political system escapes the pressures for change and the demands of necessity. Particularly in revolutionary regimes, with the passage of time and as generation succeeds generation, the ardor of buoyant and crusading political movements tends to be supplanted by the more pragmatic spirit of those who must cope with ongoing events. They find there is too much unfinished business in the daily lives of their people to warrant continuous crusades abroad. This has happened in present-day Russia, and evidences of such a movement are beginning to be visible as well in China. Requirements of national security usually prevail over ideological slogans.

The most compelling incentive to international cooperation lies in the terrible predicament raised by a thermonuclear age. Modern instruments of warfare have turned the prospects of an enemy's destruction into the possibility of self-destruction. Limited engagements and local wars are not excluded where restraint is practiced, but over them all hangs the deadly peril of the thermonuclear holocaust. Communist and open societies share the same perils. The limited test ban is proof, if any is needed, that neither side is immune to the demands of necessity. This revolution in modern weaponry may be the most far-reaching change of all, with untold consequences for the pursuit of international cooperation. It may drive men to policies and behavior that they have not otherwise been able to achieve over the centuries.

The present conflict between the Soviet Union and the United States can be seen most meaningfully in terms of the factors that lie at the roots of foreign policy. The struggle between the superpowers, now nearly two decades old, is clearly a conflict with at least two dimensions. At one level, it is a struggle for men's minds; at the other, it engages two great configurations of power that, by necessity and design, reach out to influence others. Soviet-American rivalry at root is primarily a problem in foreign relations, and as such it partakes of the age-old patterns of international politics. It will be determined by factors of national power that inevitably influence competition among states.

In the struggle, both the United States and the Soviet Union are blessed with favorable geographic situations. The United States is bordered on the north and south by friendly and less powerful states, and safeguarded on the east and west by two great ocean moats. The sheer geographic area of the Soviet Union, about one-seventh of the earth's surface, has historically swallowed up any would-be invader, although its western boundaries are exposed to the European plains. The natural resources of both powers are immense, and their technology far advanced. In conventional military weapons, Russian strength probably exceeds American, but in the production of new weapons—first of an offensive type but, more recently, of a defensive kind—the Russians, despite their progress with satellites, have for most of the cold war lagged behind. Russia's population is greater than America's, although its per capita technical skill is probably less. American political institutions should, in the long run, prove superior, but the Russians may temporarily enjoy the advantages that flow from a system in which instantaneous decision-making and kaleidoscopic initiative are possible. National morale, particularly in the hydrogen age, is difficult to measure before a crisis. The quality and potentialities of diplomacy on both sides are subject to the broad tendencies and special problems that have been described.

Americans live by the faith that other peoples will come to embrace a political creed that involves a decent respect for the dignity of man, and that an international order may be founded on respect for the rights and interests of other sovereign states. However, there are several difficulties that confound American policy-makers and often confuse our friends abroad.

The first is the difficulty of marshaling domestic support for American policies while at the same time putting America's best foot forward in the eyes of the rest of the world. To mobilize public opinion, Americans say things to themselves that, from the standpoint of other people, might better be left unsaid. (In this, the United States is, of course, not unique.) America is a vast, sprawling continent whose people display great diversity in political and religious beliefs; in its constitutional system, power and responsibility are broadly diffused, although less so in the conduct of foreign than of domestic affairs. As Americans seek to persuade one another of the right course to follow, they speak with many voices, some of them raucous and strident. The language of domestic politics is not that of political theory. It aims to unite people behind certain policies. It looks for a common denominator that can more often be found in broad principles and moral generalities than in directives for strategy that, like military policies, must be cast in practical alternatives to meet varying circumstances. It prefers militant slogans to qualified truths and a crusade to public conversation on a problem.

Above all, it is a permanent feature of the landscape of international relations that American foreign policy must draw its support from a union of experts, the public, and friends and allies abroad. History demonstrates that no American statesman can ignore any point of the triangle without courting disaster. Before World War II, public opinion lagged behind the thinking on foreign affairs of experts and allies. After the war, and up to 1950, American policy—especially for Europe—was acceptable alike to the experts, the public, and members of the postwar grand alliance. This day has passed, and the three groups have tended to diverge more and more. America's allies have increasingly come to view their national interests as not necessarily identical with those of the United States, and ironically, in the late 1950s and 1960s when American policies were being criticized by experts at home and abroad, many of them enjoyed broad endorsement at all levels of American life.

Another difficulty stems from the colonial dilemma, which since World War II has touched conflicting interests throughout the world. For the late 1940s and 1950s, the colonial problem stood at the top of every agenda for discussion of American foreign policy. Nationalism was on the march in Asia, the Middle East, and Africa; and Americans implored one another to identify their country with these movements. Responsible officials were encouraged to issue proclamations throwing America's weight behind popular revolutions. Unhappily, the colonial problem is less tractable than such exhortations would suggest. For, at the same time the fight is being waged to end the old imperialism, a new expansionism is threatening. Some feel that, in order both to contain it and to maintain a minimal system of order and a stable balance of power, America must cleave to its trusted allies with whom it has interests and military bases in common. Yet, in itself, this is unlikely to be enough. The present equilibrium of power and the sense of justice will be upset unless America supports the new nations in the so-called underdeveloped areas. The United States has over the past two decades faced a triple challenge: to stem the tide of Russian imperialism and world communism; to unite the other Western states; and to draw closer to non-Western peoples only recently emerged as independent states. It is the unenviable task of American states-men to keep all three of these balls in the air. And not all allies nor all newly independent states are equally worthy of support—but how are we to decide?

A final difficulty has its roots in the moral problem. The question of right and wrong is continuously raised in international and individual relations. Nations, like individuals, claim that they either seek to do, or have done, what is right. The values embodied in American culture ensure that, far from being an exception, America persistently aspires to bring about justice and international order. We are pained when we are told that some aspect of our national conduct cannot be justified in international terms, yet we take comfort that, throughout history, one of the most baffling philosophical problems has been whether an action can be called good if it serves merely the immediate group or primary loyalty, or whether to be virtuous it must serve a more inclusive purpose. Political morality, as distinct from pure law or justice, looks for the point of concurrence between the particular and the general value, rather than calling for the sacrifice of the part to the whole. Politics can count on a residual egotism or self-interest that represents the creative potential of individuals and groups. The nascent international community must guard against the more extreme forms of parochial loyalty that reserve the right to take steps "necessary to national security" even at the expense of accepted international morality. Moreover, it must be able to harness, beguile, and deflect the more limited national purposes, even though it cannot easily transcend them. For it remains true that the individual or the group may feel called upon to sacrifice an immediate value for the sake of the more ultimate or general interest, yet no community can demand this sacrifice as its right. It is one of the consequences of the still-existing ideological conflicts that the moral purpose and general interests of mankind cannot be uniformly defined. Even if some common goals are accepted, the differences persist in the realm of means.

The American credo of political morality, especially in recent years, has been more pretentious than this. It has often called upon others to sacrifice a limited advantage to some higher cause. Justice and international order are properly considered the broad framework of political morality, but their weight and particular content in any decision can never be determined in advance. The values of community and order are frequently in tension with the principles of justice, which are liberty and equality. If a national community cannot ensure a tolerable measure of justice, even though it maintains order, in the long run its authority will tend to erode. Similarly, if the international order lacks the power and prestige to safeguard all its members, they will be tempted to seek justice in other ways. There is an indefiniteness in political morality because

> various and frequently contradictory values are involved in political decisions, and the preference which is given one value and end over another must be determined by historical contingencies rather than fixed principles. There are fixed principles and norms in the political realm, but there is no fixed principle for relating the norms to each other. It is possible to define as "bad" only those situations in which one or more norms are completely wanting. . . .[1]

Policy-makers sometimes look for short cuts to the moral problem. They spend a great deal more time talking about the need for greater morality in political life than in determining what this would actually imply. They seize on popular expressions congenial to their tastes and interests, like "majority rule." The workings of political machinery are invested with all the trappings of a religious exercise, and political pronouncements are equated with the glorification of God. The problem of public morality calls for Christian humility rather than for moralistic self-righteousness, which can win few friends and serves only to lower the currency of moral principles.

For more than a century and a half, national security has been primarily the concern of soldiers and statesmen. Since World War II, however, public opinion in the United States has engaged in a succession of great debates on military strategy. Collective security, support of the North Atlantic Treaty Organization, and nuclear weapons policy appear constantly on the agenda of public discussions. And, significantly, no recent discussion of defense policy has omitted reference to moral issues. An example is Article 2 of the NATO Statute. It is as if people in the United States reformulated Clemenceau's classic dictum to read, "National security is too important to be left to generals," and added "and it must be approached in the context of morality."

If the recurring tensions between Soviet Russia and the West were clearly either a clash of military systems or a struggle between political ideologies, we would doubtless face the future with greater confidence and hope. However, most of us must admit that we vacillate between a military and an ideological view of the situation. Our difficulty in arriving at acceptable policies arises primarily from our uncertainty over the nature of the tension. In the early days of the cold war the majority of informed observers were convinced that the Russian threat to Western civilization was identical with the Nazi menace, and that the recipe for dealing with it was the same. It was said that over two centuries of experience had proved that a foreign policy unsupported by military strength is likely to be impotent. Nevertheless, after the World War II, as after World War I, the United States dismantled its military establishment as proof of its peaceful intentions. As Germany had done after World War I, the Soviet Union seized the opportunity to impose its will upon nations that fell within its zones of control. They succumbed not because they were lacking in morality, but because they had no means of excluding foreign intervention.

The West has carried this lesson into the atomic and thermonuclear age. There are evidences that the Soviet Union more than once marched up to the brink, threatening to engulf Greece and Turkey, Iran and Berlin, only to withdraw when it met resistance. Conversely, where resistance proved ambiguous, uncertain, or divided, as in the United Arab Republic, Syria, and the Far East, the Soviet sphere of influence flowed across boundaries that had long marked the limits of Russian power.

Those who look at the international situation from this point of view see the immediate military threat as unquestionably the gravest danger, and call urgently for the multiplication of more powerful weapons of destruction, for new strategies, and for missile bases and a nuclear weapons pool. They believe that the irreconcilable conflicts and tensions of the cold war will end only when one side or the other forges decisively ahead.

A second group urges states to display equal vision and energy in seeking

political and economic solutions and in launching expanded military programs. It pointed as early as the 1950s to technical assistance programs of the
Soviet Union, which pledged $1.5 billion to underdeveloped areas. It noted
that the tactics of Soviet imperialism have shifted from the use or display of
military power to subversion, infiltration, and indirect aggression.

The value of "ultimate" weapons in developing areas, with their great
numbers of agrarian peoples spread over vast regions, seems doubtful at best.
Crises have passed in Indochina, Korea, and the Middle East without their
being used. Because the newer nations, with the possible exception of India,
neither possess nor see the relevance of these terrible weapons, they have led
the movement to outlaw them.

However, the contradictory reactions of these states to thermonuclear
devices are revealed by the grievous blow to the United States' prestige in the
same countries when the Soviet Union launched the first satellite in 1957.
Despite criticism throughout Asia and Africa of the United States' materialism and preoccupation with technological and military advance, confidence in
United States policy was gauged by the very standards that were deplored.
Equally, when the United States, through the United Nations, held the line in
Korea, those who had been its sharpest critics (including some Indians who
had judged the United States to be rigidly anticommunist and obsessed with
the military threat), applauded the successful deployment of American power
and its rapid movement through Korea, particularly until the fateful crossing
of the thirty-eighth parallel. And the shift in India's thinking from a rather
superior and patronizing criticism of the original nuclear powers to a defense
of its own nuclear explosion illustrates a similar pattern.

The relative validity of a military and an ideological characterization of the
crises cannot be measured by a barometer registering the rise and fall of
Stalinism in the Soviet Union. If Stalinism is synonymous with the brutal and
heedless sacrifice of every other goal to those of the communist society, then
it is as alive today as ever. The Russian military threat undeniably survived
the death of Stalin; we have only to look at the sputniks and the hundreds of
divisions guarding Soviet frontiers, to recall the threats and displays of force
when crises arose in the Suez, Hungary, Czechoslovakia, and Poland, and
during the Turkish-Syrian disputes, to recognize that moves and counter-
moves on the political and economic fronts are equally real. The contest
shifts almost imperceptibly from one type of warfare to another and sometimes is joined simultaneously on all sides. It is worth noting that the Soviet
Union during the last five years of détente in Europe has relentlessly increased its military preparations by several orders of magnitude.

Three errors are commonly made in appraising the military component of
foreign policy. First, military power is often confused with national power,
and a nation's capacity to impose its will is equated with its military

establishment. But military power is like a fist, the force of which depends on the health and vitality of the body politic and the whole society. Second, the military element is often viewed in too-static terms. In two world wars, the democracies were the last to arm, but they gained the final victory. However, it is often forgotten that the United States had two years to arm in both World Wars. Third, it is difficult to analyze the most effective distribution of the components of military force. For example, what comprises a strong military force today? Is it large ground forces, hydrogen bombs, or intensive research? Is a small, highly specialized army more desirable than a large number of ground forces, or are both essential? We know that an effective foreign policy must be supported by a military program that can safeguard national security, but decisions must be made about distributing limited resources among alternative means of defense without any certainty of the kind of war in which they may be used.

Beyond this, the weapons of today may not be used in future wars because technology will have rendered them obsolete. It is said that conventional weapons are fast being supplanted by new and more deadly ones, and that therefore traditional armaments fail to provide a sound basis for foreign policy. On the other hand, some military experts question whether atomic and hydrogen weapons will ever be used, because of the prospect of mutual annihilation. Does the stockpiling of weapons that no one dares use furnish a state with the requisite military strength? These are the horns of the dilemma on which defense strategy could be impaled. The recent agreement of East and West to reduce stockpiles was based on the application of the principle of mutual dissatisfaction with this situation.

From Coexistence to Cooperation

Despite the fact that nations continue to live between peace and war, profound world forces are at work bringing about a relaxation of tension. These include the rising pressures in communist and democratic countries alike for a more abundant life, the nuclear stalemate and fear of mutual annihilation, the disappearance of first-generation bolshevik revolutionaries, and the coincidence in the leadership in Moscow and Washington of moderates and pragmatists. The breakup of great-power authority, symbolized by the Sino-Soviet split and by Gaullism in the 1960s, had the effect of contributing to the détente. Yet coexistence remains at best provisional and unstable. What has changed is not the substance, but the forms and modalities of competition. Neither side can afford to contemplate the escalation of conflict except as a last resort. Meanwhile the ideological struggle continues.

One result is that the scene of great-power rivalry has shifted to competi-

tion for influence in the developing countries. It is in Africa, Asia, and Latin
America that the merits of the various political and economic systems are on
trial. Neither system is likely to afford a completely satisfactory blueprint.
Emerging societies will fashion their own forms of government. Yet, as they
evolve, they will, like every political order before them, draw on the legacy of
the past. Having tapped the wellsprings of social and political experience,
thereby learning from the past, Americans in turn must play the role of
partner, not patron, in helping others freely to shape their future. The United
States could not escape this challenge even if it wished to do so. In an era of
peaceful competition with a rival political system, it must pursue its purpose
with dignity, restraint, and justice.

Indeed, the hope for greater cooperation and more lasting friendship
relates to the great purposes that Americans and other free peoples espouse.
At least at the level of broad principles of justice and freedom there is a
profound and lasting identity between the ends of the American people and
mankind everywhere. If this were not so, the American Constitution and Bill
of Rights would not be mirrored so faithfully in the Preamble and first two
Articles of the Charter of the United Nations. Both documents affirm the
principles of the right of men to choose their own form of government and to
be ruled through the consent of the governed, individual human rights as
against oppressive rule, freedom of speech and conscience, freedom from
arbitrary arrest, and social and economic justice. No national or international
leader can long deny or thwart the realization of these fundamental freedoms
without stirring the conscience of the international community, for they lie
at the roots of all civilized life, including relations between nations. Achieving
full realization of human rights and fundamental freedoms is of course an
endless and largely unattainable task in which judgments are continuously
made whether concrete goals, American or universal, serve the needs of other
peoples.

The attainment of an international order made up of nations that respect
justice and "the Rule of Law" is, of course, a long-run objective. Some states
must, in any foreseeable future, place order ahead of justice or give internal
security priority over, say, the creation of a multiparty political system. Their
ultimate goals and purposes and their underlying and persisting intentions can
make all the difference. If freedom for a people to select their own government is merely postponed, not abrogated, a society can be seen as moving
toward membership in a true international order. Their respect for law will
evolve internally and be reflected in international conduct. They may serve to
remind us all what a long and painful process the development of representative government has been in this country, and in England. (We tend to forget
that England fought a civil war over precisely this question.)

Some will say that national goals are more often than not unique, and that not only in the realm of concrete aims but in broad purposes nations on opposite sides of deep ideological cleavages have little in common. Even where this identity of ultimate purposes is lacking, however, the benefit of contacts across national borders remains. The peoples of communist and noncommunist states have much to gain from one another. Cultural exchanges provide fruitful channels for clarifying goals and intentions and ensure that the benefits of science and learning for a more peaceful world will be shared. People who come to respect fellow professionals in other lands are likely to help turn the tide toward more favorable attitudes based on mutual respect. Where great powers confront each other, mutual respect, while falling short of affection and goodwill, represents an important advance.

A world order, when it comes about, will result from a recognition of the infinity of common interests and ties that bind men together. Today, the threads that bind us together are a blending of fear and respect. For one thing, the threat of mutual annihilation hangs over us all. The spotlight is relentlessly focused on the risks of nuclear war. Beneath the surface, less visible and publically acclaimed common interests are being forged. Scientists around the world are dedicating themselves to the search for new and better solutions to the major problems of welfare that face all mankind. Nations are drawn together by an infinity of threads that unite them as members of a single international order: health, commerce, population, communication, transportation, science, and the war against hunger. The realization of this order will come when the forces that divide are outweighed by those that unite.

INDIVIDUALISM, NATIONALISM, AND INTERNATIONAL MORALITY

> *Those who would treat politics and morality apart*
> *will never understand the one or the other.*
> John Morley

As the last quarter of the twentieth century approaches, the United States finds itself caught up in far-reaching worldwide change. Our position is in certain respects an unenviable one. We stand at the point of intersection of a mass of forces at work in the world, none of which can be wholly ignored. Issues concerning the rights of man, national self-determination, freedom, neutralism, and communism come to a focus in Washington. Even when they are on the periphery of the American sphere of interest, they have a way of moving toward the center. This is because every nation or aspiring center of influence espousing these forces tries either to invoke American power or influence or to prevent them from coming into play.

In looking at the present world scene, the observer has the task of selecting, from myriad problems and forces, those which are the most urgent and fundamental. His choice must reflect a set of priorities and a judgment on what is both basic and operational. What is basic for one form of analysis or one point in time may be irrelevant to another. In selecting individualism, nationalism, and morality, I mean only to call attention to three important trends of thought and practice chosen from many that provide a set of organizing themes underlying the conflicts and crises of our age.

Individualism

Individualism is an ancient creed that calls for renewal and restatement in every era. Its foundation is respect for the sanctity of the human spirit. It proceeds on the assumption that self-realization depends on the right of each individual to work out his or her own destiny. In negative terms, this means that no one is willing indefinitely to be pushed around or to be made the pawn of others. Self-fulfillment is impossible where individuality is ground down by the wheel of fate. The subordination of one human will to another, if carried to its final conclusion, leads ultimately either to rebellion or to the extinction of individual personality. This fact, and not vague romantic notions about freedom, justifies a regime that safeguards individual rights.

An individualism that ignores the inescapable presence of conflict and coercion is of course illusory. Individual rights are not guaranteed by past defenses nor protected by apathy or isolation. While solitude may assure that no one infringes on my rights, it also guarantees that those rights in any full, untrammeled sense will not be exercised. Man is a social animal, and for most of us, life in society remains a precondition for becoming an individual. For us individually this process of self-realization demands that we grow and respond through human experience and emotion. We must cooperate and compete, contend and concede, judge and be judged, accommodate and struggle. It is not enough to call for one mode of conduct or the other; for individual responsibility requires that we be at home in all these realms. We must test and be tested and find or lose ourselves in experience. No copybook is open to guide our steps; the quest for individuality assures both our glory and our misery.

The notion of our affirming our nature within the calms and storms of history runs afoul of certain persistent ideas that have attached themselves to individualism, and that have tended more to confuse than to clarify the place of individualism in history. The first is that *the individual is good* and *the collectivity evil.* The second is that *each individual pursuing selfish interests will serve,* as though guided by a hidden hand, *the common good.* The third is that *history is on the side of individualism* and that political and economic systems grounded on it will ultimately prevail.

The first idea has suffered the fate of other simplistic moral views. It ignores the inevitable intermingling of good and evil in every human situation. History affords too many examples of good collective action and evil individualism to make the proposition convincing. For instance, organized programs of social justice in the twentieth century in leading Western states are hardly to be equated with the cynical ruthlessness, in the late nineteenth century, of individual "robber barons." There may well be a greater chance of collective justice than that made possible by an uncompromising individualism.

The second idea, of the individual automatically serving the common good, is no more persuasive, and the idea of laissez-faire with which it was linked has long since passed into disfavor. When a leading member of President Dwight D. Eisenhower's administration tried to resurrect it by claiming that "what is good for General Motors is good for the nation," the philosophy was questioned on all sides. Few if any present-day Americans believe that men engaged in the hard work of seeking their own fortunes automatically serve the rest of mankind. This is not to say that men pursuing their own selfish interests may not, if successful, help others to attain a more abundant life. It is rather that a too-simple mystical view that sees individual ambition and the general welfare as inseparably bound together will not stand the test of history, even though more rigorously argued theories of economic behavior have been sustained for long periods.

The third notion, which is that individualism is on the march and destined to triumph over every other social and political philosophy, flies in the face of much of the evidence. Some social systems that retain a healthy regard for the individual survive and flourish. Others have prospered while trampling the individual in the dust. At some point in the eighteenth and nineteenth centuries, individualism acquired an overlay of utopianism and optimism and, very like what happened to the prevailing peace philosophies of that day, was overrun by the forces of history. For one thing, different nations espoused conflicting versions of individualism. For another, totalitarianism no less than democracy proclaimed that its programs were designed to serve the individual. Sometimes the claim was that policies would make a better individual—the "master race" in Hitler's Germany is an example. Communist states have persecuted and destroyed individuals and groups so that the remaining mass could enjoy more social and economic justice, and continue to do so. In short, powerful social and political creeds have sought to harness individualism, bending the notion of individual needs to fit ideological purposes.

Even basic individualism in its simplest form seems curiously inappropriate to the current scene. At least this is true when present-day problems are viewed superficially. Decisions that affect individuals are made by great collectivities—the state, huge corporations, powerful labor unions. Education as well, long the citadel of creative individualism, is subject either to the facilitating action and standard-making of state and federal organs or to the policies of ever larger local bodies. In New York City, for example, a single board of education for many years formulated the policy for eight hundred and sixty schools, fifty thousand teachers, and a million students. Decisions on social welfare are those of the overall system. Productivity in the economy is increased through a vast network of interdependent units and a host of interchangeable parts.

In such a setting it will no longer do simply to juxtapose good individualism and bad collectivism. In our kind of world, collective instrumentalities are needed to serve the individual if he is to have a chance to realize his individuality. If he is to receive fresh water, good food, a living wage, and equal opportunities for education and employment, larger aggregates of responsible and representative men and women, joined together, must act in his behalf.

The paradox of our times is the fact that collectivism has been called on to support individualism. Human welfare is everywhere being safeguarded and preserved by group action. Big business is balanced by big labor; big government is called upon to protect the individual against mass actions that might otherwise override certain basic individual rights. The process is endless, and the workings of countervailing power take their main justification from pledges that this or that program will better serve the essential needs of man.

The process is, of course, fraught with the gravest dangers. The greatest risk is that the individual will be lost sight of. Apparent gains will be nugatory if Washington, Sacramento, or Albany launch programs which individuals count as losses, not gains. A self-perpetuating and self-confirming momentum builds up in collectivism that feeds on itself, losing sight of the ends which programs were organized to serve. It is here that individualism must be rediscovered, must form the true basis of collective action, and must constitute the grounds for policy review. Representative government—with its popular mandate, its capacity for renewal, and its intricate system of checks and balances—remains the best guarantee of humane collectivism yet evolved. Individualism and collectivism in mass societies must be rejoined. Failing that, each has within it the seeds that will eventually destroy the other.

Nationalism

The dilemmas of individualism are related to the rise of a second worldwide force, nationalism. The hopes and aspirations of individuals are difficult to realize in a collective age. Men seek security, recognition, and power; yet for many, the conditions of modern life conspire against them. Most of us carry unfulfilled goals and ambitions for most of our lives, if not to the grave. Some learn to live with disappointed hopes, but others seek release through a wide range of psychological responses. Self-hate and insecurity are common reactions but another is ceaseless criticism and resentment of those whose achievements more nearly match their aspirations. A third is the projection of unfulfilled goals and aspirations onto larger groups. What we cannot realize ourselves we seek through larger social organizations.

It is worth noting that group emotionalism and fervor reach fever pitch when individual disappointments and frustrations are at a maximum. Thus the dispossessed middle class in Nazi Germany—the *Lumpenproletariat*— became the most strident element supporting radical and expansionist policies. They projected personal failures into national crusades. The fervor of present-day nationalism, in both newly emergent and ancient states, may have similar foundations. A brief review of the origins of nationalism may help us to grasp its role on the present scene.

In some respects nationalism is not novel, for there have been primitive societies in which men worshipped the political community as today modern societies glorify the nation. There were few signs of nationalism anywhere in Europe during the early Middle Ages. The way was prepared for it, however, by the quickening of national consciousness inspired by the Crusades. Frenchmen, Castilians, Portuguese, and Catalans were brought into contact with others who spoke the same language or dialect. These contacts served to inspire a feeling of pride in their own nationality and a consciousness of rivalry with others. Loyalty to an area or locality and the growth of a spirit of community among a people through the spread and effects of a language or dialect were the seeds from which nationalism was to grow. The fundamental nature of modern nationalism is the demand of such a group for a state or an independent political organization of its own. The achievement of this stage in modern nationalism awaited popular revolutions in the late eighteenth and nineteenth centuries.

There were, however, signs of a precocious nationalism somewhat earlier than this. The development of contemporary nationalism was foreshadowed in the North Italian city-states of the fifteenth and sixteenth centuries. Their origin corresponded with the breakup of the seamless web of universal Christendom. In Florence, Milan, and Venice this new crop of Central and North Italian city-states revived the pagan religion of "tribalism." These tiny city-states constituted in microcosm modern nation-states. The same rules for the art of politics which Machiavelli perceived and described for the city-states have become accepted principles for the practice, if not the acknowledged creed, of politics among nations. These miniature nation-states served as laboratories for proving and testing techniques of diplomacy and power politics which present-day nation-states took over.

Subsequently, in the seventeenth and eighteenth centuries, a new form of nationalism appeared, more half-hearted and easygoing in character. If one identifies this at all with contemporary nationalism, it must be distinguished as a much weaker and more diluted form. It is in the nature of this form of nationalism that its followers were partly starved for any plausible object of worship. In dynastic nationalism, the idol had to be the vested interest of the dynasty, hardly comparing as a wellspring of emotion and loyalty with the incarnation of a sovereign people.

This is one side of the coin of dynastic nationalism. The other is the drawing together of dynastic regimes by the firm bonds of common membership in an "aristocratic international." There was often more community between two princes or rulers than there was between a prince and his own subjects. Frederick the Great of Prussia spoke French more fluently than German, which he confessed he always spoke like a coachman. Since rulers and ruled were essentially indifferent to the symbols of nationalism, it should not be surprising that this era did not produce strong nationalist sentiments among their citizens and subjects.

The late eighteenth century heralded the dawn of a new epoch. In a series of revolutionary convulsions which racked the world from 1775 to 1918, nations were substituted for dynastic states. The transitory and uninspiring figures of monarchs such as Louis XVI and George III were replaced by the effulgent images of "France," "England," and "America." These incarnations of the spirit of national communities were to acquire the same glory and splendor as ancient Rome or Athens. They furnished an object of worship which no "Prince" could supply.

A series of events mark this change. Fanaticism and ruthlessness toward foes and former friends is foreshadowed in the harsh treatment of the Loyalists by the Americans in 1783. The same emotional pattern is continued throughout Europe, beginning with the French revolutionary *levée en masse,* the German *Befreiungskrieg,* the Belgian Revolution of 1830, the burning of Moscow, and the Italian *risorgimento.* Since those days international politics have become increasingly infected with the virus of unqualified national loyalty and mutual hostility until the old forms of moderation and accommodation have almost completely disappeared. A signpost of this development is the contrast between the last moderate peace treaty of 1866 (we might say that the Japanese Peace Treaty of 1951 is an exception only because of the demands that both sides acquire allies in the cold war) and the Peace Treaty of 1871 between France and Germany. The latter treaty was a direct consequence of a German nationalism which, under the fostering hand of Bismarck, had become so strong by 1871 that it was his master rather than his servant. Because of this pressure, and against his better judgment, Bismarck was compelled to inflict a rankling wound on the French national consciousness by tearing away Alsace-Lorraine from the French body politic.

In other words, nationalism today has become a political religion. In the days of Guiseppe Mazzini, intellectual spokesman for Italian unity in the nineteenth century, and Thomas Masaryk, first president of the Republic of Czechoslovakia, nationalism was characterized by its humanitarianism and moderation. The aim of each ethnic and national group was to establish its own independent state. But correlative to this idea was the widely acknowledged view that other groups also had the right to set out to achieve this same goal and purpose. Thus Mazzini in the *Pact of Fraternity of Young Europe*, wrote, "Every people has its special mission, which will cooperate toward the fulfillment of the general mission of humanity. This mission constitutes its nationality. Nationality is sacred."

Humanitarian nationalism of this easygoing variety has been supplanted by the universalism of present-day nationalism. Three conditions have led to the almost unlimited concentration of power in the hands of the state. They are technological, psychological, and politico-religious factors. The most astounding changes of modern history, perhaps of all history, are those surrounding the Industrial Revolution. Within the past half-century, indeed the past two decades, the globe has been shrunken by changes in transportation, economic interdependencies, and communication. It is possible to circle the globe by jet in less time than it took to travel from Philadelphia to Washington in 1790. Whereas the range of most weapons was only a few hundred yards in the sixteenth century, in the twentieth century missiles have attained an operational range of more than seven thousand miles. The social-psychological development which accentuates national fervor is the increase in unfulfilled ambitions in modern society. The tasks of present-day industry are specialized and fragmentary, and the laborer who spends his days performing minor tasks in assembly-line production must realize his thirst for creativity and prestige elsewhere. By projecting his unfulfilled aims and aspirations into the world actions of the great nation of which he is a citizen, he experiences a vicarious fulfillment of his needs and desires, which contemporary society would otherwise have thwarted. The claims he makes upon his nation in world affairs are therefore less moderate than those the eighteenth-century diplomat would require. Finally, the role of nationalism has been secured by the disappearance of spiritual forces which for centuries competed successfully for the minds of men. Religion as a universal force had at one time an equal claim on men's loyalties. The doctrine of the "Two Swords" was the philosophy which ascribed equal influence to church and state, each in its own sphere. Today the emotional fervor which once characterized loyalty to the spiritual order has been united with the patriotism of the past. Combined in this way, religious fervor and patriotism have become the most powerful and dynamic force of our day, perhaps the most powerful in the history of the world.

Taken together these changes in technology, psychology, and religion have created the Leviathan. They have strengthened the state and made it nearly invulnerable to popular revolutions. It possesses a monopoly over the means of violence; and its power has become so overwhelming that over wide areas, popular rebellions can be stamped out with effectiveness. (There are exceptions in developing countries where the authority of the state is not yet fully established.) Control within the Soviet empire, for example, is easier to maintain than in all earlier Russian empires. In 1956, a massive Soviet intervention liquidated the Hungarian Revolution in a matter of a few days. Even an attempt at change was crushed almost overnight in Prague in 1968. Dissension can be crushed almost instantaneously by powerful air squadrons rushed to the scene of the trouble, whereas at the beginning of the nineteenth century, revolts in the provinces of Spain or Italy against Napoleon required oftentimes prolonged and full-scale military campaigns. At the same time, nationalism has absorbed the dynamics of industrialism in the sense that production in every country is geared to preserving the products and resources of the state for the eventuality of war. Nationalism, moreover, has played a more decisive role in determining the ultimate loyalties of workers than has socialism. For example, French laborers fought German workers in two World Wars despite the recurrent dreams of a workers' international. Finally, as in the case of Titoist Yugoslavia, loyalty to the nation outlasts allegiance to a foreign-dominated ideology. It should be clear that plans for rapid change through new international institutions must recognize the power of contemporary nationalism or suffer failure, disillusionment, and despair. We are merely deceived if we conceive of present-day nationalism as brittle, fragile, or transitory.

International Morality

The environment in which international morality must be practiced is therefore at least partly determined by individualism and nationalism. Moral action involves individual choice, while the narrowing areas of individualism limit the sphere of moral choice. Because the great choices seem to involve collective action, the solitary individual resigns himself to a state of powerlessness on the significant decisions of the day. The problems and issues are so complex and difficult that individuals are prone to conclude that they can contribute little toward solutions. Men come to see themselves as objects, not subjects, of social and political action. In such a setting, the question of a just society loses its sense of urgency. Those who once expressed concern for their neighbors no longer react with compassion to what is happening in hospitals, prisons, and schools. They develop, if not a blindness, at least apathy and inertia to injustice and cruelty. In a crowded society, there is too much suffering and wrongdoing for the individual to bear, let alone respond to. His moral judgments tend, therefore, to be held in abeyance; and when released, they reverberate with all the righteousness of a moral crusade. For example, the nation girded itself to resolve the important problem of civil rights through a nationwide social and religious movement. For long years before that, however, leaders of opinion in church and state had displayed singular indifference to the residual unsolved problems of the American Civil War. If this example is not the most appropriate, the more general question of broad swings of the pendulum in social policy remains. The individual who stands in danger of losing his identity also finds his moral concern weakened by a mass age.

Similarly, the force of nationalism tends to weaken man's sense of solidarity with the suffering and persecuted elsewhere in the world. It is obviously untrue that people in general are now more callous and indifferent than they were in the centuries of bear-baiting, public floggings, endemic disease and unchecked famine. However, in our day principles of right and wrong must be channeled through national agencies and interpreters. Here there are certain analogies between the domestic and the international scene. With the former, programs of social welfare, involving slum clearance and housing, help to the sick and aged, and widening opportunities for the poor and disadvantaged, follow laws of rational organization. A whole vast machinery of social action has been instituted with the aim of serving the needy individual. The "Good Samaritan" of our day, if he wants to help someone, must isolate himself more and more, through a whole gamut of administrative machinery, from direct contact with those he wants to help. It is obvious that the instruments of administration are abstract and dehumanized; indeed, this is a condition of their effectiveness. Acts of love and compassion must be made part of an administrative case load. The great challenge in a collective era is discovering the human significance of anything that might otherwise become just another case. Organized social action hovers dangerously near the brink of the routine and procedural. The one antidote is remembering that while the methods of social welfare are a system, the object remains an individual. The system's justification is the individual. This attitude and spirit must penetrate the organized structures of social action if deterioration and decay are to be avoided.

On the world scene, the need for a civilizing and informing moral attitude is equally urgent. In international affairs it is difficult to talk about ethics in general or single out national policies that are wholly and unqualifiedly good. Nor is it always clear that on all questions in dispute the organized international community embraces justice. The root problem is the near impossibility of defining international justice in terms that are acceptable to all the parties. There is an ancient saying, "What is just on this side of the Pyrenees is not just on the other side of the Pyrenees." No international body has yet escaped this dilemma. Those national leaders who declare that the United Nations, for example, embodies what is right and moral may, when confronting issues sensitive to the national interest, find their conception of justice at odds with that of the United Nations. In debates over political ethics, the real issue usually arises in the realm of means, not ends. There is unlikely to be substantial division over ends, but differences appear nearly inevitable on the methods and means. This is why it is difficult and often pointless to talk about ethics in general, whether in terms of peace or justice or international order. Decisions in foreign policy seldom involve simple and tidy choices. Actions stem from on-balance judgments. What is usually called for is an evaluation of the elements involved in a decision and the consequences likely to flow from each alternative course of action. In choices that are made, the best may be the enemy of the good. Not absolute truth but practical morality must be the guide.

In Jacques Maritain's words, "Means must be proportioned and appropriate to the end, since they are ways to the end, and, so to speak, the end itself is in its very process of 'coming into existence'." Prudent views of foreign policy must give heed to the call for restraint and a sense of proportion. No one who claims to be pursuing moral ends can disregard the choice of means, for with John Dewey we can say that "means and ends are two names for the same reality." Proximate morality is usually the highest practical attainment in statecraft.

The focal point of moral purpose in international relations is the interests and goals of a nation. We start with the tacit assumption that responsible men will, generally speaking, view national interests in broadly similar terms. If this were not so, bipartisanship would be impossible. Former Secretary of State Dean Rusk observed that he had appeared before committees of Congress in executive session more than two hundred times during his term of office. He was able to recall only two occasions when the discussion of important issues was cast in partisan terms. On both sides of the aisle the controlling viewpoint was "what is right for the country." Congressmen off the hustings seek the best interests of their country. T. H. Healy wrote to Lord Hugh Cecil, "Nationalism is what men will die for. Even the noble Lord would not die for the meridian of Greenwich." If the national interest does not exhaust the possibilities of ethical principles, it is always the necessary starting point. This is not to deny that on many controversial issues, responsible people may interpret the national interest in conflicting ways. The concept, however, provides a discipline and a framework for their debates.

This fact ought never obscure the need for "a decent respect for the opinions of mankind." If it is possible for political leaders to think responsibly about the national interest, they can also be expected to search for common interests with the spokesmen of other national states. If national interest is a fact, so is the possible mutuality of national interests. There are common interests transcending narrow national interests. They form a network of shared relationships that draw together men of different national creeds and aspirations. For example, no one expects the divisions between divided countries such as East and West Germany to dissolve overnight. Yet change can be expected from a continued series of "little steps" or technical changes in trade, cultural exchange, and limited tourism. This process, if practiced with patience and restraint, may draw the two together and unlock the doors to greater unity. Even when existing political systems divide, common social, cultural, and economic interests may in time serve to reunite them.

No division is more profound and no cleavage greater than that separating present rivals in the arms race. Looking out over the chasm that divides East and West, the late Secretary General of the United Nations Dag Hammarskjöld put forward a design for "disarmament by mutual example." He queried whether the United States and the Soviet Union did not have a common interest in limiting their armaments and checking their spread to other powers. History will show that the great powers have inched ahead in the limitation of armaments. Bilateral disarmament in certain fields proceded the nuclear test ban treaty, which in turn led to arms limitation. There have been tacit agreements to limit at certain points the further accretion of particular forms of military preparedness. In recent years a corresponding respect has developed by both sides for territorial boundaries in Western and Eastern Europe. While negotiators failed, or did not try to arrive at an overall peace settlement following World War II, the crises and subsequent responses in Hungary, Cuba, and Czechslovakia demonstrate a rough-and-ready acceptance of the other's hegemony in its own sphere of influence.

Finally, international society is not bereft of certain broader principles of justice, freedom, and order, however difficult their application in concrete situations. Their form may remain embryonic in a half-organized world, but their existence is understood. In formulating their foreign policies, states seek points of correspondence between their actions and certain broader principles. In foreign policy the concept of elemental right and wrong is never fully realized, but it can be approximated. Even the fact that states possess an awareness of injustice indicates the possibility of justice in foreign affairs, for a sense of injustice presupposes categories of justice to which leaders have recourse. Anticolonialism is firmly rooted in certain general and inchoate notions of what is right. Often the right is but dimly perceived. Frequently, distributive justice is the highest attainment of states. The right may be as hazy and unclear as the shadows in Plato's cave, yet these shadows represent the beginnings of the necessary conditions for greater justice in the relations between states. As Reinhold Niebuhr once observed:

> Our position is not an enviable one. Yet from an ultimate standpoint it need not be regretted. For a nation which cannot save itself without at the same time saving a whole world has the possibility of achieving a concurrence between its own interests and the general welfare; which must be regarded as the highest form of virtue in man's collective life.[2]

Order is the framework for the healthy growth of viable nation-states. A respect for national independence demands an international order to safeguard it. Freedom and justice presuppose order. If the world and its staunch supporters cannot preserve the international order, an early casualty is bound to be the survival of new and independent states.

Thus, there are layers of ethics in politics and international affairs. They deserve study, especially when the strongest voices are crusaders and cynics. The ethical dimension is comprised of shades, not of black and white alone. Grays predominate; and practically speaking, the characteristics of political ethics may be discoverable in a recognition of the relativity of all ethical judgments. The centers of morality and religion in the land cannot stand aside from man's needs in this realm. For example, the church, which teaches patience in all things, should strive to inculcate this attitude toward world affairs. Foreign policy all too often is like "women's work"—it never ends. As every long-suffering homemaker knows, despite the introduction of dishwashers and freezers, the unending drugery of housework remains. And in much the same way, the shining United Nations buildings, multilingual translation apparatuses, and instantaneous communications systems around the world have not prevented one challenge or conflict from following close on the heels of another. The consequences of actions that are noble in themselves are seldom fully anticipated. For example, a well-deserved homeland for suffering and persecuted Jews has led to tensions and wars in the Middle East. The French Revolution brought in its wake Napoleon's armies marching across Europe. Independence for the newer nations in our day is only the beginning of new trials and testing. "It is provided in the very essence of things," Walt Whitman declared, "that from any fruition of success, no matter what, shall come forth something to make a greater struggle necessary." Most of life is lived on the ground of successive crises. Peace and prosperity in an "America sailing on a summer sea" never provided the acid test of character. Rather, moral and spiritual resources are put to the test when peoples or nations teeter on the abyss of disaster or when decisions have to be made for which there is no present consensus nor future certainty. Ethical judgments, however painful and difficult, often reach a high point in clarity and resolve at the moment of moral crisis.

THE SEARCH FOR A WORLD BEYOND THE COLD WAR

Right conclusions are more likely to be gathered out
of a multitude of tongues than through any kind of
authoritative selection. To many, this is and always
will be folly; but we have staked upon it our all.
                                        Learned Hand

One taproot idea of Western civilization is faith in freedom and the *free marketplace*. Americans tend to believe that truth will win out over falsehood, right over wrong, reason over unreason in free and open debate. In the interplay of forces of justice and injustice, justice rules the future and behind the dim unknown stands God keeping watch above His own. Another taproot idea is faith in the inevitability of *progress*. History is on the march. Even the Marxist heresy prophesied that history was moving irresistibly through thesis and antithesis toward a new synthesis, the classless society. Capitalism foresaw the day when increasing production and rising living standards would transform the spiritual no less than the material lives of everyone. A third credo is faith in *science*. Science has its own momentum and inner logic. It provides the framework and the terms for decisions, taking the place of old-fashioned moral reasoning. It can save man because it leaves nothing to chance. It is grounded in facts.

The world crisis is upon us because all three of these regnant ideas—*freedom, progress,* and *science*—have come under question. What seemed indisputable and irrefutable a generation ago is no longer self-evident. Two-thirds or more of the world's people in the developing countries appear willing to trade freedom for order or for order coupled with economic growth and national prestige. We have learned that unbridled freedom in national and world assemblies leads to impasse and chaos, and to a shift in the locus of decision to other agencies: the executive in national governments and the great powers in world politics. Freedom of speech and assembly unbalanced by respect for the freedom of others brings pressure, not for freedom but its restriction. We hear pitifully little talk of freedom in certain quarters: whether among the most hard pressed and beleaguered nations of Africa and Asia, or among the defenders of the status quo, the rich, and the powerful.

If freedom has fallen under a cloud, however, progress as the dominant belief of the culture is yet more in eclipse. Indeed its antithesis, an all-pervasive sense of powerlessness, has spread throughout the land. All too many of our people see mankind and the world not as "growing better and better every day in every way," as Coué put it, but the very opposite. They have doubts about a society that brings us consumer goods but not happiness. But more serious than this, they doubt their ability or their government's or the world's to turn things around. The Club of Rome Report is unnerving not because of its stark and pessimistic diagnosis of present trends of overpopulation, pollution, resource depletion, and famine, but for the implication, however, intended, that nothing can be done about it. The end of the era of progress has left us, apparently, not with a steadier and more realistic grasp of our prospects but with a failure of nerve and a sense of impotence. How ironic that, in the most powerful nation in the world, people should feel so powerless vis-à-vis the great problems of the 1970s, their governments, their families, and across the broad front of threatened individualism. And the more they talk of "people power" or personal potency, the less convincing are their words to themselves or others. It is as though so many words had been uttered in the era of progress about inevitable advancement or invincible man or the transformation of human nature (most recently the process of the "greening of America") that we no longer believe our own words. Could it be that the age of overkill and oversell has left us satiated and immobilized? Are we alternately the victims of too much and too little faith? Do we vacillate between the role of true believers and total cynics? Is there some profound and as yet unexplored connection between the death of the idea of inevitable progress and the birth of McLuhanism? Have we found greater difficulty coping with our discovery that life is more often a rollercoaster than an escalator precisely because electronics and technology have made us observers glued to the tube, not actors in life's drama?

I do not know the answers, nor perhaps even the proper questions to ask, but I am persuaded that one aspect of the present crisis is our response to the demise of the idea of inevitable progress. A discovery that had to be traumatic has paralyzed our will to act in a new age of uncertainty, and this as much as objective factors lies at the root of the crisis.

We must seek the fountainhead of the moral crisis beyond the problems of freedom and progress. It is bound up somehow with the elevation of science to an autonomous, self-contained, and all-controlling force in civilization. Our predicament is illustrated in a dispatch from Canada reported in the *New York Times* for August 26, 1972, about Peter Pollen of Victoria, British Columbia, a successful car dealer turned mayor, battling to turn back urban sprawl built on the premise that big is good and bigger is better. The specter of row on row of billboards and crowded apartment buildings and cars sucked into the cities by capital funds overconcentrated on highway development prompted Mayor Pollen to ask: "Who is the enemy?" He answered: "It's the American scene basically. You guys are screwing up your world in the United States, but we're not going to screw up ours." His critics, Canadian developers, struck back by saying: "You can't stop growth"—in other words, the irresistible march of science and technology.

Herein the moral problem. We live in a culture that tends to translate and resolve every issue of moral and social choice in technological terms. If science and technology can build a larger and faster airplane, build it. If research and development, to which we devoted twenty-two percent of our defense budget in 1970, can create more lethal weapons, we must have them. If the SALT talks put constraints on quantitative increases, we shift to qualitative refinements. If the family is in travail, the answer isn't in the substance of love but in the techniques of sex manuals. And in the final illness, when neither the doctor nor the family can face the moral choice of prolonging life or accepting death, the availability of techniques and treatment makes the decision for them. Science has become an autonomous force and, by its dramatic advances, coupled with the retreat from moral reasoning, in this age of numeracy tends to preempt the field.

The message is not that science will destroy us any more than it is that science can save us. Nor is the solution to be found with those moralists who frame every issue in the vocabulary of absolute right and wrong. The challenge we face is to rediscover the habits of moral reasoning that reduce social choices neither to techniques nor to moral absolutes. Professor Paul Freund of the Harvard Law School speaks of the need to look at values not as abstractions but in the context of living social problems. In our fantasies, and particularly at election time, we look at the world in categories of simple right and wrong or good and evil. In real life, values cluster together, compete, and are in conflict, and can lead, depending on the choice of one or the other, in utterly different directions. Value choices are seldom if ever between good and evil. They more often involve a choice among rights and rights; evil or lesser evil; free speech versus crying fire in a crowded theatre, intellectual curiosity versus the right to privacy, freedom versus order, peace versus justice, freedom of scientific inquiry versus the right of a student to build nuclear weapons in his kitchen. Moral discrimination in human life is less mathematics or science than a juggler's act—keeping eight or ten values in view and in balance.

The problem is twice compounded in foreign cultures. How are values that had not previously existed in the culture stimulated and inculcated? The new nations face problems not only in balancing values in a social context but in inculcating new values toward work, time, achievement, status, and perseverance, which may have no cultural roots. These are not simply behavioral matters but grow out of the fundamental conception people have of the meaning and purpose of life. Status in countries such as Indonesia is a product not of hard work but of inner perfection. There is no Protestant ethic. Hard work is secondary to a more elemental factor, the condition of the soul. Or take birth control. In many areas large families are highly valued and so is the economic well-being and symbolic immortality achieved through the work and lives of many sons. Science may offer new and efficient techniques of birth control, but their acceptance or rejection depends on cultural values.

Or consider violence. The problem in part arises because basic human drives long dormant and controlled can break loose. In Indonesia, young people flood the cities so that fifty percent of the population is urban youth below seventeen. Development in cities such as Jakarta is phenomenal and prices skyrocket. For example, Jakarta has a per capita income of $300 and the rest of the country has less than $100 per capita. This has a profound effect on social cohesiveness within the nation, for an elite lives at an international level and the poor far below it. But also within the cities youths wait for jobs that never come. The juxtaposition of affluence and poverty, hope and despair, lead to reactions of anger and fear. Violence remains close to the surface; there are naked expressions of pent-up frustration and greed. The great problem is how to keep despair from erupting into violence and stay on top of the problems of living in huge metropolitan areas. It also involves the need to think about the underlying sources from which violence springs.

The point is that, at home or abroad, we need to look beyond science to the aspirations incarnate in man and embedded in culture. If we look only at what man is now, there is little hope for the future. Man has the capacity to be both more and less than he was and is. There are strengths and resources in every man and society that can help them to move ahead. For example, traditional Javanese society embodies the values of self-restraint, sharing, and moderation. Americans are generous, voluntaristic, and responsive to a mission. The task is to cast these values in ideological terms so they can take on behavioral patterns and generate social action. But neither freedom nor progress nor science can do this. It requires leadership and an act of will—but in a context more complex than commonly understood.

This brings us to the United Nations and our underlying faith that "right conclusions are more likely to be gathered out of a multitude of tongues." With the breakdown of the ruling dogmas of freedom, progress and science, and the attendant uncertainty and powerlessness that many feel, the United Nations may be more vital than its founders dreamed. The crux of the problem is the need for limited, proximate, and interim faiths less vaulting than progress and science but more durable and lasting. More than a century ago, President Lincoln spoke of Americans as a people "destitute of faith but terrified by skepticism." Because so much of ancient faith was shaped in a more simple time of sheep and shepherds, we cast about for substitute faiths. Some find it in the political religion of nationalism, others in the bitch goddess success, and still others, among them some of our young, in a curious blending of nihilism, asceticism, and moral superiority. Others suffer because their dream has indeed come true but has left them bereft of true satisfaction.

Wilfred Jenks, the late head of the International Labour Organization, observed that our dilemma was in believing in the United Nations while awaiting the emergence of something better, something which would grow from experience and not the drafting of world constitutions. This kind of faith is never easy to sustain, but we had better grow accustomed to it. The alternative, as we have seen with science or progress, is to link hope to a singular purpose, achieve or fail to approximate it, and fall into despair when utopia is not forthcoming. There may even be some virtue in the fact that the United Nations is as fragile an institution as it is, thus saving its members from self-righteousness and pretentiousness. For it is a fact that the structure of the world reflected in the United Nations General Assembly bears little relationship to political realities. Canada and the United States are outnumbered forty to two by the votes of the African states. China, with eight hundred million people, can be outvoted forty to one. Is it any wonder that the great powers have tended to act outside the United Nations? Yet in doing so they run the risk of weakening the framework of the only world institution within which global peace can be pursued. It is understandable that the United States and the Soviet Union, for example, would be impatient with the delays, the demands to which they are subjected, and the checks to their power within the United Nations. But would these demands be any less outside a constitutional framework? Have the great powers felt any more powerless in seeking to impose their will, say, on Vietnam or on Cuba? And how is one to compare the reactions of the rest of the world to American actions in Korea undertaken within the United Nations framework to those in Vietnam pursued outside the United Nations, and what lessons can we learn?

The crisis in the United Nations is but a reflection of the moral crisis outside its halls. Its actions are no better and no worse than those of its members. And its strengthening and weakening occur as regnant themes and ideas ebb and flow. The United Nations at birth was undergirded by the same dogmas of freedom, progress, and science at work in the culture. It was illusory then to speak of "open covenants openly arrived at" or of diplomacy under klieg lights. Dag Hammarskjöld left mankind a legacy of what could be accomplished through "quiet diplomacy" that demonstrated how fruitful and complementary free debate and the healing processes of private diplomacy could be. *Progress* was proclaimed by Cordell Hull, who spoke of the new international organization as eliminating alliances, the balance of power, and those ancient rivalries among states that congealed in power politics. Yet the living United Nations, while failing to eradicate these primordial forces, has discovered ways, at its best, of controlling them, bringing them under scrutiny, and ameliorating their most damaging effects. The great powers have more leverage in world politics in bringing about settlements but the United

Nations has greater authority in legitimizing them. And whereas *science* was rather naively enshrined in UNESCO and other United Nations agencies, its wisest practitioners have recognized the need to go beyond science, to organize and use it, as was done in Stockholm at the UN Conference on the Human Environment, and to mobilize all the moral force inherent in "the conscience of mankind" to keep science's destructiveness in check.

I believe in the United Nations because it is a far more pragmatic institution than some of its early spokesmen made it out to be. Primarily because it provides a forum for a multitude of tongues to be heard and a process through which a multitude of interests can be accommodated, it is more indispensable now than in the innocence of its infancy. Interest can be balanced against interest and claims and counterclaims registered through voices and votes, not bombs and bullets. The greatest challenge in the 1970s is for men and nations to live with uncertainty, with the decline of old certainties and dogmas. We need one another, yet we fear one another, we hurt one another, turn to aggression, and walk a collision course. Because the first order of business of the United Nations is to harmonize interests, maintain international peace and security, and deal with the underlying causes of conflict, its task is an unending one.

In this task and through its manifold activities in social and economic programs, the United Nations is building a stronger world system. Its movement in this regard is bound to be evolutionary, not revolutionary; glacial, not millennial. If we can help it to carry out this mission, defend its credibility, reinforce its strengths, and remedy its weaknesses, and above all not abandon it in isolation, we may yet save ourselves and the world.

NOTES

1. Reinhold Niebuhr, "Theory of International Politics," unpublished manuscript (n.d.), p. 11.
2. "The Conditions of Our Survival," *Virginia Quarterly Review* 26 (Autumn 1950), p. 482.

3: THE PROBLEMS
AND THE PROSPECTS

The most urgent problems which face the world, as seen by an American observer, begin with his nation's search for identity, called on to give world leadership whether it wills it or not, involve the growing threat of world hunger and famine and the dire prospects of the population explosion, and conclude with the grim specter of world destruction through a possible thermonuclear war. Characteristically, only the first and last of these problems are normally included in overall international relations study and analysis. The other two fall more naturally to the skills and insights of agronomists and geneticists or to scientists in medicine, public health, and demography.

The demands for international cooperation in each of these areas invite serious inquiry, not only into the substance of the scientific problems, but also the functions of cooperating bodies and the forces that shape their actions. It is as national bodies that they must cooperate, subject to all the possibilities and constraints of other national and international bodies. It will be crucial in looking ahead to anticipate the role they can play. For this, international relations approaches may prove relevant. It is with such a focus that these urgent world problems are considered in the pages that follow.

AMERICA'S QUEST FOR IDENTITY:
PROMISED LAND OR WASTELAND

Driven from every other corner of the earth, freedom of thought and the right of private judgment in matters of conscience direct their course to this happy country as their last resort.

Samuel Adams

Hamilton Fish Armstrong, the late editor of the influential quarterly *Foreign Affairs*, wrote in its fiftieth anniversary issue (October 1972): "Not since we withdrew into comfortable isolation in 1920 has the prestige of the United

States stood so low." Lest his judgment be construed as political rhetoric, it should be noted that Armstrong was an adviser to both major political parties. And if anyone doubts that there is cause for this critique, he need only consider the following: the United States, which in the 1940s and 1950s had an "automatic majority" in votes at the United Nations, learned in the 1960s what it means to be outvoted in this same assembly. Americans, who during and after World War II trumpeted the cause of anticolonialism and the end of aggression, are today condemned as imperialists and aggressors. And while we have been heralded since 1946 as the most powerful nation in the history of the world, a tiny and divided nation among the less developed of Southeast Asia has fought us to a standstill. Is it any wonder Armstrong wrote of the decline of America and pointed to the loss of our prestige in the world? Or that Hans Morgenthau can say, "America no longer sets an example for other nations to emulate; in many respects it sets an example of what to avoid."[1]

For those who would make sense of this decline and seek to understand it, without affixing praise or blame, the saga of America can be read in two conflicting portrayals of America's place in the world. There is ample historical evidence that we have seen ourselves, and been seen, in turn, as the Promised Land and as a barren and materialistic Wasteland. Each of these visions has its roots in mind as much as in matter. Each takes on meaning from the power of the spirit, of ideology and of the national psyche. For men and nations, profound psychological and sociological forces shape who they are and how others see them. In the end, the mystique of prestige is made up of intangible and impalpable factors that have reality and growth and which no one manufactures with Madison Avenue shibboleths and slogans. At their best, such visions are dreams—the American dream. At their worst, they become nightmares from which men seek escape but which haunt and hold them as do those distressing images that torment us in our half-waking hours.

The Promised Land

To understand the American dream, a dream of a people set apart, we must return to the days of our birth as a nation. Through the miracle of history, we can be "present at the creation." The Founding Fathers and those who embraced their credo had as their goal the building, in the wilderness, of a home in which values they had inherited, not invented, could be enjoyed and experienced. These values were the legacy of two thousand years of experience: Greece, Rome, and Israel; Great Britain and all of Western civilization. They sought to give expression in a new land to the goals Pericles attached to Athens in his immortal funeral oration: "Our form of government does not enter into rivalry with the institutions of others. We do not copy our neighbors, but are an example to them. . . . I say that Athens is the school of Hellas. . . ." Or Rome, the cradle of lawful government, of which Virgil proclaimed:

> But Romans,
> never forget that government is your medium!
> Be this your art: to practice men in the habits of peace,
> Generosity to the conquered, and firmness against aggressors.

And for Americans who saw themselves as God's chosen people and an eighteenth-century Israel given by God to the new world, Isaiah's words portrayed their mission: "I will give you as a light to the nations, that my salvation may reach to the end of the earth" (Isa. 49:6).

But there was more than that, more than professions and proclamations. The colonists had turned their backs on Europe. A sense of freedom informed their thinking. They fled Britain and the Old World not because they doubted the historic values such as freedom but because these goals could be realized only in the New World—or so they thought. Europe was wallowing in wars, tyrannies, and abortive revolutions that were fostering pessimism, violence, and despair. It was true that Britain had given the world the common law, the Magna Charta, the safeguarding of individual rights against the state and religious freedom. But Englishmen were cribbed and confined in a tight little island; religious conscience was threatened by a religious system hardened at the margins by time and authority. Dissenters had no place. By contrast, the United States looked westward on a vast and relatively uninhabited continent. Structures of political tyranny had not yet formed. Poverty was forced on no able-bodied citizen. For the poor and the disaffected, there were open frontiers—the society's safety valve about which Frederick Jackson Turner was to elaborate the frontier theory of American history. America was for him God's highest human revelation to date. "We are the chosen people," Josiah Strong wrote. "Can anyone doubt that the result of this competition of the races will be the 'survival of the fittest'?"[2] Charles Pinckney arose at the Federal Convention on January 25, 1787, to say: "Our true situation appears to me to be this.—a new extensive Country containing within itself the materials for forming a Government capable of extending to its citizens all the blessings of civil & religious liberty—capable of making them happy at home." As the noted church historian Philip Schaff was to observe after the event: "I doubt whether the moral influence of Christianity and Protestantism has more deeply and widely affected any nation. . . ."

The political and psychological consequences that flowed from all this were threefold and persisted throughout our early history: optimism and hope, equality, and national self-righteousness. The first two were the wellsprings of early greatness. The third carried seeds of strength and weakness and was to persist well into the twentieth century.

Optimism and hope on the colonial scene were more than an illusion. They stemmed from the objective situation in which people found themselves. Americans were enchanted with their world and their communal existence. American artists in the nineteenth century, at least those of schools such as the Native School, painted as if the world were serene, as if there were no sorrow in the world. They sincerely believed that the world had been created for the greater happiness of all. They reflected the national optimism of the Era of Good Feeling and the Jacksonian era. William Sidney Mount, who painted "The Power of Music," jotted in his journal, "I wrote with my finger on the bridge in the white frost; God is good." And this faith helped men to survive suffering and deprivation as they pushed ever westward into the harsh and unknown reaches of a land they fervently believed flowed with milk and honey.

Yet optimism was anchored in the *egalitarian* character of the new society—a quality often conspicuously missing today in the new societies of Africa and Asia. Read *Letters from an American Farmer;* for Crèvecoeur the new society

> is not composed, as in Europe, of great lords who possess everything, and of a herd of people who have nothing. Here are no aristocratical families, no courts, no kings, no bishops, no ecclesiastical dominion, no invisible power giving to a few a very visible one; no great manufacturers employing thousands. . . . The rich and the poor are not so far removed from each other as they are in Europe [or, one might add, in the less developed countries today] . . . . We have no princes, for whom we toil, starve, and bleed: we are the most perfect society now existing in the world. Here man is free as he ought to be; nor is this pleasing equality so transitory as many others are.[3]

"The truth is," wrote Benjamin Franklin,

> that there are in [this] . . . country few people so miserable as the poor of Europe, there are also very few that in Europe would be called rich. . . . There are few great proprietors of the soil, and few tenants; most people cultivate their own lands, or follow some handicraft or merchandise; very few rich enough to live idly upon their rents or incomes. . . .

Or to return to Charles Pinckney: "The people of the U. States are perhaps the most singular of any . . . there are fewer distinctions of fortune & less of rank, than among the inhabitants of any other nation." And Walt Whitman, speaking of equality, wrote: "By God! I will accept nothing which all men cannot have the counterpart of on the same terms. . . ." It mattered less that words like these obscured the distinctions between freemen and slaves, or elites of talent or property who enjoyed comforts the average citizen could not conceive. What mattered was that there were neither permanent rulers nor permanent subjects. Equality meant equal access and equal opportunity. The ideal affirmed that every man had the freedom to seek political power—

and this ideal sent out echoes around the world. And perhaps more important for the health of the body politic, it stirred mankind from all walks of life to take a hand in the governance of society. Participation is the corollary of equality and voluntarism is a handmaiden. Tocqueville sensed this when he wrote: "To take a hand in the regulation of society and to discuss it is his highest concern . . . if an American were condemned to confine his activities to his own affairs he would be robbed of one half of his existence."

The third consequence of the fact that Americans saw themselves as living in the Promised Land as a chosen people was a pervasive national self-righteousness that persists to the present day. We were a new nation in a new world beyond the seas. Immigrants had found release from the anxious and painful strife, the wickedness and poverty and the frustrations of the old world. Europe was the prison house from which they had fled. The sense of escape and freedom from evil was reenforced by a religious ingredient shared alike by pilgrims and puritans, deists and secularists. The religious version led Edward Johnson, in his *Wonder Working Providence of Zion's Saviour* (1650), to find in New England the place "where the Lord would create a new heaven and a new earth, new churches and a new Commonwealth together." The secularized version comes through in Thomas Jefferson's affirmation: "Before the establishment of the American States, nothing was known to history but the man of the old world crowded within limits either small or overcharged, and steeped in vices which the situation generates."[4]

Strikingly enough, these affirmations seemed confirmed by our early history. In the first phase, the frontier saved us from the acrimony of class struggle and later a superior technology gave the adventurous and ambitious new outlets. Beyond this, we were freed from international responsibility by the fortuitous coincidence of geographic isolation and the workings of a European balance of power. In such a world, it was natural to assume that Americans were indeed a chosen people and, even with the passing of these conditions, the psychology lingers on. This American state of mind, and sense of mission, has sometimes been a source of strength, as in rallying men to defend their country, but it has also made for that peculiarly American version of self-righteousness about which Tocqueville wrote:

> If I say to an American that the country he lives in is a fine one, aye, he replies and there is not its equal in the world. If I applaud the freedom its inhabitants enjoy he answers "freedom is a fine thing but few nations are worthy of it." If I remark on the purity of morals . . . he declares "I can imagine that a stranger who has witnessed the corruption which prevails in other nations would be astonished at the difference." At length I leave him to contemplation of himself but he returns to the charge and does not desist until he has got me to repeat all I have been saying. It is impossible to conceive a more troublesome and garrulous patriotism.[5]

America as Wasteland

How distant and remote all this sounds as we think of the present. Pause for a
moment to reflect on the present century: the first decades with the nation
struggling to find itself, combating bigness, rallying to Teddy Roosevelt,
Bryan and the populists, Robert La Follette and the Wisconsin Progressives,
inspired by Woodrow Wilson to join in the War to End Wars and then
repudiating his League to Enforce the Peace. Next, the twenties and the era
of normalcy as the nation, weary of two decades of "the strenuous life,"
sought to regroup and reconstitute itself—albeit through self-indulgence. Then
two more decades of severe challenge and testing in the 1930s and 1940s: a
grim depression that spread across the globe, the nightmare of fascism,
worldwide warfare and unimagined destruction, the holocaust with its savage
mass murders in gas chambers and concentration camps and then, most
fateful of all, the bomb. But there were more than challenges: there were
responses as well that constitute some of mankind's "finest hours"—ending
fear, restoring the economy, turning back fascism and providing hope where
there had been despair—all by pragmatic governments that satisfied wholly
neither the right nor the left. War-weary and uncertain about reform, the
nation, as it moved through the 1950s, having known in McCarthyism the
noxious and poisonous effects of "a house divided against itself," sought
healing in the steady and calming presence of its most respected war hero. It
retreated in the 1950s, as it had in the 1920s, to renew and rebuild itself, to
gain a second wind before pressing on. But even a Dwight David Eisenhower
could not wholly calm the storm. War clouds darkened in Berlin, Southeast
Asia, and the Middle East. Economic growth slowed down, and despite the
settling effects of "an era of tranquility," a sense of restlessness and unease
pervaded the land. When a young Senator promised to get us moving again,
we were ready, despite the immense personal popularity of his predecessor.

But what are we to say of the 1960s? What kind of an era has it been? Has
it expressed once again the historic pattern of reform following retrenchment,
of the cycle of a great leap forward building on the stabilization of the era
that went before? The 1960s began, according to pattern, with the New
Frontier and the Great Society, and it seemed that history was repeating
itself. But the accidents of history that have shaped the world intervened—
assassinations of three strong leaders, domestic violence, the grotesque horror
of Vietnam, social decay in the cities, pollution and overpopulation, dramatic
advances by one minority sparking reactions by other minorities and ethnic
groups. In the aftermath of all this, the people—and in the end it is they who
have the say—called for a pause, a breather from too much change. It was as if
they had had enough; the world of complexity and uncertainty was too much

with them. They were weary of sacrifice, skeptical of intellectuals, saturated by the media, and dubious about reigning ideologies and dogmas.

But most fateful of all, the Promised Land came to be viewed as a Wasteland—a landscape of endless problems, of strategies piled on strategies, resentments and racism, recessions and inflation, and technologies advertised as panaceas that became "part of the problem." For a century and a half, we were a shining example to others. New nations slavishly and often naively patterned their doctrines of self-determination after our Declaration of Independence and their constitutions after ours. Woodrow Wilson's Fourteen Points were a rallying cry to the enslaved and the oppressed throughout the world.

Then suddenly the spotlight focused on us—critically, sharply, unrelentingly. The phrase we heard more and more was that "others were determined not to repeat our mistakes." Those who came to visit left not applauding our successes but reciting a litany of unsolved problems: the cities, consumerism, minorities, and Vietnam. We reacted, resented and then withdrew, a pathology as common to nations as to individuals. And deep down we knew, however painfully, that there was truth in the criticism—and the truth hurts. Not long ago, an Indonesian colleague on an international commission told me that the one thing Indonesia needed least was our films and our television. He feared the consequences of Indonesia having more than one national television channel, for, if they had more, they would be obliged to fill the time with programs which he felt had corrupted and weakened American society. To preserve indigenous culture they would resist the spread of plastic culture. And Robert Penn Warren complained that when he returned to his birthplace, passivity and self-indulgence had replaced participation in civic and school board affairs as the people turned first to watch and then act out the less ennobling things they saw on television.

Americans fear, deep down, that through technology they have conquered new worlds while losing their souls. We sense that things are in the saddle, riding mankind. We can describe the problem, but thus far have had little success in outlining the answers. We know things are not right, but who can say confidently he knows ways to remedy them? And our stage in history, the era in which we live gives us little incentive to be bold.

Or does it? Is there significance in the fact that President Nixon drew political strength from his China and Soviet policies? Was the reservoir of goodwill America enjoys around the world refilled more by "the green revolution" and the 1971 Nobel Peace Prize to Norman Borlaug than by all our rhetoric about defending the world against communism? Does the Peace Corps do more to validate the capacity of young people to exercise responsibility than those rather frenetic and self-conscious demonstrations which give political ammunition to the foe? And beyond all the public initiatives, what about the many private ones that go unheralded and unsung: scientists in their laboratories, teachers in ghetto schools, minority leaders filling positions of great responsibility? These spread far beyond science and learning. According to the Talmud, heaven is held in place by the virtue, love, and integrity of not one, but twelve great men—including the doctor, engineer, laborer, teacher, and farmer. Differences in talent, interest, and development mark the contrasting biographies of our leaders. The American philosopher William James observed that most of us use only ten percent of our capacities. As a great power and affluent people we suffer not from a shortage of capital, industrial potential, or technical prowess. It is primarily courageous leaders that are in short supply.

The way back to the Promised Land is to recover the truths history teaches about our past and present so we can live courageously in a very uncertain but exciting future. The way out of the Wasteland is to learn to live with uncertainty, not by escaping it through the many forms of latter-day "opiates of the people," but through the proven route to self-fulfillment, which is taking hold of a worthy purpose. No honest man can say in the seventies: "I have nothing to do." Our problem is quite simply that we live in a world where good and evil intermingle and it will no longer do to speak as though one individual—myself—or one nation—my country—is unqualifiedly good and right. But neither will it do to obscure the many good and positive forces at work in the nation and the world. It may well have seemed plausible to the children of the new Israel in 1776 that they embodied all virtue, but how sad it would be if, history having proved this untrue, their heirs in the 1970s were blinded to their own not inconsiderable virtues.

For on the one hand there is much that is good in all mankind—generosity, self-sacrifice, a spark of the divine. It is possible to speak realistically of the solidarity of mankind. The late Albert Schweitzer wrote of a universal desire "to consider not only our own personal well-being but human society as a whole." This impulse bears fruit in worldwide campaigns against hunger, ignorance, war, and disease—the Four Horsemen of the Apocalypse. It expresses itself in immediate responses to catastrophe anywhere on the globe. It is kept alive in countless little acts of kindness and charity enriching our lives. The rich and powerful are stirred by the winds of change when the poor, who are two-thirds of the world's people, ask who would not rather be fed than hungry, housed than destitute, free than enslaved, educated than ignorant, healthy than sick, rulers than ruled. Man everywhere has said "no" to life on a treadmill and has moved decisively to throw off the shackles of illness, suffering, starvation and early death. It should not exceed our capacity or wit to join our less privileged friends in pursuing this dream—remembering the principle of *equality* that from the beginning has undergirded our strength as a nation. Indeed, what I find so surprising and saddening is our failure to communicate to the world our constancy and determination in pursuing this goal. For example, we speak despairingly of inequality in education, yet forty-five percent of all minority peoples of college age in New York City are in institutions of higher learning in that city. The financial aid budget of most leading colleges and universities is very heavily weighted on the side of assistance to the poor and the disadvantaged, most of whom are performing well indeed. Yet little is known and less is said about these important advances. Equality is of course an unending quest, and today the hopes of middle-income families are threatened because the very rich and the very poor have come to enjoy a substantial advantage especially in equality of education.

There is no gainsaying the fact that evil is equally embedded in the same men and nations. Envy, greed, self-righteousness, and jealousy prevail in our personal and collective lives. Our goodness seldom breaks through regard for self. Baffled by this riddle of man, Pascal wrote: "What a monster, what a worm is man, yet judge of the whole universe." Every major religion and philosophy has tried to get rid of the fact of good and evil: the Enlightenment through the idea of progress (man was becoming better day by day) and communism through a classless society in which the domination of man by man would be replaced by the administration of things—a dream largely refuted by history. Religion, through the dual concept that the mind is good and the body evil, sought to dispose of the problem only to find that reason no less than body is harnessed to selfishness. Ironically, the illusion that one can be good and the other evil persists in all the fashionable movements today that reverse the principle and see the body as good and the mind as the source of evil.

Knowing this good and evil, is it surprising that restlessness pervades the land? New aspirations and vitalities are testing old limits; old ideals are being set aside and new and realistic ones are not yet born. In such a world, the scene is confused and the circumstances complex and baffling. Every choice is hedged about with uncertainty. With facts unclear and consequences nearly always in doubt, it will not do to paint one another as moral heroes and moral villains.

Yet neither will it do to withdraw to safe havens for, in fact, there are no hiding places. At home and abroad, civic participation is an absolute necessity, for the price of its neglect is a slow erosion of freedom and the common good. Pericles' warning has universal meaning: "Each fancies that no harm will come of his neglect . . . and so, by the same notion being entertained by all separately, the common cause imperceptibly declines." We all crave freedom but shrink from responsibility. Yet experience teaches it is better to light a candle than to curse the darkness. The forgotten truth about civic participation is that the missing ingredient is frequently stamina and endurance, a truth that our rivals in the communist party apparatus have grasped with diabolical fervor. There is a current and prevailing notion that good behavior and noble conduct occur on the mountain peaks of experience, but that the valleys of daily decisions are an ethical morass. Nothing could be further from the truth. In John Gardner's words: "Making a bad world better is hard, grinding, never-ending work. It is not for people whose interest is in posturing or striking attitudes or bandying words or venting the anger of youth."

The way to the Promised Land is through tragedy, frustration, and failure, especially for a proud and affluent people. There are no once-and-for-all solutions. By extending life, modern medicine has bequeathed a whole new set of social problems. By splitting the atom, scientists have delivered to man the power to destroy the globe. This suggests a new form of hope and calls for a new breed of American, someone who seeks virtue knowing he is at best only partially virtuous, who strives for social equality and justice knowing he will only approximate it. But he can take heart from the fact that those we celebrate are those who, as Lincoln, did their best in the very ambiguous and uncertain choices they faced and left it to history to judge. There is more serenity, inner peace and, yes, hope in this than in either the self-righteousness of a chosen people who see themselves as forever right, or those passive men who withdraw to little islands either of purity or pleasure. And more promise in it, too!

WAR AND THE ABSOLUTISTS

By prudence, we understand the practical knowledge
of things to be sought, and of things to be avoided.
                                                                Cicero

No problem facing contemporary world leaders tests political intelligence and moral imagination more severely than the issue of nuclear weapons. The awesome question of what is a viable armaments policy perplexes men no less today than it did in 1945. What are responsible governments to do with instruments of lethal destruction? What programs can international institutions devise that will broaden the narrow spectrum of security that nations have enjoyed since World War II? Who is prepared to gamble on another's restraint with the growing stockpiles of ever more deadly weapons that nations possess?

If there is no security in national weakness, can states find safety in national strength? If so, what has happened to criteria of national power

when thermonuclear devices can in a single strike wipe out whole populations, armies, and industrial potentials? How is the moralist to find his way
between the shoals of a heedless compassion that asks too much of collective
virtue and a harsh cynicism that denies the prospect of national suicide and
mutual annihilation? What are the points of convergence of justice and
security and how can they be kept in balance when crucial elements in the
equation constantly change?

To approach the armaments field through a set of baffling questions is in
no way reassuring, for no other realm of international relationships more
desperately requires clear-cut answers and solutions. Yet our approach to
armaments is undeniably full of paradox. We reassure one another that
reasonable men can find a way out of the present impasse if they but contrive
more imaginative policies. Those who admit stalemate or protracted uncertainty in political, economic, moral or social conflicts instinctively prefer
more precise designs and overall blueprints for the armaments problem. For
example, many who see no abatement in political tensions between Moscow
and Washington affirm that one action or another will assure an early end to
the arms race, for failing this all men will perish. Arms control commends
itself as a sensible way out when the problems of the Middle East, Latin
America, or Eastern Europe seem insoluble. To this approach most lend
assent up to the point at which our policy-makers carry new programs into
the international arena. When their efforts fail, however, we question their
goodwill, motivation, or intelligence, but rarely the stubborn quality of the
problem itself. Fifty years of disappointment and frustration in negotiating
an end to the arms race are apparently inconclusive for the vast majority of
dedicated observers.

Yet if men like General George C. Marshall or Prime Minister Winston S.
Churchill had been trusted, we should have devoted greater energy and
attention to preparing to live for a generation or more with the terrifying
risks of nuclear destruction. It must be recalled that a handful of wise leaders
recognized that demands for an end to armed tension showed little sign of
realization without a more basic shift in the international climate. Believing
this, their prescription required more intellectual and moral effort than most
moralists or cynics are prone to accept. The notion that "states arm to
parley" is at one and the same time offensive to pacifists and to extreme
militarists, whose diagnoses are inevitably more convincing and satisfying to
broad sectors of public opinion. Furthermore, when any problem as intractable as that of armaments resists every attempt at solution, more radical
approaches take the field. If warfare persists, men seek to outlaw it. When
great power negotiations break down, the public at large demands that
"people speak to people." The unquenchable faith in reason by which
Western civilization has made its greatest advances generates the belief that no

issue that divides men can long remain outside the boundaries of genuine understanding. Failure to solve a problem means we must therefore seek a scapegoat, whether imperfect institutions, ill-prepared negotiators, or laggard policy-makers.

Any analysis which places the accent on elements of the armaments problem that up to now have denied success to serious and responsible leaders is bound to evoke hostility and deep distrust. Critics will ask if the observer intends to leave millions of helpless men and women to their fate. What has happened to his sense of moral revulsion to war, to a renunciation of the acts and means of violence, or to the compelling lesson that man should love, not seek to destroy, his brother? Moreover, doesn't the student of international conflict move unconsciously and imperceptibly from describing the facts of international life as he sees them to a posture of belaboring those who condemn him for his callousness and immorality? Then too, the further risk is always with him of developing vested interest in the status quo, with all its tragic failures and shattered hopes. The more he observes the cancerous state of affairs brought about by such profound divisions as the rift between East and West, the more he comes to accept it, at least in the short run and barring fundamental changes, as a permanent condition to be relieved, temporarily alleviated, but never fully eliminated or cured.

Yet the moral risks of facing reality cannot excuse the diplomatist any more than the doctor from accepting the distressing burdens that are inherent in his task. If all patients were free of disease at all times, the doctor's place could appropriately be filled by someone with other training and skills. If the international stage were not plagued by rivalry, distrust, and suspicion, negotiators who have learned to take conflict in stride would quickly become obsolete. Incidentally, no diplomatist worthy of the name believes that warfare is inevitable. It is conflict and rivalry, particularly among those who contend for influence and authority, that is taken for granted; and the search is unremitting for ways and means to limit rivalries and prevent the struggle for power from crossing over into open strife and war.

The vocation and the commitment of the negotiator compel him to believe that war is not inevitable. When the inflammation caused by tension and rivalry grows too intense, he must apply a poultice to relieve the infection until time and circumstances can restore health to the body politic. If he were to act as if the infection were imaginary or could be "reasoned" away, he should have failed in his calling, however humane and civilized his motives might be. The doctor can hardly assume that health will supplant disease once and for all; neither can the diplomat proceed as if virtue were obliterating sinfulness or cooperation had superseded conflict.

For any sensitive conscience the need to recognize the dual reality of good and evil can be profoundly distressing. Few liberal Christians and humanists deny the reality of imperfect virtue and they labor faithfully in social reform and aid to the oppressed to reduce, not eliminate, human suffering. They accept the necessity of charity even within blatantly oppressive and unjust social systems whose purposes they must ultimately condemn. Within national societies, liberals and particularly pacifists link the "incompatible" forces of an ethic of love and coexistence with tyrannical regimes. Because I believe they are right in striving to bring aid and comfort to victims of an unjust political order even at the expense of strengthening that order, I am puzzled by their austere rejection of ethical pragmatism in confronting the armaments problem. Surely limited war is morally superior to total war, and the cold war is to be preferred to a shooting war. Yet moral relativists who see some justice in the most tyrannical regimes become moral absolutists in the claim that there is "no other course for the Church but the final rejection of war as an instrument for achieving justice." No one should ask men to form an unholy alliance with evil nor justify what is wrong, but it might be hoped they would consider that cooperation with evil in the interests of the good cannot be defended in political and social relations and utterly condemned in the military realm.

If moral certainty in the control and elimination of nuclear weapons and other armaments exceeds the wit and attainment of man, no one who would responsibly serve his nation and the world can abandon the search for more viable policies for limited problems. The irony of the nuclear age is that all-out war has lost its inner logic; but no major power across the vast chasm of mutual distrust can afford to be the first to found its policies upon this premise. However, the first level at which moral compulsion properly takes the stage is at the point where man's necessity to control and eliminate warfare conflicts with his insufficiency to do so. Those who assert that the practical man must "accept war in the abstract as a fact of life" are doubtless correct, as are those who point out that most choices the statesman makes are practical ones at several stages removed from the moral issue. Yet moral man faced with mankind's extinction has an obligation by virtue of common humanity to resist in every practical way the unfolding of a chain of events leading to disaster. Moral responsibility for others no less than himself requires him to act with moral and political discrimination in an unending process; and those who would restrict it to outlawing war and the instruments of warfare confine it within too-narrow limits. The compulsion to seek moral distinctions across a wide spectrum of war and peace is generated by a morality comprehensive enough to embrace both means and ends.

Secondly, the moralist is entitled to speak not merely about war in the abstract but about particular wars and the military and political conditions that either increase the likelihood of war or threaten to carry a struggle beyond the point of self-defense or legitimate national or international interests. We know enough about the tendencies of men and nations to assert that great weakness has almost always invited expansion and aggression by those possessing great strength. The duty of statesmen is to reduce the temptation for dynamic expansionist movements to spread their influence and their cause. At the same time, under circumstances of present-day technology, nations can ill afford to build defense systems capable only of wars of last recourse. Despite repeated claims that conventional wars had been rendered obsolete, outbreaks since World War II have all been conventional in nature. Military conflict and the threat of conflict in Korea, Hungary, Suez, Vietnam and the Middle East have followed the conventional pattern as is evident in the ninety-seven wars referred to by Kende in his paper mentioned earlier.

Neither national necessity nor military logic excuses American diplomatic and intellectual leaders from considering principles defining the limits of military preparation and conduct. An armaments program aimed at overwhelming nuclear superiority must be questioned both on military and ethical grounds, for the purpose of thermonuclear strength is to confront an adversary with the certainty of severe retaliation, sufficient to make the adventure too costly. The goal under present-day conditions cannot be the organizing of the means of victory, since the real defeat is the war itself, for it involves a common fate which will be visited on all who have anything to do with it. Yet reasonable prudence in establishing limited nuclear strength may prove a deterrent to those who might otherwise dare to use weapons they monopolize. Even a great and humane people succumbed to such a temptation, and we are constrained to speculate over what course we might have followed at Hiroshima if others had possessed the bomb.

The United States can ill afford to reject cavalierly the principle of proportion. Whatever the difficulties of enforcing restraint, the ancient truth holds good that grave injustices may not be repressed by means bringing greater injustice than the perpetuation of the injustice. The reexamination of the classic texts on the conditions of a just war or of defensive war are by no means outmoded in our time. Had they been followed more faithfully, the war in Vietnam need never have reached its tragic proportions. The greatest publicists of the past were more inclined than are some of our latter-day international lawyers to view law and justice in context. They searched their souls and the practice of states to ascertain when and how states and princes should be expected to keep their commitments. Circumstances led them to write less of enforcement systems and more of conditions of self-interest and mutual trust. They talked of levels and orders of justice and were not above accepting the compromises the prudent statesman was compelled to make if a tolerable order was to be preserved. I find in such writings, and in much of the historic Catholic literature, partly because its precepts are rooted both in "heaven" and "earth," a greater sense of moral discrimination and attention to proximate orders of justice than in the writings of many Protestant or Jewish perfectionists.

Our most discerning brilliant philosophers, viewing war and the contemporary scene, ask, "Where are the ethical principles to fix the appropriate limits?" If they broaden the question to read "where are the ethical *and political* principles," they might obtain an answer. Any system of limitation must serve the national interests of all parties. We are told that an armaments agreement will be self-enforcing if compliance serves such interests better than evasion or violation. The underpinnings of every international arrangement are, of course, moral in character. There must be a minimum of mutual trust. The basic problem in East-West relations has been and remains the conspicuous absence of such trust. If this trust is to be created, however, it must grow from the discovery of mutual interests so overpowering as to transcend sharp ideological cleavages. Do Russians and Americans have a common interest in attacking the problem of wheat-borne virus? Do they share a mutual interest in restricting the spread and diffusion of atomic weapons among lesser powers? Do they have an equal stake in restraining buoyant and reckless powers who on ideological or political grounds would plunge the world into a deathly atomic holocaust? The truth is that answers will come as part of a slow, gradual process, the direction of which cannot be measured by momentary successes or failures.

Modern man could look to an uncertain future with more assurance if civilization provided surer intellectual and moral footing. On one side we are endlessly disposed to downgrade the awesome burdens of political leadership and the tragic choices that political reason imposes on the statesman. In his heart, he would prefer freedom to slavery, peace to war, and love to power, yet in his official duties he is forever reduced to accepting the lesser evil (or greater good). Because the main stuff of his vocation is political calculation, his actions carry a bad name. From all sides, friends and critics call on him to pursue justice, but because he must often be an honest broker of conflicting moral claims, he ends in some measure failing them all. He must gauge the political consequences of every political and moral act and with Lincoln accept as his guide the words:

> I do the very best I know how, the very best I can, and I mean to keep doing so until the end. If the end brings me out all right, what is said against me won't amount to anything. If the end brings me out wrong, ten angels swearing I was right would make no difference.

In this sense, a political ethic is "future-facing" and good intentions or noble manners will not excuse the statesman for moral or political failure.

Yet it also remains true that every political calculation has its moral components; we remember as our greatest statemen those for whom a tireless conscience preserved the tension between the practical and the good. Prudence stands between a judgment of present reality and some higher and objective good. Incidentally, both cynics and perfectionists are inclined to undervalue the full scope of moral conduct inspired by the tension between these two poles. Thus when pacifists write that Christian conscience in wartime seems to have chiefly the effect of making Christians do reluctantly what military necessity requires, they close their eyes to a range of conduct many of us have observed: charity to helpless victims of the struggle, aid to the suffering and the wounded often at great personal risk, and, following the conflict, a lifetime of dedication to peace as the supreme goal. A profound concern, often unarticulated, with the conduct and purpose of war runs deeper in many sensitive hearts than this indictment would suggest.

Nevertheless, students of political ethics are correct in calling us back to "the moral tradition of civilized warfare" and to re-creating the military and material circumstances that may foster it. We have need to reflect on right and wrong conduct in war as in peace. The United Nations, particularly in parts of the world where suspicion of Westerners runs rampant, can be a limiting and restraining force. Yet given the immense hazards of the clash between the great powers who hold in their hands forces of mutual destruction, we should also have, with Lincoln, a sense of throwing ourselves on the mercy of Providence. In the end this may prove a greater support than political calculation or the resurrection of concepts of a "just" war.

NOTES

1. Hans J. Morgenthau, "Nixon and the World," *New Republic,* January 6 and 13, 1973, p. 20.

2. Strong, *Our Country: Its Possible Future and Its Present Crisis* (New York: Baker & Taylor, 1886, rev. ed. 1891).

3. Crèvecoeur, *Letters from an American Farmer,* Everyman's Library edition (New York: E. P. Dutton, 1912), pp. 40-41.

4. Jefferson, letter to John Adams on natural aristocracy, October 28, 1813, *Writings* (Washington D.C., 1904), 13:401.

5. Alexis de Tocqueville, *Democracy in America,* the Henry Reeve text (New York: Vintage, 1954) 2:236.

Part Two:

Education:

Understanding the World

ROUTES TO THE STUDY
OF WORLD AFFAIRS

International relations, wrote the late Frederick S. Dunn, requires the collaboration of twenty-one disciplines if the tools for perceiving its multi-faceted character are to be made available. Dunn acknowledged that an important core for such study was political science but insisted that more was needed for comprehension. It required education in the broadest terms to analyze the massive, many-sided, and ever-changing pattern of factors and forces at work on the national and international scene. All of the liberal arts were involved, as were science and technology. Philosophy and theology were essential to a comprehension of man as the maker of history. There was no single route to knowledge because what counted most was the aspect of the problem to be explored and the usefulness of the findings.

In keeping with this approach, let us examine the problems confronting the educator, the insights and knowledge to be gained from education and from those disciplines less often called into play in discussions of international relations. It could be that they will provide us with perceptions not readily apparent in more conventional approaches to world problems.

4: THE EXPLOSION
OF KNOWLEDGE

*If a nation expects to be ignorant and free, it expects
what never was and never will be.*

Thomas Jefferson

The distinguished columnist James Reston, writing in the *New York Times*,
observed:

> Change is the biggest story in the world today, and we are not covering it
> adequately; change in the size and movement of our people; change in the
> nature, location, and availability of jobs; violent change in the cities and
> on the land; change in the relations between village and town, town and
> city, city and state, state and nation, and, of course, change in the
> relations between the empires that are falling and the empires that are
> rising, the old states that are going down and new ones that are coming up.

The significance of the present era of change lies in the fact that it is
worldwide. Some writers compare the present era with that of the rise of the
European state system more than three hundred years ago. From all stand-
points, we live in a world in turmoil, reshaping itself.

The magnitude of this change becomes clearer if we think back on
conditions which existed at the turn of the century. Many of these are
obvious, yet few are discussed in the daily press. Reston goes on to say: "It is
not the earthquakes but the tides of history that are bothering us. It is the
slow quieter changes of the family, the scientific laboratory, and the elec-
tronic computer that are changing the fabric of the world, and it is the
reporting of these changes that leaves so much to be desired." Yet these are
changes difficult to comprehend and unlikely to appear in headlines. Our
newspapers, as Mr. Reston has argued, tend "to transfer the reporting habits
of the police court and the county courthouse to the great capitals of the
world." They concentrate more on the violence of the world, much as they

74

focused on the violence of the police station, leaving a vast uncovered area of change.[1]

Newspapers, however, are not alone in leaving part of the story of change untold. Looking back to 1900, we note that the world then seemed more orderly, predictable, and manageable. No general war had occurred in eighty-five years. Between 1815 and 1900, the world experienced only eighteen months of warfare in which five or more major powers participated. The balance of power, the British Empire, and the system of international trade contributed to a general atmosphere of confidence. The Enlightenment had liberated human reason from the tutelage of church and state and led men to believe that evil stemmed from ignorance, superstition, and dogma and would disappear. The growth of a technically skilled citizenry held out the promise of freedom from poverty. New democratic governments promised to rid the world of tyranny and authoritarianism. Darwin's laws of evolution had prompted the conclusion that history, like nature, could rise to higher levels. Taken together these factors led to a climate of opinion in 1900 which was one of supreme optimism in an orderly world that promised to become even better and more advanced.

Yet it is sometimes forgotten, looking back on this international system of 1900, that it often provided more order than justice. The world then was primarily a white man's domain. Half the world's peoples lived in colonies and protectorates governed by Western European nations. In all of Africa, three times the size of the United States, there were two independent countries, Abyssinia and Liberia; in Asia, three. China had no effective central government, and for most of the world the melancholy wheel of fate governed life from birth to death. No one, except for a handful of anarchists or Mensheviks who wielded little influence, questioned the distinction between "the powerful rich and the powerless poor." For most of the world, ignorance, poverty, and disease were accepted as foreordained. For a majority of the people the eternal human aspirations for a better life were limited and constrained.

These circumstances were shattered by several far-reaching revolutions. The first was the revolution in education and public health. Poverty and disease were still rampant in the early 1900s even in developed countries. In the United States only one or two of every hundred households had electric power. Public health programs in rural areas were for the most part lacking. Malnutrition was often the cause of death. Dysentery and typhoid were commonplace. Smallpox was ever-present, and hookworm took an enormous toll in human life and energy, especially in the South. Malaria and venereal infections went unchecked. Of one hundred ninety thousand homes inspected in the rural South, more than half had no sanitary facilities at all, not even an outdoor privy. In 1910 Abraham Flexner's study of 155 medical schools, revealed that for a majority the faculty comprised a few practitioners, who pocketed student fees and, in the words of the study, "a few bones." Only 50 of these schools required a high-school education for admission, and 89 asked for little more than a grammar school education.

The illiteracy rate in the United States at the turn of the century was seven percent. Nine percent of the population were high school graduates. The average expenditure per pupil per year of the schools was thirty-two dollars. Teachers received the munificent salary of five hundred dollars per year. One out of twenty young people went on to colleges or professional schools. Lawyers and doctors more often than not served apprenticeships as the sole basis for professional training. State welfare budgets exceeded the federal budget; state, local, and federal welfare expenditures taken together were less than one billion dollars for seventy-six million people. Thus the government expended about thirteen dollars per capita for the human needs of the population. In 1960, health, education, and welfare on a governmental basis accounted for twenty-one billion dollars a year, or in the neighborhood of one hundred seventeen dollars per capita. In the 1960s federal research and development grants to education totaled one billion dollars, and the National Science Foundation alone awarded 4,791 fellowships.

At the turn of the century 35 percent of the United States population lived in cities, contrasted with 73.5 percent in 1970. The telephone was a simpler form of communication than crossing the village to deliver a message—but not necessarily as private. No one called coast-to-coast for a few dollars. There was no income tax, no social security, and few labor unions. There were no laws against poisonous drugs or spoiled meat.

The United States in 1900 still was a horse-and-buggy society. Trains traveled at the reckless speed of forty miles an hour. It was nearly thirty years before the radio was to become a common household possession and fifty years before television appeared. Between the American Revolution and 1900, the pace of technological change had been slow and gradual. Then, beginning with the first air flight in 1903, the time distances between nations shortened in a dramatic and significant way. In the 1950s we drew comparisons between travel time from Washington to Philadelphia in the American Revolution with the time required then to circle the globe with modern aircraft. While we were making these comparisons, Sputnik and its successors were shattering all known conceptions of time and distance. Today we have reached the moon and interplanetary exchange seems inevitable. The technological revolution has worked a profound effect on every aspect of our relationships with other parts of the world.

This becomes clear through the force of a single example. Thomas Jefferson, then Secretary of State, wrote to a friend that he had not heard from his consul in Madrid for nearly two years. If he received no message from Madrid in the coming year, Jefferson vowed he would take some kind of action. This contrasts with the schedule of the current British ambassador to the United Nations, who files his cables at the end of each day. His colleagues at the Foreign Office the next morning labor over the questions and issues that are raised and send return cables, which await the British ambassador on his arrival that same morning in New York. Technology has transformed the map of the world and the ways of men and nations.

A third great transformation lies in the military field. In the seventeenth and eighteenth centuries war was primarily the business of mercenaries. The Swiss were proud of their military men, who served successively friendly and rival sovereigns. Combatants often changed sides. Generals wrote of waging wars all their lives without giving battle. With the French Revolution, Napoleon, and World War I, warfare became a matter of total populations and total philosophies. Today it is a matter of absolute weapons. Bombs five thousand times as destructive as those which fell on Hiroshima threaten the existence of the world. Because of the threat of thermonuclear weapons, war can no longer be defined as the continuation of diplomacy by other means.

Another momentous change results from the rapid growth of population on the face of the earth. The population explosion threatens to become the most far-reaching trend among the tides of history of which Mr. Reston spoke. In 1900 life expectancy in the United States was forty-seven years. Today it is over seventy. In 1900 one out of every four or five children died at birth. Now one out of forty perishes. Industrialization and technology have created a civilization within which the death rate has fallen sharply and the consequent growth of population climbed steeply. It has taken mankind one hundred thousand years to reproduce a billion people (1850), seventy-five years for the second billion (1925), thirty-five for the third (1960), and, according to the best available projections, it will take only twenty years for the fourth (1980) and ten years for the fifth (1990). The world's population doubled from 500 B.C. to 1650 A.D., doubled again from 1650 to 1850, doubled again from 1850 to 1935, and once more from 1935 to 1970. The rate of increase is five thousand an hour, or about fifty million a year. This rapid multiplication of the human species over the face of the earth means that population is outrunning scientific and educational progress.

At the moment in which these other tides of history are manifesting themselves, the world has also experienced a revolution of rising expectations. It has witnessed a surge of claims by people all around the world for their rights to a place in the sun. Over a billion people have become independent since World War II. Practically all colonial peoples have achieved independence. This tide of history is reflected in United Nations membership, which has climbed from fifty-one to a hundred thirty-eight. At the United Nations, spokesmen of the new nations daily proclaim their hopes. Their statements reflect the general awakening that has swept across the underdeveloped world. Men no longer see poverty, ignorance, or disease as foreordained. They measure the world community against principles that once were applied largely in the developed world. The world is moving ahead on a broad front, seeking improved conditions of life and striving for equal opportunities for all.

The irony of the population explosion coinciding with the rise of national and individual self-consciousness is that the two tend to go in opposite directions. The great force of an expanding population magnifies all the ancient problems of food and public health. As population soars and expectations rise, man has at hand the technical means capable of assuring the good life. He has within reach capacities that were undreamed of in 1900. He can point to a vast improvement and broadening of education, great new storehouses of knowledge, better tools for applying it, and more profound willingness to pay the price for human advancement. Through present methods, leaving aside the question of new resources and new energy, man could produce from the earth three times as much food as he now obtains. Yet every night half of the world's people go to bed hungry and malnourished. The disparity between rich and poor nations grows apace. At the crest of man's achievement, therefore, the dread specters of pestilence and disease, famine and war, continue to threaten existence. There is a worldwide need, in short, to which the explosion of knowledge and understanding must be addressed.

The task of the next fifty years is one of extending progress to the developing countries. Some have reached or will soon reach what economists describe as "a take-off point." Others will require far longer periods for development and growth. The developed world lacks the capital to transform all the poor nations into rich ones. However, the more experienced nations, through technical assistance, can help provide resources and chart the course for partners in the underdeveloped countries. To an ever-growing extent this is the work of a substantial portion of the one million Americans now living and laboring abroad and of their counterparts from other developed nations. The newest and most meaningful frontiers may be those separated from us by water. The young men and women in the Peace Corps have helped open up these frontiers. The professional staff of public and private assistance agencies are similarly and continuously engaged.

There are no simple answers to the problems of the developing countries. In one place population growth must be slowed down before any other progress is possible. In another, there may be ways in which other forms of assistance can precede progress being made upon the population problem. Mexico is not the same as the Philippines, and neither can be equated with India. For example, from 1940 to 1950 the population increase in Mexico was thirty-one percent. In 1940 Mexico imported much of its food, at a great cost in foreign exchange. Yet through the efforts of Mexican agriculturalists and the Rockefeller Foundation this Latin American country was transformed from a food deficit to a food surplus country. The daily diet of Mexicans increased from one thousand seven hundred calories to two thousand seven hundred calories. In the process Mexico came to see its responsibilities to other countries in Latin America. Whereas it had earlier hesitated to share its technological know-how with its neighbors, it is now the home of the International Corn and Wheat Improvement Center, which played a key role in the "green revolution."

Therefore, within regions and on a worldwide scale, international cooperation in education and understanding broadens out from experience to experience and precedent to precedent. Institutions are frequently the children of necessity. New nations come to have a stake in organizations that serve their ends. The explosion of knowledge has meaning only to the extent that it is geared to living problems that concern growing societies and nations. Knowledge for knowledge's sake is a luxury which especially the developing countries cannot afford.

The explosion of knowledge in itself assures neither advancement nor retrogression in societies. The key question is its use. Purpose in a world of expanding knowledge is of central importance. Unfortunately, our culture is not distinguished for the depth of its thinking about goals and purposes. We live today in the aftermath of an era of extravagant optimism and in a period of profound disillusionment. The ideal of progress was thrown into question by two world wars and two revolts against Western civilization, national socialism and communism. We have witnessed brutality that few could have imagined possible. The optimism of the Enlightenment has been shattered, and our philosophers have been forced to reexamine the relation between knowledge and virtue. For a century and a half the status of man was linked with his conquest of nature. It was somehow forgotten that every advance in control over nature has both its creative and destructive possibilities. Not infrequently, it has been the scientific leaders among the developed nations who most threatened security and order. In Nazi Germany and Communist Russia, education did not and has not guaranteed restraint or assured political wisdom. Greater knowledge can be accompanied by the shrinking of moral imagination. Those who confidently anticipated a parliament of man following World War II have learned instead to live with the balance of terror.

What is the source of this decline in sense of purpose? What are the roots of our age of political and moral skepticism? What are the causes of the succession of conflicts which society has experienced? Partly, the failures of the past may account for the temper of our times—the failures of the Victorian Age, the "War to end war," and national self-determination. Our situation may also be linked with the growing skepticism and doubt regarding individual moral and political responsibilities heightened and confirmed by the appalling events and disclosures of the 1970s.

Beyond this, there is the element of tragic irony in history and human relations. We seem destined to do the greatest harm to those we love. This is true of loving parents and trusting children, as well as wider national communities. There is a peculiar insufficiency to human virtue. On one side, we are never as virtuous as we claim to be. The taint of self-interest colors every generous act. The parent who acts in the best interest of his child is never unmindful of his own aspirations and needs. Nations which help other nations do so both from noble intent and out of the drive of national security and national self-interest. This is why the newly independent states are often less grateful than their former masters would like them to be. On the other side, the very intensity of devotion to helping others carries moral risks. The morally self-sufficient and close-knit family can be oblivious to wider community needs. The righteous nation may be so dedicated to its own virtue that it runs roughshod over the virtue of others. The route in foreign relations from isolationism to an internationalism that amounts to inverted isolationism has about it a certain inevitability. From having nothing to do with the world, nations move to having everything to do with it—but on their own terms.

These human and moral considerations shape and limit behavior among individuals and states. The wise use of knowledge requires an awareness that they make up the context and circumstances of much of the human drama. It may be that part of the problem with statements of towering national goals is their divorce from context. This is an irony of our times, for Western civilization has as one of its most ancient virtues an awareness that conditions of society and people affect the use they make of knowledge. Social circumstances and habits either support, reinforce, or resist the good life. It is imperative that we understand this clearly and face it boldly as we proclaim noble principles for the use of knowledge.

Examples are writ large in history of the limitations circumstances place on virtue. The list is a long and significant one. Aristotle and the Bible condoned the practice of slavery. The recognition of the rights of women has come only gradually with changing customs and attitudes. The history of the realization of good purposes is the history of their coincidence with propitious circumstances, preceded by long delay in realization when circumstances were not favorable. Opposition to usury in Greek, Islamic, and Christian societies stemmed as much from the fact that they were agrarian societies and needed more trustworthy credit as that usury gave moral offense—both necessity and morality were considerations.

The coming together of two independent strains of thought and belief may produce a new set of circumstances and make possible the achievement of noble purposes. The Judeo-Christian tradition is a part of the background of American democracy. So is the liberal democratic thought. The one fostered the notion of higher law and rules of the game within which politics could go on. The other avoided making sacred every political measure that was necessary for the progress of society.

On the worldwide stage this same confluence of forces occurred and made possible the Marshall Plan. Winston Churchill described American aid to Europe following World War II as the single most generous action of statecraft in all history. However, while magnanimity played a part, it came about no less as a result of the threat of the Red Army poised on the borders of Europe. In short, American self-interest and magnanimity coincided. A more enlightened Southern attitude toward Negroes may have resulted from the work of the church, but surely no less a factor is the enlightened self-interest of businessmen who wish to maintain or increase profits. The United Nations is another stage on which the merging of virtue and self-interest occurs. It is a place where good intentions and necessity meet. It has been said that the role of the historically despised two-thirds of the world whose spokesmen are the Asian and African states is "to keep the rest of us honest."

Thus knowledge has greatest meaning when it is linked with circumstances that make possible actions that serve mankind in and out of season. It remains of course the business of education, at the same time as it participates in the extension of knowledge, to foster an awareness of purpose and the goals of a better life. The beginning of wisdom may be an awareness that men serve best when they act from a sense of cosmic humility, recognizing the limitations of good intentions. Yet those partially realized acts of goodness can help to pull us up by our bootstraps. For men and nations without a sense of purpose all too easily accept national and international structures that are, in the words of Thomas Hobbes, "solitary, poor, nasty, brutish, and short." Yet any worthy purpose has its time and season and those who have grasped what is true and right must have the patience to await the season.

NOTES

1. *News* is by definition something that is new and/or different. Thus when people complain that the news is all of disasters, crimes, and unpleasantness, and say "the world is not really like this" they are correct—and it is because the world is not all like this that such matters are reported. The risk is that those who gain their main picture of the outside world from the media and the news may conclude that the world is indeed a place of crime and disaster, that all politics is Watergate, and that deceit and cruelty are signs of the times.

5: EDUCATION FOR WHAT?

*The aim of education is not to make men clever for a
day but wise forever.*

Axiom

A great philosopher in another age proclaimed that survival was a race
between education and destruction. Yet to restate this leaves unanswered the
question "education for what?" The Germans under Hitler were a highly
cultured people yet wreaked destruction on the world; our own consciences
are uneasy after Hiroshima, Nagasaki, and Vietnam.

The question turns in part on the meaning and purposes of education.
From the standpoint of a democracy, we have linked education to the open
society and to open minds on whom it depends. The educated man, we say, is
sensitive to alternatives and aware of consequences. He is an agent of change
and an instrument of progress. This notion of education for responsibility
presupposes both process and purpose, for openness is based on some form of
commitment, whether to science, progress, or truth. We can afford to be open
because there are moorings and benchmarks. With William James we can say:
"It is not thinking with its primitive ingenuity of childhood that is most
difficult but to think with tradition, with all its acquired force. . . ."

The answer, from this viewpoint, to the timeless question, "education for
what?" has been "sufficient to the day." It has accorded more or less with
the trends of the time and the spirit of the people. Now we find ourselves in a
world rent by social and biological revolutions, sweeping alterations in interpersonal and national moods. We have less time to ponder and less willingness
to forgive or forget or to practice restraint. Life styles for many have visibly
changed, and for many more there are far-reaching questions and doubts
about who we are and where we are going. This growing movement presents
us with questions that outnumber answers. We cannot be clear which aspects
of change are transient and which will persist. Having witnessed the demise of
the nineteenth-century idea of unending progress, we may be misled if we
assume that world forces today are driving mankind, though not without risk,
toward a higher moral and political plane. Yet men live by faith.

I would answer the question, "education for what?" with four necessarily over-simple propositions. First, education, while fostering individualism and equal opportunity, must help give us a sense of identity of who we are as a people and as a part of mankind. When we were less knit together by technology and communications, we could afford to have many nations within the one, and different levels of opportunity and citizenship. Today a house divided cannot stand. If this is a counsel of perfection, it may also be a guide to survival. With all the stress on cultural pluralism and ethnic diversity, emphasis on union may seem quaintly old-fashioned, but not if we believe in the proposition *E pluribus unum.*

Achieving equal opportunity is always socially disrupting. It feeds on its inner dynamics and momentum. We jostle one another as we seek to be equal. If the pain and offense are too great, it may arise from the poverty and narrowness of our view, for "one is not rich but poor, when one can always seem so right" (Marianne Moore). This surely touches both those who provoke and those who are provoked. The stages of growth of every society include periods of deep contradictions and schisms. Every action and counter-action must be viewed in this light. The end of the story, in periods like ours, is seldom itself in the event. In such times "the deepest feeling shows itself in silence, not in silence but restraint." Miss Moore's wise words may also appear utopian but following them we might discover that whatever our differences, there were deep-running tides of unity which strident debate had but tempo-rarily obscured.

Second, there is urgent need in education to avoid the apocalyptic view. Martin Luther's affirmation still has relevance: "Even if I were told that the world was going to pieces tomorrow, I would still plant my apple tree today and pay my debts." For modern man, it may be asking too much to cling to this faith. In personal and national life, we almost daily are driven to the precipice of despair, so continuous and all-consuming are the crises we face. As with the man who is grievously ill, we cannot accept the "learn to live with" admonition. Instead of bearing our burdens, we are told there are only two choices: either the apocalypse or the new man—and with him, a new world. But the new man does not walk among us yet, nor are there any discernible comprehensive or total solutions in sight.

Third, education must help us return to the marketplace and conference table. It must help fashion capacities for public and private decision-making. The trouble with silent majorities or marching minorities is that while they are silent or marching, someone else moves in and makes the great decisions. We need to add that it is not participation as some kind of aimless and noisy activity we seek. Nor is it self-righteous factionalism seeking only to divide and destroy. It is participation at the point of leverage on policy. The guideline is still to act responsibly. With Bonhoeffer we need to say: "It is easier to act on abstract principle than from concrete responsibility." And to be concrete, we must immerse ourselves in matters however limited, where we have earned the right to be heard.

And, fourth, the greatest need of all, whatever one's temper, is for precise and definable targets to follow patiently discovered and determined routes. We must adapt and build social institutions, cope with population, produce more food, curb inflation, improve the environment, limit and circumscribe conflict—and on and on. None of these steps will bring a new world, but they may contribute. And as Jonathan Swift wrote in *Gulliver's Travels* (which often comes at our problems more directly than much of current writings), "And he gave it as his opinion that whoever could make two ears of corn, or two blades of grass, to grow upon a spot of ground where only one grew before, would deserve better of mankind, and do more essential service to his country, than the whole race of politicians put together."[1] Who has stated the moral grounds for feeding mankind or responding to basic human need better than this?

You will say I have tried to untie the Gordian knot, to link processes of continuity and change, purpose and action, and I plead guilty. But so did Alfred North Whitehead, who wrote: "It is the first step of wisdom to recognize that the major advances in civilization are processes which all but wreck ... society. ... The art of free society consists, first, in the maintenance of the symbolic code; and, secondly, in fearlessness of revision. ... Those societies which cannot combine reverence to their symbols with freedom of revision, must ultimately decay. ..."

NOTES

1. *Gulliver's Travels,* Part II, Chapter VII.

6: EDUCATION AND CHANGE

I cannot say
Of any condition of human life "This is fixed. This is
clearly good or bad."

Change is the first law of the universe. No one disputes this, at least not in the abstract. The rub comes when change confronts us in our homes, in the universities, and on the streets. Change as an idea is comprehensible; as fact and reality it shatters our picture of the world and the sense of identity we carry into the world.

Change, if it comes too abruptly, destroys personal security, social stability, and the effectiveness of institutions. Then we are in trouble—grave trouble—because, too often, change leaves us bereft of accepted values, workable policies, and accustomed life styles. The new world is not yet born. And even if it were no one can be certain that the new is the better world. This is the underlying cause of the debates and controversies that rage all around us.

Like Vietnam, the crises in education leave some among us with a deep yearning for a simpler, more peaceful day. One is reminded of Arnold Toynbee's poignant wish that "America would retreat again into the isolation from which we once were so eager to see her emerge." Some feel that way about a return to student apathy and the little red schoolhouse. Yet history makes mockery of nostalgia, and there are rewards from continuing a dialogue joined in protest and grievances that may just be sustainable in reason. Four issues, among others, deserve a place on future agendas; they include relevance, governance, new institutions, and the balancing of science and service.

First, the issue of relevance is both the most urgent and complex problem on the educational agenda. It is no longer enough to dish up a diluted version of warmed-over graduate school lectures. However, as Professor Paul Freund of the Harvard Law School has observed, if in the 1930s he had studied only what was relevant to the years of economic crisis, he would have studied the economics of depressions. Yet nothing would have been less relevant in the 1950s and 1960s. Too often relevant studies are the products of short-run assessments.

85

Yet it is also the case that our colleges and universities are the homes of our best minds. We would plead not for irrelevance but for sufficient vision to anticipate what will be relevant in intellectual endeavors. Who can say that basic science and fundamental theory are less relevant in coping with emergent problems? And who, viewing the broad sweep of intellectual history, can reject out of hand the thesis of study entitled *The Usefulness of Useless Science.*

Second, we stand at the threshold of a new era in the governance of universities. What is called for above all is an open mind. There is need for the same type of concentrated intellectual endeavor that culminated in the *Federalist Papers.* Educators and students must accept the fact that participation by all major concerned groups is a prime requirement if educational institutions are to survive. Yet participation must serve the primary functional objectives of education, however they may be reformulated in the days ahead. Hundreds, even thousands, of experiments are needed, geared to local needs; and the guiding criteria must be the unfolding of quality education sufficient to a world in change. National reviews like those of the Kerr Commission and the American Academy of Arts and Sciences are also needed.

Third, higher education is no longer the province of an elite; equal opportunity is the watchword for learning and for life. Yet social invention and innovation, which have been a national trait and unique American strength, must be called into play. If we rest on our oars and merely load on more and more novel functions to institutions created for given historic purposes, the losses will exceed the gains. A world of change demands new institutions at all levels. Innovative institution building, as emerging community colleges attest, is not beyond the wit of our best educational architects. Their mission is not that of protectors of vested interests. Their handwork must be as imaginative and enduring as their predecessors', and their task no less noble.

Finally, science and service, or learning and social need, while often in tension are not inevitably antagonistic. One need only consider the rise of our great land-grant colleges. Or one can reflect on the contribution of geneticists who set aside pure research to bring about the "green revolution" in agriculture. Those who place emphasis on service are not second-class citizens in the educational establishment. Still, universities must preserve their quest for excellence and roles as havens for free and unfettered thought.

With stringent budgets and clashing social philosophies, the pressures to narrow free discourse will be great. Yet, long ago some of our wisest political philosophers, such as John Milton, John Locke, and John Stuart Mill, prophesied that truth would emerge only in the marketplace of free ideas. If we are to gain our footing in a new world, we cannot cast aside this ancient faith.

For if our problems and perplexities are great, the resources that can be let loose by a free people may be sufficient unto the day.

THE IRRELEVANCE OF RELEVANCE AND THE
USELESSNESS OF KNOWLEDGE

It would be a shame to die without winning some
victory for humanity.

Horace Mann

We would approach the debate between those who sound the trumpet for relevance and those who raise their voices for more knowledge with greater understanding if their respective extravagances and excesses were made clear. The trouble with most arguments for relevance is that they rest on fallible human appraisals of what is relevant, which history all too often refutes. Even when the first judgment of what is important rings true, history has a way over time of outstripping our best observers. That is one reason why in free and democratic societies the people turn out their leaders whose wisdom has been sufficient to the day—but not to the days which follow. Winston Churchill was the foremost wartime leader in the West but hardly had the guns ceased their fire in Europe than "an ungrateful electorate" drove him from office. In part they did so because the Labour Party spoke more convincingly to peacetime issues and the rebuilding of the economy. But also his appeals to wartime unity within Britain and the British Empire had lost their relevance.

The call for relevant action is addressed primarily to the educational system. Yet the students for whom a more relevant education is invoked are the leaders of tomorrow, not of today. Their education, like that of tomorrow's generals, is all too often structured "for the last war." The more unqualified the emphasis on relevance, the more likely this will be the case. A student in the 1930s whose prime concern was to study the problems of economic recession would hardly have prepared himself for the urgent problems of the 1950s or '60s. The first element in a rational foreign policy of the 1950s was a credible deterrent, while in the 1970s the SALT talks have brought new means of arms reduction. The burning world issue of the 1940s was the building of an international order, while in the 1960s and 1970s it has become development and world poverty sharply accented by too little food and too many people.

The point is that the relevant all too soon becomes irrelevant and for education to place all its bets on relevance is likely to breed illusion. Yet to move to the opposite pole and erect a theory of education based on knowledge for knowledge's sake alone is no less a mistake and a delusion. Knowledge is inextricably linked up with purpose. As John U. Nef pointed out in his classic study of war and inventions, a disproportionate number of scientific breakthroughs with peacetime no less than wartime consequences have had their origins in war. Arnold J. Toynbee, in applying the concept of challenge and response to civilizations, has shown that necessity and adversity—in his terminology, "hard ground"—produced major social and political inventions. The history of science finds nature disclosing its truths to man, but only when man asks of nature the questions he wants answered.

It will not do, therefore, to see either in relevance or in the free and undifferentiated quest for knowledge the single answer to education's mission. There is value in mobilizing and redirecting educational resources to meet society's most urgent problems. When educational institutions become too isolated, self-satisfied, or self-contained, someone must reenlist them in this task. But he who does must remember that the building of educational structures involves more than the preparation of fire fighters. It involves the search for knowledge—but knowledge to some end, whether the pursuit of truth and virtue, scientific discovery, or beauty.

GOVERNANCE AND THE DILEMMAS OF CHOICE

Perfectionism is too simple for the problem of carrying each other's burdens.
                                                                    Reinhold Niebuhr

Every age and people has its social and cultural ethos or *élan vital,* its values and virtues, personal and collective devils, hallowed and haunting memories, its own peculiar vision and blind spots, and characteristic strengths and weaknesses. We are no exception. What may set us apart is our diversity: a vast sprawling continent of almost every faith and race, united in crises but divided by regional, ethnic, religious, and racial loyalties. Therefore, anything one says about culture or values is subject to refutation at some point by someone in the land. We are not one culture or society, but many. We are, in Walt Whitman's phrase, "a nation of nations."

Differences notwithstanding, there are tendencies and traits that cut across all our differences, and tides in the nation's history that carry us along. The marketplace is one part of our social ethos reflecting the value we assign to free and open discussion. No institution is more deeply rooted in the American soil, whether it takes the form of the town meeting, open hearings at school boards, public commissions, or legislative assemblies. Or in another realm, the economy operates, in theory at least, as a free marketplace.

Friends abroad who would identify policies within the American system ask "who speaks for the nation?" Sometimes they turn away in sorrow, not finding a simple answer. The workings of the marketplace mean that Americans speak not with one voice but many voices, as often strident and discordant as reasonable. The price of continuous public debate is seeming disunity, which confuses our enemies and dismays our friends but protects us from the more fateful errors that occur when only one mind is at work. If nineteenth-century Americans believed that truth, contesting with error in the marketplace, inescapably would win out, the twentieth century has taught that the latter-day marketplace serves as a safety valve against turbulent upheavals, fosters responsibility through participation, and broadens public understanding of issues.

Linked as an underlying value with the institution of the marketplace is the idea of public responsibility, writ large in such bedrock concepts as the general welfare and the common good. Rarely does one find in other cultures a more steady devotion to such broad and all-encompassing principles. Instead, in most societies, the public official owes primary allegiance to himself, his family, and his particular group. O. D. Corpuz, former Minister of Education in the government of the Philippines, writing at the time of the Garcia scandal on "The Two Faces of Philippine Morality," observed that within the Philippine hierarchy of values, attention to the needs of the extended family took precedence over the needs of the society and state. Corpuz discovered that this was true in other Asian and African cultures. Not for one moment in offering this example is there any intent to prove that corruption is uniquely the province of the developing countries or to conceal the strengths that flow from family solidarity. We merely suggest that the moral ordering of values gives ultimate legitimacy in existing value hierarchies to the family and its extensions when there is no concept of the common good.

If the concept of public responsibility has saved us from a too-narrow individualism or communalism, the ideals of individual rights enshrined in our Bill of Rights have guarded us against a mindless collectivism. It was the unexampled political wisdom of the Founding Fathers, and particularly of the authors of the *Federalist Papers,* that they saw values inescapably in tension with each other, existing in pairs: the general welfare and individual rights; the rights of states and the federal system; freedom and order; peace and justice; and the interests of the majority and of minorities. Students of politics around the world go back to these early writings and find in them enduring insights for politics everywhere. You have only to hold up to these writings, as to a mirror, present-day writings with their prevailing appeals and stress on simple, single values, whether the welfare state or local rights, peace or justice, minority rights versus the new majority, to see how far we have fallen from the more comprehensive insights of early leaders and writers. How ironic that the republic should have witnessed so rich a flowering, not in its maturing but at the outset of its history.

As Edmund Burke expressed the real issue:

> To make a government requires no great prudence. Settle the seat of power; teach obedience: and the work is done. To give freedom is still more easy. It is not necessary to guide; it only requires to let go the rein. But to form a free government; that is, to temper together those opposite elements of liberty and restraint in one consistent work, requires much thought, deep reflection, a sagacious, powerful, and combining mind.[1]

On governance we have been throughout much of American history mildly schizophrenic, wanting the fruits of governance but uneasy and perplexed by the moral burdens and ambiguities accompanying it. For governance and its distinctions between rulers and ruled collides with the *élan vital* of the frontier. The concept of levels of responsibility clashed with radical egalitarianism. The exercise of power conflicts with freedom and individualism. And whereas we are able, however deep-seated our egalitarianism. to accept excellence as the basis for status in the military, or in science, or in business, we resist it to the end as a working principle in governance. Instead, we talk in the most pejorative terms about the power elite, interlocking interests, and establishment men, forgetting that public responsibility for most is a brief and transient experience, and usually means the expending of energy, money, and personal interests.

We dress our personal devils in false garb if we see them as evil practitioners of governance or government We have had so much talk on all sides about the evils of governance, we run the risk of losing sight of its nobility. One side speaks disparagingly of government as blind paternalism while the other views government as the last refuge of the rich, the old, and the corrupt. Yet none would survive in the absence of governance.

Indeed the great danger today is not from those who hold power for a brief moment or hour and willy-nilly are destined to be overturned or replaced. It is not even from those who are corrupted by power—for who among us, looking at himself and his leaders, would not acknowledge with Lord Acton that power corrupts and absolute power corrupts absolutely. The greater danger is that we, sometimes with reason, have cast so dark a shadow over the acts of governance wherever practiced that the great majority are content to criticize, denounce, and condemn instead of testing themselves in the harsh battlefield of decision-making. With the Watergate scandal continuingly before us, this danger is greater as we approach the mid-1970s than any time in recent history.

If you believe I have overstated my case—and perhaps I have—will you ask yourself such questions as the following: What is the prestige and standing today of the college or university president? Of boards of trustees or regents? Civil servants? Cabinet members? Presidents of large corporations? If one can feel the pulse of the people through opinion polls and public expression it would seem that their prestige has never been so low. And we cannot but ask, in the aftermath of Watergate, have we reached the nadir?

If we ask the reason for this long-term decline, I at least would find it in the curious ambivalence and the sweeping and fluctuating moods of Americans toward the problem of power. For most of the past four decades, Americans have fled from the exercise of power, particularly American power in the world. You may ask how this can be when twice the United States entered world wars to preserve some measure of international order. Its entry, however, was always at the eleventh hour and both before and after the conflict Americans tried to withdraw from world affairs. Minorities in particular, with the possible exception of labor, remained on the sidelines throughout the early twentieth century. This was an era of a retreat from power because power was assumed to be evil, especially in world politics.

In the last three decades, we have witnessed an almost complete reversal of this stand. Groups everywhere, beginning with civil rights groups, have sought for themselves the benefits and trappings of power. Through protest and demonstration they have achieved leverage in the political system. Yet somehow the impression persists that, as with the nations of Africa and Asia before independence, their exercise of power is in the framework of the politics of protest, not the politics of governance. (Even within the Congress, the committee assignments sought or accepted by many minority leaders seem to reflect a desire more to display than exercise power.)

Yet governance is the process that brings to fruition the goals and objectives that protest has proclaimed. It is the testing grounds for moving ahead—by increments. John Milton, in *Areopagitica,* wrote: "Assuredly we bring not innocence into the world, we bring impurity much rather; that which purifies us is trial, and trial is by what is contrary." Somehow, many Americans have in recent years grown more enamored of proclaiming their dis-ease with things as they are than with having a healthy part in shaping a better society. It may be that we suffer more at certain points on the social and political spectrum from this disease than any other. Nihilism, criticism, and negativism are the best assurance of nongovernance in the system.

But the disease runs deeper than this. It has its roots in an American tradition of individualism, described by Quentin Anderson in *The Imperial Self,* that acting directly on others was wrong and even destructive, an invasion of the other person's right to realize his own potential. For Emerson, Whitman, and Thoreau, man's traditional roles in society or the family were clearly subordinate to the development of the self. Emerson believed it was right to provoke awareness in others but not to instruct them. Whitman explained that he tried by indirection to make us feel as he does that we possess the whole world. In Anderson's words:

> I found in all three men a striking contradiction: their passivity to experience, which was the inevitable consequence of their refusal of active roles, was complimented by an extraordinary, an almost megalomanic, assertion of their dominion over the whole of experience. I concluded that in these men the conditions of action had been fractured; that they could not see action on the everyday social scene as anything other than destructive of the potentiality of the self.[2]

It would be a corruption of great minds such as Emerson and Thoreau to speak of them in the same breath with the spokesmen for today's more fashionable social patterns that seem more likely to be remembered as aberrations than as dominant social trends. However, the same passivity to experience and rejection of active social roles as a means of self-realization is present in much of the human potential, sensitivity, and encounter group movements. Their watchword is "What have I done for myself today," not "What have I done for others, whether my family, the nation, or the world?" It could not be farther removed from the ancient maxim: "I must lose myself in order to find myself." To achieve dominion over myself, I create little islands apart and leave mankind's social and collective needs to others. Yet this is to ignore the great issue of how self-interest and group-interest relate. How different in the levels of understanding from Paul Freund's counsel: "To remain immersed is to run the risk of becoming bemused and sentimental; to remain aloof is to court the danger of obtuseness and pedantry."

In viewing the problem there is another attitude that persists at the opposite pole on society's broad spectrum. It is the notion that governance in the American style resembles the divine right of kings and that executive power lies beyond the reach of the public, free of those historic constraints that come into play whenever men act in society. To turn once again to Quentin Anderson, he speaks of an opposing literary school represented by James Fenimore Cooper, Ernest Hemingway, one strain of Norman Mailer's work, and the classic cowboy movie (it is significant that Secretary of State Kissinger was quoted shortly before his appointment as describing himself as the lonely cowboy riding into town with his six-shooter and observed that this was what Americans wanted their leaders to be). In Anderson's view this opposing approach thinks of action as self-supporting, of individual actions as creating reality, almost as if the protagonists were one-man societies who by their vitality could lift us all into a new social world.

And this literary trend is reenforced by the most powerful force in present-day society, the autonomy of science. Lord Snow has written: "The only weapon we have to oppose the bad effects of technology is technology itself;" but Stuart Hampshire in the *New York Review of Books*, challenges him in these words:

Nor is the distrust of accelerating technology always unrealistic. Certainly starvation can be mitigated and prevented only by technology. . . . But it does not follow that the application of technologies without limit ought not to be obstructed; for different technologies destroy one another each feeding on scarce skills and capital resources, and the more innocent and useful often, perhaps usually, go to the wall. . . . [Thus] faith in technology may result in ever better methods in Massachusetts General Hospital and ever greater medical poverty in outlying places which lose their few remaining doctors to centers where progress is made. Or, more frivolously, the journey from London to New York becomes shorter and shorter, and from Oxford to Cambridge longer and longer, until after a few more years of "advance," the first will be shorter than the second.[3]

Because we cannot solve our problems close at hand, we sometimes turn to those far away. Yet for problems everywhere there is need to recall Robert Kennedy's injunction the last day of his life: "We can never solve social problems, we can only work to reorder our priorities."

Governance, in short, involves the capacity of living with the dilemmas of choice. In preparing for this, young men and women receive pitifully little guidance and direction from high places. They lack in recent political texts the inspiration they could draw from earlier ones. Compare, for example, in this regard, what our Presidents have said in inaugural addresses in the past twenty years with Lincoln's Second Inaugural:

On the occasion corresponding to this four years ago, all thoughts were anxiously directed to an impending civil-war. All dreaded it—all sought to avert it. While the inaugeral [sic] address was being delivered from this place, devoted altogether to saving the Union without war, insurgent agents were in the city seeking to destroy it without war—seeking to dissol[v]e the Union, and divide effects, by negotiation. Both parties deprecated war; but one of them would make war rather than let the nation survive; and the other would accept war rather than let it perish. And the war came.

One eighth of the whole population were colored slaves, not distributed generally over the Union, but localized in the Southern part of it. These slaves constituted a peculiar and powerful interest. All knew that this interest was, somehow, the cause of the war. To strengthen, perpetuate, and extend this interest was the object for which the insurgents would rend the Union, even by war; while the government claimed no right to do more than restrict the territorial enlargement of it. Neither party expected for the war, the magnitude, or the duration, which it has already attained. Neither anticipated that the cause of the conflict might cease with, or even before, the conflict itself should cease. Each looked for an easier triumph, and a result less fundamental and astounding. Both read the same Bible, and pray to the same God; and each invokes His aid against the other. It may seem strange that any men should dare to ask a just God's assistance in wringing their bread from the sweat of other men's faces; but let us judge not that we be not judged. The prayers of both could not be answered; that of neither has been answered fully. The Almighty has His own purposes. "Woe unto the world because of offences! for it must needs be that offences come; but woe to that man by whom the offence cometh!" If we shall suppose that American Slavery is one of those offences which, in the providence of God, must needs come, but which, having continued through His appointed time, He now wills to remove, and that He gives to both North and South, this terrible war, as the woe due to those by whom the offence came, shall we discern therein any departure from those divine attributes which the believers in a Living God always ascribe to Him? Fondly do we hope—fervently do we pray—that this mighty scourge of war may speedily pass away. Yet, if God wills that it continue until all the wealth piled by the bondman's two hundred and fifty years of unrequited toil shall be sunk, and until every drop of blood drawn with the lash, shall be paid by another drawn with the sword, as was said three thousand years ago, so still it must be said "the judgments of the Lord, are true and righteous altogether."

Is there anything more to be said about governance and the dilemmas of choice? Has an approach which is faithful to reality been as clearly drawn? Has anyone held so firmly the dual forces political and moral that come into play in a conflict? Lincoln's words are a classic expression of practical morality.

ELITISM AND EQUALITY

Sir, your levelers wish to level down as far as them-
selves; but they cannot bear leveling up to themselves.
Samuel Johnson

Two concepts, both essential to education, are perennially at war with one another within every democratic institution. The one is the concept of an elite, or to use Thomas Jefferson's more felicitous phrase, an "aristocracy of talent."[4] Leadership involves the identification of talent, chosen by the people or selected by those who in some form or another are accountable, whether in the political or economic marketplace. If a society is to cope with the succession of problems with which it will inevitably be confronted, it has no alternative but to search for leaders—identify them, train them, use them. They will be the channels for information and skills for social purposes. Their strengths are likely to fall into certain broad categories such as generalists or specialists and operators or conceptualizers. The generalist sees interrelation-ships and interconnections, comprehends the whole no less than its parts, and holds to values that emphasize coherence and the wider social good. The specialist, ever more essential in a technological society, displays both the strength and limitations of his intense and narrow training. Yet both have unique capacities for leadership.

If generalists and specialists are a different breed, each with his own mission to perform, so are conceptualizers and operators. No one has written with greater insight than Robert K. Greenleaf, former industrial leader and presently educational adviser and writer, who in an unpublished paper defines the skills of the *conceptualizer* as "the ability to see the whole in the perspective of history—past and future—to state and adjust goals, to evaluate, to analyze, and to see contingencies a long way ahead. . . . Leadership, in the sense of going out ahead to show the way, is more conceptual than operating. The conceptualizer, at his best, is a persuader and a relations-builder." By contrast, the *operator* has "the ability to carry the enterprise toward its objectives . . . from day-to-day, and resolve the issues that arise as this movement takes place. This calls for interpersonal skills, sensitivity to the immediate environment, tenacity, experience, judgment, ethical soundness, and related attributes and abilities." Greenleaf sees the problems of most institutions as keeping the right blend of conceptualizers and operators. Each is generally lacking in qualities required of the other and in large institutions the operators tend to drive out the conceptualizers. The latter need to achieve a certain critical mass and to constitute themselves in some form of mutual protection society if they are to survive.

However we describe our leaders, whether as generalists or specialists, conceptualizers or operators, it is assumed they have certain talents and skills by which they differentiate themselves from others. In a word, they are not as other men. The notion of an elite clashes head on with the idea of equality, and the tension between them is not simply and easily resolved. Equality, in Western political thought, is the regulative principle of justice: it means giving each man his due. This in turn has translated itself operationally into equality of opportunity. Men are not equal but this ought not to preclude each man developing his God-given talents to the full. The doors should be open wide but the question immediately follows "what doors?" Unfortunately there is always a lag between the broadening of opportunities and the building of new institutions appropriate to individual needs. In the interim, the struggle goes on between those now qualified by law to enter the gates and those who question whether old structures can and should be transformed to meet new needs. It is sometimes forgotten that Harvard College was built in the seventeenth century to respond to certain educational and religious needs. Is it beyond the wit of man to construct new institutions more appropriate to the needs of what is potentially a new elite? Harold Howe, former U.S. Commissioner of Education, has noted that the community college is the one bold new educational invention of the twentieth century. Some would add that so are lower level leadership training programs in urban centers such as Chicago: Fifth City, the Kenwood Community Organization, and Better Boys. There must be others in other spheres if society is to adjust its institutions to train new elites and satisfy the goal of equality.

What is healthy in the debate over elitism and equality is that America has had no permanent elite. Plantation owners and Federalists, settlers and successful prospectors, robber barons and political bosses, one after the other have had their day and been supplanted. Power and wealth are transient. There is movement in and out of any given elite and today's establishment often becomes tomorrow's forgotten men. (Where, for example, are the fifty families who were said to govern New York City as recently as a quarter century ago?)

Nevertheless the controversy between "elitists" and "egalitarians" will go on. Populists of widely differing views—compare William Jennings Bryan, Theodore Roosevelt, or Robert La Follette with Congressman Patman or Governor Wallace—will rise up against the possessors of too much wealth, influence, or power. The tension in any given moment will be great and the arguments credible within themselves. It would be foolish to pretend the conflict was not present—yet out of conflict new and creative relations may emerge.

WHAT IS A UNIVERSITY?

> *The University in a developing society must put the emphasis of its work on subjects of immediate moment to the nation in which it exists, and it must be committed to the people of that nation and their humanistic goals. . . . We in poor societies can only justify expenditure on a University—of any type—if it promotes real development of our people. . . . The role of a University in a developing nation is to contribute: to give ideas, manpower, and service for the furtherance of human equality, human dignity and human development.*
>
> Julius Nyerere

We have taken it for granted that universities stand at the center of enlightenment and progress in this country, and it would be surprising if this viewpoint had not been carried over in our relations with the rest of the world. The role of universities may be understood by looking at their place in developing countries. A debate has raged between those who maintain university development is premature in the developing countries and those who give it primacy. The former argue that first priority should be given to the building of elementary and secondary schools and to the fashioning of relevant vocational programs. They would have those who would assist turn their attention from higher education to primary and secondary education, which is, they contend, the cornerstone of any emerging educational system.

For various reasons this viewpoint has not prevailed. First, universities already exist in many areas of the developing world. They are a fact—however much they may be a fledgling fact—of life. Second, some national leaders argue that, in their role as responsible political leaders, they cannot afford to turn over to outsiders responsibility for educating the very young. It will not do, they say, to acknowledge any weakness in their own ability to train and bring forward young men and women in those years where education is most formative to intellectual and moral development. The President of Tanzania, Julius Nyerere, in a conversation with the author, said, "If I leave to others the building of our elementary school system, they [my people] will abandon me as their responsible national leader." Third, universities and colleges, for better or for worse, have become a primary requirement of a new nation. In the beginning it is a matter of national pride to have an undergraduate institution just as most states insist on having their own airline. In recent years, even within such interdependent nation-states in a particular region as Kenya, Uganda, and Tanzania, national leadership has felt obliged to call for the building of indigenous professional schools in essential fields such as medicine and agriculture.

All of this means that higher education is going forward in the developing countries and that no force within or without is likely to change this fact. It is nevertheless relevant to ask with respect to these new universities, "Education for what?", "Education for whom?", "What are the priorities?" Each country must inevitably apply its own criteria, and the answers to the question, "What kind of education?", will depend on which of various possible criteria they see fit to emphasize. Some nations looking at their universities may stress the relevance of education to urgent national problems. According to this approach, new universities cannot afford to give priority to anything but immediate national needs. Based on these criteria health or food production or engineering are likely to be primary fields of interest. The training of technicians will take priority over the training of humanists. The development of paramedical personnel is considered more important than the preparation of fully-trained medical personnel.

Another criterion sometimes stressed is that of excellence. According to this view, quality should take priority over every other concern. It must be the task of institutions to train national leaders, in every field, of such quality that they may hold their own anywhere in the world. The universities must be a school for statesmen, whether in science, education, or statecraft. And they must prepare the best managers of industry, not merely a few such leaders.

A third criterion is concerned with the three levels of education which might be given the most immediate emphasis. A country can give primary stress to higher education, to elementary-secondary education, or to vocational education. It can seek to bring about job training at the most practical possible level. It can build a scheme of apprenticeships for work in the fields of immediate importance. In fact it must at some point pay attention to all sectors, but with limited resources and urgent needs it must make certain critical choices at various stages in its development. Whichever of these fields is singled out will affect the overall educational system. The choices made as to which level of education is given priority are probably the most fundamental choices of all.

A fourth criterion which influences choice arises when the question is asked, "Education for whom?" In one form or another every country is confronted with a choice between mass education and the training of an elite. False as an either/or selection may be, the educational system chosen will reflect the stress that is placed on basic literacy as opposed to leadership, on training in the basic skills as opposed to training in fundamental knowledge.

Another point at which selection and choice become pertinent is in determining the purpose of education. Is the goal some specific form of educational competence or is it wisdom and judgment? Is it specialists that are sought or generalists? Is it sending men into society well stocked with information and detailed knowledge as against providing them with the tools for deciding important questions?

Another criterion develops in response to the character of a society. It makes considerable difference whether training is designed for the public or the private sector. Where the public sector constitutes a major portion of economic and social life, education must somehow register this fact. Obviously, the choice in the end is not one or the other but some combination of both. The real issue involves how the system is ordered and how its totality shapes the particular aspects of the educational organization.

Most universities in developing countries are at best fragile and delicate emergent institutions. They have not yet been tested and tried as have developed institutions. Their success is thus not easy to measure. Almost everyone is caught in the severest kind of political and economic cross fire. Student enrollments have multiplied so dramatically that faculties which were designed for small-scale education have been thrown overnight into large-scale efforts. This trend is bound to continue. Institutions are unlikely to grow rapidly enough to fill the vacuum. It is expecting too much that universities which might have done their jobs with skill and distinction under optimum circumstances can be as effective under great financial and political pressure. University systems which attempt to maintain costly elitist patterns in time of urgent necessity may be an effective preparation for social upheaval.

Moreover, there are, inevitably, hard times ahead. The developed countries which have had a primary role in international cooperation are already reducing their commitments. Britain's overseas efforts have already been reduced. There are also signs in the shift of emphasis from international to domestic programs in the United States. What the effect will be if withdrawal and termination of international educational cooperation occur prematurely is not easy to say, but it is almost certain that there will be problems.

The future of the new universities is also bound up with their ability to look realistically at their economies. Every nation and every university must provide for itself some forms of professional training. The status of international cooperation remains too unpredictable to entrust all advanced training to others, and yet few of the fledgling nation-states have the resources to undertake advanced training in all fields. At some point they must make a choice. They must choose to do some things and leave others undone. While medicine is essential, perhaps not all its branches (such as open-heart surgery) are. If agriculture is required, veterinary science may not be essential for each independent country within a region. The balance will have to be struck between the desirable and the essential, and along the way painful choices will have to be made.

Yet these choices will inevitably reflect needs and requirements that lie at the heart of national development. It can hardly be said that the growth and development of a nation can take place in the absence of higher education. This being the case, developing universities can afford very little which smacks of luxury, while much will be exacted which involves harsh necessity. Faced with necessities, responsible leaders in difficult times have come forward with solutions. Perhaps it is not asking too much to hope that a new breed of leaders—emerging in the new countries, in part as a result of developing universities—will do the same.

NOTES

1. Edmund Burke "Reflections on the Revolution in France" (1790), *Works,* 12 vols. (Boston: Little, Brown, 1889), 3:559-60.

2. Letter to the author.

3. Stuart Hampshire, "Suspect Sages," *New York Review of Books,* September 21, 1972, p. 12.

4. Letter to John Adams, October 28, 1813.

7: THEOLOGY
AND INTERNATIONAL RELATIONS

Theology is but our ideas of truth classified and arranged.

Henry Ward Beecher

Over the years religious leaders have concerned themselves with issues related to war and peace, periodically expressing deep concern and anguish. Journals and sermons abound in testimony for or against particular policies: World War II, Suez, Vietnam. Leaders have rushed to the barricades in defense of deeply held convictions about such matters as conscientious objection, disarmament, the United Nations. These interventions have influenced the trend and character of American thought, especially among the ethically sensitive and socially conscious of each generation. From them, the young and the dedicated in every age group have drawn inspiration. Yet the combined effect of this thinking has had no more than occasional influence on policy-makers, whose work has gone forward largely divorced from the thinking of religious leaders. While religious and moral witness has touched the American conscience, it has not shaped the practice of foreign policy. Down to the present day a wide gulf separates the great bulk of religious witness from diplomatic practice.

However, a handful of theological leaders has demonstrated a sustained, informed, and generalized interest in international relations, backed by solid study of the field. The most conspicuous examples from Protestantism—and while I have drawn examples familiar to me largely from Protestant writers, I have no doubt similar if not identical trends can be found among Catholic and Jewish theologians—are found in the work and writing of Reinhold Niebuhr and John Bennett. Each lived and wrote during periods of ferment and change in religious thinking. Each had "the courage to change" perspectives and viewpoints as conditions and circumstances varied. Their work can best be understood against the background of four major stages in the development of theology and international relations, stages from which other religious traditions are not exempt but which were peculiarly a product of

100

American Protestantism. By understanding these periods, we can appreciate and understand the contributions of these men—contributions which have a continuing and generalized importance.

THE THEOLOGY OF IDEALISM

American thinking in the period between World Wars I and II was strongly isolationist. This attitude had deep roots in the unique geographical position of the United States and in the backward state of communications and transportation. We were a far-flung continental land mass capable of economic growth and political development with a minimum of "entangling alliances." We were relatively free of the commitments so familiar in Britain and Europe. On the surface it seemed that there was little need for involvement in the struggles of Europe or for preserving some measure of equilibrium in the power situation there or in Asia.

The major thrust of the theological writing in this period was outspokenly idealistic. It was marked by a self-conscious indictment of American isolationism and indifference. Journals such as *The Christian Century* and organizations such as the National Council of Churches struck out boldly against the prevailing trend of American withdrawal from the problems of the rest of the world. But even the theologians did not see as clearly as they should have that the United States had far more international involvements than most people realized.

In this period, the American people rejected membership in the League of Nations. The major architect of the League, Woodrow Wilson, had been repudiated by his own people and had given his life in an ill-fated defense of internationalism. His message fell on deaf ears and there was lacking a concert of national political movements capable of providing legislative and popular support for his "Grand Design." He himself had become, particularly in his later years, a theologian of sorts doing battle against "the forces of evil." His allies in death became more numerous than his supporters in life, particularly among religious leaders, international lawyers, and idealists in all walks of life.

Furthermore, there was a natural convergence of thought between the bold and simple tenets of Wilsonianism and the idealistic temper of theology. Both dealt in essentials. Both saw the world as it ought to be, not as it was. Both found distasteful political give-and-take; both eschewed compromise and concessions; both resisted ambiguous means. Therefore, many theologians in search of a credible international program which was not offensive to nobler ends found it in the doctrines of Woodrow Wilson. With Wilson, they affirmed that the evils and high costs of international relations would be mitigated by turning to transnational institutions.

The trouble with this approach was not its error but its insufficiency. Mankind through the ages has tirelessly searched for new machinery for improving the conduct of interstate relations. Procedures and institutions, however, are no more effective than the environment permits. They are limited by the social and political setting that determines what commitments and loyalties men will have to the goals and practices of institutions. Those who called for a new world order found it comforting to point to symptoms that would be removed, to forms that would be changed, and to legal tenets that would be altered by adoption of these plans. The underlying political and social realities, however, are the determining forces for nations as they operate within their institutional frameworks. If nations cannot afford to depart from ancient practices, no new constitutional arrangements will alter this fact. If leaders are in the habit of giving priority to their own national security, no amount of rhetoric concerning international security will change their primary need.

Another circumstance that prevented responsible political leaders from accepting the theology of idealism was the fact that this nation had already made commitments and undertaken responsibilities that were departures from isolationism. It was true that the foes of Woodrow Wilson had overturned his particular version of American participation in the world. It was not the case, however, that the United States had retreated and pulled back on every front from assuming international obligations. Indeed, our representatives were continually linking us economically, culturally, religiously, and politically with peoples in distant areas. We participated in international naval and economic conferences, in disarmament negotiations, and in commerce and trade around the world. Our action or inaction played a vital role in deterring or encouraging ambitious leaders bent on expanding their influence in Europe and in Asia. The history of the Stimson Doctrine and American vacillation on the question of our guaranteeing the security of weaker nations in Asia provides a case in point.

The effect of the United States on the rest of the world, and conversely our response to events far from our shores, can also be seen in the sources of our worst economic depression. It was brought on by economic events in Europe and in turn influenced the economies of all of Western and Central Europe and Latin America. One of the largest banks in Central Europe, the Credit Anstalt in Vienna, closed its doors in May 1931. The panic spread to Germany and the ensuing massive unemployment prepared the social and political conditions for Hitler's rule.

Thus the issue was not so much whether the United States had a moral obligation to involve itself in world affairs but what form that involvement should take and on what social and economic arrangements it should be based. A United States indifferent to the fate of countries in other parts of the world would hardly be more helpful within the League of Nations than outside. Theoretically, at least, it would have been possible for the United States to participate in world affairs wisely and consistently outside the League of Nations no less than inside it. In any case, the distinction that was drawn and disseminated by legal and spiritual idealists between a good American policy based on involvement in the new international organization and a bad one based on separating us from the League ignored two important realities. It ignored the setting of international politics in a state-centered world. At the same time it overlooked the network of commitments this nation had made, quite unnoticed, in far-flung corners of the world. In doing so, both its diagnosis of the international problem and its prescription for transcending it proved more confusing than helpful.

On one side, as practiced today and in the past, the theology of idealism asks too much of the United States. It calls on policy-makers to transform the international environment in one sweep by ridding the world of the time-honored instruments and actions that nations have always employed to safeguard their national security—military strength, alliances, and security arrangements. Idealists forget that even a bold and heedless state acting upon these premises would have limited influence on others. It might offer itself as a sacrificial example to the harsh realities of the international jungle; but nations have done this before without exerting effects on others. Before World War II Belgium and the Netherlands sought not to offend their more powerful neighbors by the display of even minor power or strength, but their weakness had little influence on the mighty juggernaut the Nazis unleashed upon all of Europe. The United States, following World War II, set an example of the wholesale dismantling of a massive military establishment, but no historian can show that this led to comparable steps by Soviet military planners. Nor did it evoke worldwide disarmament within the framework of the new United Nations. And with the mounting threat of Soviet might at the center of Europe and the subsequent conflict in Korea, the trend for the United States as well was overturned.

On the other side, the theology of idealism asks too little of nations by minimizing the importance of meeting international responsibilities and commitments around the world. It has next to nothing to say about security guarantees, particularly when they take on a less than universal character. It speaks in derogatory terms of the maintenance of a balance of power. It questions policies that involve coming to the aid of a threatened and embattled nation-state. In short, its very idealism and internationalism are profoundly isolationist where the use of the existing and limited instruments of international order are involved. It is willing to be wholeheartedly internationalist and responsible for security everywhere in the world, if and when an idealized international system comes into being; but its sense of responsibility verges on the irresponsible where peace and order depend on the existing machinery of international order.

These failures and limitations led to the call for a new theology—a theology more attuned to an age of crisis and conflict. In the wake of questioning the dominant theology, new thinkers appeared on the horizon, some of the ablest clustering around the journal *Christianity and Crisis.* Their influence redirected American approaches by theologians to war and peace. They included the principal architect in this country of the theology of responsibility, the senior editor of the journal, Reinhold Niebuhr. Among Catholics, Father John Courtney Murray came to occupy in the years which followed a position not dissimilar from Niebuhr's.

THE THEOLOGY OF RESPONSIBILITY

There is tension, if not contradiction, in the fact that theologians must stand in judgment on those who wield power without themselves being forced to carry this burden. The degree of tension is minimized on the domestic front because most of the functions within national governments involve orderly constitutional processes and rational and routinized bureaucratic procedures. Actions are carried out within a broad constitutional framework where law and justice are generally defined. On the international front, however, there is no consensus among states as to the framework within which foreign relations are conducted. Some states pursue policies aimed at maintaining the status quo. Others are dedicated to overthrowing it. Law and justice are filtered through national aims and interests that largely determine their content. Whatever the lip service states may give them, the rules of the international system are frequently in dispute since somewhere in the world there are states bent on changing them. There is division between the haves and the have-nots, oil-producing and oil-consuming nations, colonial and nationalist powers, communist and democratic states, new and old nations. Even if the circumstances were such that no important nation or group were bent on overturning a particular international order, the interpretation they give it would put them at odds with one another at certain important points.

What is the role of the responsible state or statesman, or for that matter the theologian, in this kind of international system? This question was posed in the 1930s, not in the abstract but in brutal and crushing military terms. Talk of law and justice proved impotent in deterring the sweep of the mighty armies of Adolf Hitler and his allies across the face of Europe. The League debated and passed resolutions, but in the end it was powerless and unable to halt the march of German and Italian power. Chamberlain's Britain tried appeasement, but the appetites of the aggressors were only further whetted.

Neither world public opinion, which proved to be a collection of divergent voices from the international community, nor the appeals of essentially reasonable leaders were able to deter Nazi or Fascist imperialism.

What did the theology of responsibility have to say in these circumstances? How was it to address itself to the violent and irrational impulses that generated a series of imperialist thrusts that soon left almost the whole of Europe within the grasp of a single aggressive power?

The spokesmen for a theology of responsibility were first and foremost Christian or Jewish realists. They knew that civilized nations cannot responsibly stand aside while one power, or a consortium of powers, gains hegemony over an entire continent. Men such as Reinhold Niebuhr had learned this in the crucible of local politics. They knew that justice on the local scene was a product of some form of equilibrium of power. (The Liberal party in New York had in fact grown up to balance the monopoly of power that otherwise would rest in the state Democratic party.) But these spokesmen of a new theology of responsibility were also students of history and sociology. The lessons of the past had taught them that whether the threat was Napoleonic France, monarchist Spain, or present-day Germany, the challenge of a power to control the whole of the European continent must not go unanswered. Their theology was derived in part from Augustine, who had written classically about the power dimension of moral decision, and in part from the sociology of Max Weber, who had written convincingly on the ethics of responsibility.

Responsibility in an age of crisis meant more than a retreat to institutional or legal affirmations. It required will and commitment, blood and treasure ("blood, sweat, toil, and tears" in Churchill's words). There came a time when invoking the prestige of the League was not enough; nor was talking of compromise and accommodation enough, although responsibility required that all these remedies be tried and exhausted. At some stage, tragic as it seemed, there could no longer be any alternative to meeting power with power, force with force, commitments with commitments. Once the aims and objectives of the Nazis and Fascists were seen as unlimited in character, there was need for more than words or threats if their worldwide mission was to be turned back.

For those who espoused a theology of responsibility, the judgment of their colleagues was harsh. Idealists invoked the Sermon on the Mount and the historic creed of religious and secular pacifism. Others called into play the doctrines of the world community. Not the Grand Alliance but the agencies of world law should be the deterrent. Yet none could show that turning the other cheek had protected the helpless and powerless from Hitler whether in Central Europe, in the Low Countries, or in the Scandinavian countries. An individualistic ethic that offered reasonable guidance for relating man to man was largely irrelevant where great and massive collectivities fired by national passions were involved. Nor was it reasonable to call on an international assembly whose strength had been sapped by defections and by failure to pose a responsible deterrent to aggressive powers. If the League of Nations had proven unable to protect little Ethiopia from the overextended power of Mussolini, who could expect it to resist the mighty German juggernaut?

In the end, it was clear that what counted was not so much what the League declared or resolved, but what its leading members were willing and able to do. France and England had vacillated and finally gone their separate ways in successive crises facing the League. If either or both had been prepared to resist aggression early in the crisis, the image of the allies as defenseless and unable to stem the tide might not have encouraged further adventures by aggressors in Europe. At the eleventh hour the United States had the choice of reacting in kind or of belatedly joining its allies in halting a military movement that had gained enormous momentum and power.

The theology of responsibility postulated that power in the world presupposes responsibility. The failure of will and responsibility had invited aggression. Now the task of those who had the means of restoring the peace of Europe was to join together in the defense of those whose freedom was being snuffed out. Failing that, the freedom of those who had the power (whether latent or in being) to assure national survival would in turn disappear. France and England, having slept as the threat appeared and mounted, would be overrun unless there was a revival of national responsibility against aggression.

This particular story of the defense and preservation of freedom is a closed chapter in the history of mankind. The theology of responsibility has been tested by events. While few would be bold enough to claim the relevance of this approach for all time, it proved the best guide for statesmen and ethicists of the day. It was clear that the relative security which came with the defeat of Hitler could scarcely have been gained in any other way. And those who sought to relate ethics to international politics then helped men to understand that the price of peace was the responsible use of countervailing power.

THE THEOLOGY OF PLURALISM

The global situation after World War II differed from that with which the prewar theologians of responsibility had been obliged to deal. Not two world systems—aggressors and peacemakers—but a great variety of political regimes came into being.

At first this world was viewed through the perspective of those who spoke of communist and noncommunist states. Indeed, the only states that mattered at the outset of this discussion were the two superpowers, the Soviet

Union and the United States. Each of them had in the past pursued policies which led to rivalry and conflict. They were both centers of enormous power and influence, possessed far-flung geographic empires, had governments that provided models for the rest of the world, and were the capitals of strongly held political ideologies. It was tempting to substitute the Soviet Union for Nazi Germany, and the United States for the Allied powers, and to apply tenets of the theology of responsibility in evaluating them. This way of viewing the struggle was plausible to anyone studying postwar foreign relations. The Soviet Union emerged from World War II possessing great military and political power and newly acquired prestige. Its ideology under Stalin was that of first-generation revolutionaries who looked forward to a comparatively early communization of much of the world. Whereas prior to and during World War II, Russian survival had required emphasis upon the preservation of communism in one country, following victory the Soviet Union found it reasonable to expect the stabilization of its system within and the expansion of its influence beyond its historic confines.

The Red Army was stationed in the center of Europe—on the boundaries of a divided Germany and within the territory of an expanded Soviet empire. It seemed clear that unless this expansion could be arrested, the Soviet Union would replace Hitler's Germany as the principal hegemonic power in Europe. Therefore circumstances called for the building up of "situations of strength" to replace power vacuums into which Soviet influence could flow. The basic principle underlying the Marshall Plan and the Truman Doctrine was the need for a reconstructed Europe in which free and independent nations could work out their destiny without having to be politically and economically dependent upon the Soviet Union.

All this had the ring of sound moral and political thinking. It grew out of earlier experiences with threats to peace in Europe. It reflected what sensitive students of politics and religion had learned from the study of the interwar period. Moreover, the application of a firm and responsible policy of deterrence to the spread of communism as organized and led from Moscow proved to be a largely successful policy in restoring the economy and the security of Europe.

Before much time had elapsed, however, the necessity of widening the horizons of this approach became clear. The evidence soon mounted that the Soviet Union was both more and less of a threat than Nazi Germany had been. It was more of a threat because it possessed a persuasive political ideology. It had a program that offered some kind of salvation for oppressed people. In particular, men and nations existing on the borderline between starvation and survival found it an appealing doctrine. Soviet communism was less of a threat in the military field. Whereas Nazi Germany pursued a military strategy from beginning to end, the Soviet Union, perhaps because it foresaw the eventual triumph of communism, was more apt to be patient and use nonmilitary techniques, holding in reserve its massive military establishment. Thus the risk of outright global conflict was a serious but not an immediate threat. Responses on the part of other nations required strategies more complex and varied. These included economic and social programs as well as military preparation. At the same time, Soviet imperialism remained a threat because the USSR since 1945 has occupied the heart of Europe (expansionism has been part of the Russian heritage since the sixteenth century), Stalinism pursued a hard line in Iran and Central Europe, war by proxy has characterized Soviet policy in Korea, Vietnam and the Mideast, and the last few years have witnessed an unprecedented increase in the absolute and relative strength of the Soviet army and navy.

In addition to communism, a richly varied pattern of nation-state development grew up elsewhere in the world. The new states of Africa and Asia, whatever their constitutional arrangements, bore little resemblance to the older states of Europe and America. New concepts such as "guided democracy" and "one-party democracy" came into everyday political parlance. A blending of various liberal and collectivist methods and techniques was developed in these new states. A country like Tanzania drew economically, politically, and educationally on approaches and people from Western Europe, Britain, the United States, and the Communist world. It was not surprising to find in developing universities two or three acting heads of departments recruited from Poland working alongside other heads of departments who came from the United States or Canada.

In other words, it was difficult to use traditional Western political or ideological terms in talking about the characteristics of these new regimes or their objectives and intentions. What was common and self-evident in their development was the immense variety they reflected. To build an international order it was no longer enough to resist the expansion of one or two nations or to keep the spirit of one or more ideologies within bounds. The real issue became one of assisting the orderly and peaceful development of new societies along some kind of internationally acceptable course, of minimizing poverty and illiteracy and of encouraging opportunity for education, of giving assistance to those who sought constructive national development, and of keeping in check a growing sense of alienation and despair that could only breed extremism and military adventurism.

A plural world required plural approaches to peace and order. It was no longer enough to talk of resistance to this or that imperialist force. There was need for human and material resources, new and innovative technologies, wiser allocation of limited resources, extension of cooperation within regions (including regional trade), and the growth of a sense of responsibility by those most directly concerned.

This kind of world required that something be added to the doctrine of responsibility, resulting in a theology of pluralism. A more complex set of concepts was needed; a greater appreciation of variety was called for. Theologians such as John Bennett and those whom he encouraged in the journal *Christianity and Crisis* gave increasing stress to these considerations. They were outspokenly critical of statesmen who failed to recognize the diversity and pluralism of world society. They denounced those who spoke as though all Communist states were the same. They were no less impatient when leaders acted in recognition of a pluralistic world but did not account for their actions by setting forth new doctrines that reflected the facts. In this the theologians performed their historic, prophetic function of challenging men to reach out for new principles that were ignored or unarticulated in practical politics or diplomatic encounters. (Perhaps if the theologians had experienced more of the anguish of having to interpret their actions to not one but many publics and being held accountable for them they would have been more forgiving.) In any event, a new world had come into being, and the theology of pluralism sought to grant it legitimacy for citizens and leaders alike.

THE THEOLOGY OF CHANGE

The several trends that are reflected in earlier stages of evolving theological approaches have come to a head in the recent expression of a theology of change. Beginning in 1946, the world experienced profound change. Upwards of a billion people found that political realities and the legitimacy myths under which they had lived had been changed. New nations came into being; old empires came crashing down. (It is worth noting that the pragmatic and liberal British Empire accepted change and gave independence to its colonies voluntarily. The Soviet empire, a product of World War II, has felt the winds of change within its satellites but has not chosen to loosen the bonds and grant them autonomy.)

Other profound and far-reaching changes were at work. The maxim that war is an instrument of national policy, or that war, in Clausewitz's terms, is a continuation of diplomacy by other means, came into question. The incredible destructiveness of thermonuclear weapons guaranteed that victor and defeated nation alike would both be victims. The equation of rational warfare was upset if not overthrown.

At the same time other forces were at work transforming modern thought. Young people who had witnessed the legislation of moral purposes in the civil rights crusade called for a similar attack on the problem of war and conflict, but justified this as a means of overthrowing a corrupt society. Much as the pressures before World War II had mounted for eliminating war, so in more rational and persuasive terms young minds called for the elimination of war in the late 1960s. As they saw it, war was the servant of unjust causes: witness Vietnam. War was a product of the military-industrial establishment: note the gains that privileged groups enjoyed. War was a diversion from civil pursuits: witness the neglect of the problems of the cities. Whereas young men in the 1930s had called for the outlawing of war, they asked in the 1960s that man put an embargo or boycott on it. The use of demonstrations and mass appeals came to be the basis for influencing the course of history. These movements for change were not the product of a few young people in one country. They were the expression of a worldwide phenomenon having deep roots in the rebellion of youth against the wrongdoings of society.

The theology of change called for a spirit of impatience with both past and present. It needed its scapegoats and found them in leading decision makers. It ignored writers who were less prepared to see the world as wholly new and transformed. It required slogans reminiscent of those after World War II which saw war as the product of a handful of munitions makers.

But the movement went farther and struck deeper roots. It was geared to a growing awareness that thermonuclear war would be an act of madness. It generated support from young people who wanted to get on with the business of improving society. It came at a time when the worldwide trend of abandoning all ideologies for a more pragmatic approach to our problems was being challenged. The benefits of pragmatism and realism lie in their under-standing that problems can be tackled on their merits; their liabilities are that they offer little inspiration or uplift, for their approach calls for patience, routine, and trial and error in confronting each successive problem.

Of even greater moment, a vacuum had grown up in the realm of ideals. For a time young people found a way of filling it with commitments to civil rights causes. As time went on, however, there was need for something more. They searched for a more generalized theory. Someone had to be held accountable for the gap between the ideals men proposed and their failure to realize them. This was possible in our society because never before had there been such freedom of expression, never such affluence and abundance for those who labor, including those who read and write, never such concern among conservatives and liberals alike for helping the downtrodden and the oppressed. In order to go beyond the pragmatic efforts that were thus made possible by the world of change, young people and the new theology felt compelled to judge reform by more absolute goals. There was, in fact, a return to moral absolutism of the kind Reinhold Niebuhr had challenged over a lifetime of thinking and writing.

The theology of change tends to be a one-directional approach. It looks forward from things as they are to the ideal of what things ought to be. It has little taste for measuring backward to things as they used to be. In short, it has little sense of history. Nor is it willing to measure its assumptions laterally against the conditions of other societies elsewhere on this earth. By and large, theologians of change know less about history and the rest of the world than might be expected. Therefore, while their thought is attuned to the time and to the forces of change, it fails to provide the internal standard against which to judge its own doctrines.

In this context the philosophy that can boast the strongest sense of history and the wisest perspective of change is still the theology of responsibility. Perhaps the challenge for tomorrow is to find ways of marrying the wisdom of this approach with the vitality of the theology of change. There is wisdom and relevance in each emerging theology. It would be misleading to say that one theology is universal and the others geared solely to the era in which they have prevailed. Yet each partakes of qualities that belong to a particular moment in history and a given complex of problems. Each is a response to a set of issues. Each is intended to give meaning to a complicated and baffling set of facts with which men have been obliged to come to terms.

THE CALL FOR A NEW SYNTHESIS

Theologians of the future, therefore, will face the challenge of sorting out and defining the points at which earlier theologies have relevance. They cannot long escape the need to relate and reintegrate historic approaches. It should be within the reach of our ablest and boldest minds to lay down certain guidelines or working hypotheses concerning the timelessness of these great historic adventures in thought. This task is the unfinished business of the theology of international relations. It constitutes the agenda of the future.

A few concepts and proposals for the future may be worthy of enumeration in the form more of questions than of conclusions. First the shape of the future will be a design for change. We face vast and far-reaching transformations in the numbers and makeup of the world's population, the circumstances under which men live, the pressures for survival and a better life, the relationships between rich and poor, young and old, the privileged and the oppressed. How will theology deal with these changes? What will it have to say about life in the twenty-first century? How can it avoid, on the one hand, automatically sanctifying forces and peoples who represent the pell-mell rush toward change or, on the other hand, dignifying time-encrusted factors from the past? Where should it direct the main thrust of its judgments? How can it avoid both neutrality and self-righteousness respecting the good and evil embedded in both the new and the old? Where is the balancing force that will prevent beneficiaries of change from becoming its high priests? Who will speak against praise of novelty for novelty's sake? And with the explosions of knowledge that have both great civilizing and great destructive potential, who will turn revolutionary movements from destructive drives to civilizing effects while preserving the dynamism of change? And through it all, who can speak both to and for the poor, the young, and the alienated and in doing so maintain the dialogue for peace?

Second, where are the moral and intellectual resources that prepare men for living in a pluralistic world? How can one find the route to and basis for peace and understanding when the differences between societies loom larger than their commonalty? How can points of community be found between societies that live on their differences, whose polities depend for their strength and survival on accentuating what distinguishes them from the others? We need to remind ourselves that the fuel of nationalism is the self-consciousness that societies are different, that tutelage is contrary to human nature, and that social cohesiveness requires an external threat. Totalitarian leaders justify elaborate superstructures of power by the claim that outsiders are plotting their destruction. And finally, how can we reconcile respect for differences without obscuring the fact that within all systems of government there are better and worse regimes? In short, does pluralism indicate that man's quest for the good society and the best political regime is a mere illusion?

Third, is it possible that responsibility is a concept of a different, more universal quality than either pluralism or change? Must not responsibility, with its emphasis on the wise and prudent exercise of authority and the clear recognition of the limitations of institutions and men, be written somehow into every political doctrine and every theology of international relations? I believe profoundly that this is the case, and no amount of rhetoric about new problems and more contemporary approaches can change its enduring fact. The older theologians seem to perceive this more clearly than some of their younger followers who, caught up in the challenge of a new theology, may not yet understand it fully.

Finally, must not idealism continue to be the broad and overreaching framework that inspires each emergent theology? Is it not the "higher thought" that can lead men to the stars? Is it not the ultimate task of theology to blend idealism and responsibility, to glorify and humble mankind, and to channel and examine human aspirations? Must not idealism be the molder of the dreams of all men, whatever the limits of human achievement?

There is need then for the old and the new, the inspirational and the practical, and the creeds that are relevant for the present and for all time. Theology, which has addressed itself to the stark issues of international relations, must learn from the Reinhold Niebuhrs of our time who have had the courage to take hold of many strains of thought in order to meet many versions of one problem: What is the nature of man, and how can he live with his neighbor, whatever the context of the challenges that confront him?

8: IDEOLOGY
AND CHANGING PICTURES OF THE WORLD

The idol is the measure of the worshipper.
James Russell Lowell

OLD AND NEW IDEOLOGIES

Ideology is a philosophical concept, recurring throughout the history of contemporary political thought, which communicates itself to philosophers, statesmen, and citizens, albeit at different levels of inquiry and purpose. For the philosopher, ideologies are systems of political action and theory inviting rigorous study and comparison. For the statesman, an ideology is customarily the context within which he communicates and works. Ideological aspects of policy are among the tools of the trade. For the citizen, ideology is a source both of clarification and confusion. It helps him to locate himself in the world and to generate and focus his loyalties. It affords vicarious satisfaction that escapes him in his personal life. At the same time, as he brings to the surface the reality and functioning of the ideological process, he suffers confusion and disillusionment. There is something about ideological warfare that offends his respect for the rights of the individual. The use of ideologies to make the worst appear the better cause or as a rationalization and justification for actions otherwise motivated may be inevitable in politics but repugnant to the simple but honest citizen. In his lexicon, ideology is a concept to be used in describing the nefarious practices of others, less often as a rallying cry for his own political faith.

To compound the confusion, we are told by the extraordinarily able sociologist Daniel Bell that we are witnessing "the end of ideology" in the present era. More and more decisions are being made in pragmatic and practical terms. Will a policy serve a nation's interests, promote "socialism" in one country, lead to "more goulash," increase production, raise incomes, or improve the prospects of a political leader or his party? The man in the street has grown skeptical about high-sounding proclamations and asks instead of a policy or action "what will it do for me—today."

It is also true that the waning of ideologies is related to particular examples deriving from particular historical circumstances that no longer obtain. Liberal democratic dogmas of the eighteenth and nineteenth centuries corresponded to the political interests of a rising middle class. The ideology of free trade was linked with the goals of mercantile and trading groups. The circumstances which produced the ideas and energy that fired these powerful political and international movements have changed. It would be surprising then if the ideologies themselves had not lost much of their intellectual and political power. The Colombian political philosopher Mario Lasserna has suggested that the present moment in history is one in which old ideologies are dead and new ideologies have not been born. He looks forward to the birth of new and more relevant systems of thought that take account, for example, of the need for practical solutions by technocrats and specialists to the problems that confront every society. Communistic and democratic societies share common problems and seek comparable answers for agriculture, industrial production, price policy, inflation, and unemployment. Problem-solving more than class interests provides the basis for new and realistic ideologies.

It is important to observe, nonetheless, that ideologies are essentially the work of the "great simplifiers." They rarely if ever comprehend the full scope of a society's problems. One is reminded of the characterization of political platforms in the American political process. Platforms are similar to the portable railroad platforms used in boarding passengers—"something to get in on which is pulled in by the passenger after he boards the train." There are complexities and problems involving hard choices that go on within every political order. An overarching ideology can provide a broad framework for considering these problems without facilitating any of the working guidelines necessary for the political or economic process. It may be requiring of an ideology what it can never perform to expect it to function in this way.

Nevertheless, the question must still be asked whether present ideologies are obsolete and outmoded. Are they anachronistic models for present-day societies born and matured in another age? If so, the question poses itself "What can be put in their place?" And to what extent, when men talk of exporting revolution or democracy, are nations engaged in a futile and hopeless endeavor? In what ways are the problems of ideology within separate nation-states transferred to the international arena, to major problems such as war and peace?

RHETORIC AND REALITY

Rhetoric . . . is like the flowers in corn; pleasing . . .
for amusement, but prejudicial to him who would
reap profit from it.

Jonathan Swift

The American scene in the 1960s was a study in conflicting ideologies. Some called for sweeping changes and others for maintaining the status quo. The word revolution was on many tongues: the black revolution, youth revolution, women's liberation, and the white ethnic revolution. Taken together, the calls for revolution suggest that society is in dire straits, urgent problems are being ignored, and the political and constitutional system is breaking down.

No one can question the severity of the crisis or the grave threats hanging over the future of the land. Too many problems have too long been tabled and set aside. Too many groups have a hundred-year legacy or more of suffering and broken promises.

Yet this being true, it is helpful to distinguish between rhetoric and reality on the American scene. In the 1960s, the woods were full of rhetoric— rhetoric intended to put to rest problems and abuses, evil and injustice. Depending on one's choice of rhetorician, we were told that policies need supplanting, the nation was lacking in leaders, and the social and political system was beyond redemption. The sheer weight of our problems and their resistance to solution seemingly confirmed the prognosis. In every sector, we lack the resources—human, material, and moral—to deal decisively with the great issues.

In this context, clear and unambiguous philosophies and proposals fell on willing ears, partly because the best efforts of pragmatists and those schooled in ambiguity had not done away with problems. We have listened to a steady drumbeat of popular thinking. We were told that efforts to improve the political system have not changed the world; therefore, let us do away with the system. Similarly, the democratic process has failed to produce unrivalled leaders; let us be done with democracy. Dissent breeds violence and division; are we not justified then in throwing up barriers to freedom of speech and press?

In a confusing and turbulent era, it is important to remember the inevitable gap between rhetoric and reality. There is always a distance between what men say and do in political matters. It is tempting to explain this by saying that politicians deceive us and cloak their partial truths in absolute moralistic terms. They deal in ideologies and strategies through which the lesser is made to appear the greater good.

Yet politicians have no monopoly on rhetoric; it is the common possession of all who seek to order and dramatize complex events. Yet bold formulations in words are often far removed from actions. The closer rhetoric moves toward the concrete, the less absolute is the moralism it can sustain. When rhetoric is forced to cope with reality, it must come to terms with conflicting values, ambiguities, and the balancing out of political judgments.

One example is the regnant populism inherent in much of student protest and in New Left doctrines. It holds out against large-scale collective action legitimized and mandated by the state; it protests against bigness, ironically, at a time when the left seeks diligently to enlarge its effective constituency. More importantly, the problems that appear at the top of the left's agenda are national and worldwide. Poverty, racial balance, and environmental destruction are problems that call for concerted action by the entire social system. As large issues, they require large responses.

Thus those concerned with poverty or racial injustice must contain and keep in check those populist views that express suspicions of every large-scale social action. In the same way, concerned individuals who seek to preserve the quality of the environment must recognize that larger efforts are needed than the handiwork of a dedicated few returning to nature. Only a nation-wide mobilization of government, industry, researchers, and the public will meet the challenge.

Yet these expressions of political rhetoric were less ominous, self-serving, and far-reaching in the threat they posed of confusion and misapprehension than those of the 1970s. As the United States moved into the seventies, an administration consolidated its power and enlarged its mandate by reciting a litany of moralism and pieties apparently drawn from the reservoir of American idealism. It spoke of constitutionalism, law, and order. It appealed to a people weary of sacrifice and too-rapid change. It threw a blanket of suspicion and doubt over anyone who questioned its policies. It enlisted religious and moral spokesmen such as Billy Graham who, whatever their commitments and motives, became "house theologians," rather than keeping the line taut between politics and morals. Although the policies it pursued were unqualifiedly pragmatic—for example, in espousing Keynesian economics and opening up channels of diplomatic and cultural relations with China—it posed as the defender of high principle and of the status quo. If ever a country has had its pendular reaction to the turbulence of the previous decade, the United States came to know it in the Nixon administration as one excess was followed by another.

From the standpoint of the rhetoric to which Americans were exposed and the reality of actions pursued, the practices and ethos of the White House were at least as widely separated as in any comparable period in history. At the same time as its leaders spoke of law and order, it sought to overturn the normal processes of constitutional government and politics by burglaries and deception. It rejected the most time-honored principle of American democracy that the channels of political competition must be free and open to assure the test of the marketplace wherein today's minority can fairly compete in the hope of becoming tomorrow's majority. It violated the most sacred principle of American government by which constitutionally appointed officials are answerable to representatives of the people by setting up a wide-ranging "dual system" of extraconstitutional government removed from congressional scrutiny. And it did all this in the name of constitutional government. It claimed executive privilege for all civil servants without distinguishing whether their actions were criminal or integral to the functions of government.

Thus from the right and the left, from protesters and their government, the mass of hard-working and heretofore trusting citizens have been subjected to political rhetoric which has had the effect of deceiving and confounding their judgment. The new ideologies—in contrast with such historic ones as liberalism and conservatism—have widened the gap between political proclamations and practice to the point that democracy itself is strained and threatened. Far from helping the citizen to understand, they have bred distrust and disillusionment. For the first time in recent times, the doubts and suspicion citizens characteristically have for local officials have spread to the federal level. We are in dire need of a renewed study of the limits and roles of rhetoric and ideology if the ideas of a "virtuous republic" is to survive.

Confusion results when the roles of rhetoric and policy-making are too readily interchanged. Each has its proper sphere, its function, and limitations. Rhetoric can point the way to the stars and set goals and ends worthy of man's noblest efforts. By comparison, confronting reality means bringing goals and values into the marketplace; it means putting them alongside ends and purposes that may compete. Yet the two must never be wholly divorced if either is to retain its credibility. For almost every man who seeks to legislate rhetoric into policy, it means living in a world of compromise and contradiction. For some this is excruciatingly painful; for most it involves living in two worlds; for all it involves a perception that rhetoric and reality, while interconnected, are also separate and distinctive. Above all, living with rhetoric and reality calls for understanding and integrity, knowing and acknowledging the realm of discourse in which one is engaged, and confessing—with statesmen such as Lincoln and Churchill—that in this ambiguous order, one can only strive to do one's best.

THEORY AND PRACTICE:
LIBERALISM AND CONSERVATISM

What is conservatism? Is it not adherence to the old and tried, against the new and untried?
                                        Abraham Lincoln

Reformists and Realists

One of the failures of the intellectual community after World War I was its reluctance to deal with politics in a world system neither ordered nor controlled by an all-powerful central authority. It chose to abjure the rigors of power politics—a luxury in which practitioners can rarely indulge—which it considered a passing phase of an international society that was about to disappear with the birth of a brave new world. According to this point of view, the end of power politics was to be brought about in three ways. Ultimately, power politics would be eliminated through instituting a world government. Practically, power politics would be abolished when its main practitioners, the totalitarian states, had been erased. Provisionally, this evil system would be progressively and decisively undermined through the example of a moral and upright nation forswearing relations with corrupted and power-seeking nations, pursuing policies of neutrality, and abstaining from the morally ambiguous exercise of influence or coercion in world politics.

The irony of this period in American foreign relations stems from the fateful influence that such a philosophy exerted on the conduct of foreign policy. If one reads the personal papers and memoirs of men like President Franklin D. Roosevelt, Sumner Welles, or Joseph Grew, their profound embarrassment over the implications of this creed is plainly apparent. However, the gap between their thinking and that of the intellectuals who fathered such views tended to be swallowed up in the spirit of the times.

It is not by accident that, until the past decade, the United States has vacillated in its policies among three courses of action. Before both World Wars, Americans tried to abstain or withdraw from the impure and corrupted politics of the European continent. We refused to give guarantees against German expansionism, especially to France, partly because to have done so would reduce the force of our moral example. Similarly, an intervention in the affairs of Europe in order to bolster and strengthen democratic forces in the Weimar Republic might have weakened our moral position. But neutrality and abstention from the unhappy rivalries of the world lost any justification when Germany threatened American security and Japan attacked us at Pearl Harbor. We turned then from neutrality to a holy crusade against the evil incarnate in fascism. We engaged in the world struggle not selfishly or for political advantage but in order that conflict might cease once and for all and the evil men who had been responsible might be destroyed. These wars were not ordinary struggles for territorial adjustments or specified political objectives. World War I was the "war to end war" and "make the world safe for democracy." World War II was a holy war of "unconditional surrender" against infidels and troublemakers who had caused the catastrophes and with whose demise rivalry and aggrandizement would cease.

After World War II, it was essential that what had been undertaken and achieved in two wars be sealed and perfected in peace. Secretary of State Hull and others proclaimed that in the new commonwealth of the United Nations the problem of power could disappear. What this meant in concrete terms was that the status quo—with its prevailing lawfulness based on the relative satisfaction of the victorious powers—must be made permanent through the regularized procedures of new international organizations. Thus, through the policies of neutrality, holy war, and the substitution of organization for world politics, the philosophy of the interwar period made itself felt. By World War II, the barrenness of this theory made it imperative that there be a point of view that would explain the war and the preconditions of peace to Americans as Winston Churchill and particular British intellectuals had done for their people.

This was the legacy that the political realists were called upon to provide. For this group, beginning with Niebuhr, rivalry and some form of strife among nation-states came to be viewed as the rule and not a mere accident of the past. There are harmonies and disharmonies among states, but the failure of every scheme for world peace in the past must be sought in the stubborn conditions out of which disharmonies emerged and not in deviation from a blueprint of a commonwealth of perfect harmony. In all social groups, whether the state or smaller, more intimate communities, a contest for influence and power goes on. On the international scene, rivalries among states remain largely uncontrolled by effective law or government. The task of statesmanship and diplomacy under these conditions is to limit the struggles and restrict their scope. The means available are a mixture of military power and diplomacy employed in the unceasing pursuit of new balances of power and rough equilibria among contending parties. The aims include adjustment and accommodation on the basis of mutual recognition that an equilibrium does not exist. The realist strives to mitigate the rivalries among nations through checks and balances and by compromise and bargaining. Abstract moral principles may be the ultimate object and purpose of the bargain or agreement, but an abstract principle is not an essential part of the bargain itself. In President Wilson's words, "There is indeed an element of morality in the very fact of compromise in social undertakings." Realism would prepare men for the tragic and stubborn discrepancy of means and ends in international politics. It accepts as the guide and premise of its thought the permanence and ubiquity of the struggle for power. But it strives unceasingly, through every means at its disposal, to contain and limit concentrations of power and to compose and relieve tensions which could lead to war.

Liberalism and Conservatism

The political and philosophical molds in which popular approaches to domestic and international politics are cast in most Western countries are neither reform nor realism but liberalism and conservatism. One reason for this is doubtless the instrumental and procedural nature of the former. Realism or reform give appraisals of the nature and dynamics of the political process, its requirements, limits, and laws. Liberalism and conservatism, by contrast, partake of the character of political ideologies. Quite commonly they provide moral justification for the claims of interest groups; they may also in more general terms constitute a philosophy. In Acton's phrase, "Liberalism is not only a principle of government but a philosophy of history."

One of the difficulties with liberalism and conservatism issues from their alternating meaning as philosophy, political ideology, or public mood. In addition, they plainly lack fixed meanings; consider, for example, that liberalism has meant at various stages Manchester laissez-faire, moderate state-interventionism to safeguard liberty and equality (e.g., the liberalism of the New Deal), and utopianism in world affairs. Nevertheless, public policy, including foreign policy, has been influenced by these living political doctrines, and, while recognizing with Erasmus that every definition is dangerous, we may usefully explore their place in Western civilization. Their political currency from the founding fathers to the incumbent President suggests they are perhaps the prevailing Western political creeds. If this be true, a discussion of America's foreign relations should give heed to the meaning of these philosophies.

Liberalism and conservatism, as they have been used in political debate, appear at first glance to be simple and straightforward terms. "What is conservatism?" Abraham Lincoln asked. "Is it not adherence to the old and tried, against the new and untried?" Others tell us that conservatism seeks to defend the status quo while liberalism aspires to leave it behind. Conservatism finds its treasures in tradition, custom, prejudice, and prescription. According to Chesterfield, "the bulk of mankind have neither leisure nor knowledge sufficient to reason right; why should they be taught to reason at all? Will not honest instinct prompt, and wholesome prejudices guide them, much better than half reasoning?"

The English constitution is, to the conservative, the arch-example of custom and prescription, for "its sole authority is that it has existed time out of mind." Conservatism, with its abiding veneration of the past, need not be aligned irrevocably against change as such, although this is its besetting danger. In Denis Healey's apt phrase: "The Conservatives have a congenial grasp of the rules of thumb for protecting British interests as defined in the Victorian heyday. But they are slow to recognize changes in those interests and even slower to understand changes in the world within which their rules of thumb must be applied."[1]

Conservatives oppose too-rapid social change because of its consequences. Burke essayed to distinguish profound and natural alterations and the radical infatuations of the day. He preferred a gradual course in order to prevent unfixing old interests at once: a thing which is apt to breed a black and sullen discontent in those who are at once dispossessed of all their influence and consideration [and at the same time] . . . prevent man, long under depression, from being intoxicated with a large draught of new power. . .[2]

Insights such as these into issues of interest and power have given conservatism an historic relevance sufficient to evoke Harold Laski's remark: "Burke has endured as the permanent manual of political wisdom without which statesmen are as sailors on an uncharted sea."

Nevertheless, this wisdom has been judged and found wanting in the face of rapidly changing conditions in industrial societies. For conservative movements, the exercise of power easily becomes an end in itself and an exclusive aim of political activity. In Karl Mannheim's words: "The Conservative type of knowledge originally is the sort of knowledge giving practical control. It consists of habitual orientations toward those factors which are imminent in the present situation."[3] Thus it makes obsolescent administrative techniques serve as a substitute for policy in a world that is ever changing. The demands of a technical society for new institutions, status and power for rising social groups, and far-reaching national programs have brought the more inflexible conservative points of view under question. In modern societies, liberalism, being less disposed to defend uncritically every status quo, has enjoyed certain a priori advantages. Moreover, liberalism in its various stages has been linked with industrialization and with democracy. Initially, it rallied its followers, especially in Britain and France, to the goal of overturning feudal aristocratic authority, including the authority of the mercantilist state. As the political ideology of a rising middle class, it sought

to free the individual from the traditional restraints of an organic society, to endow the governed with the power of the franchise, to establish the principle of the "consent of the governed" as the basis of political society; to challenge all hereditary privileges and traditional restraints upon human initiative, particularly in the economic sphere, and to create the mobility and flexibility which are the virtues and achievements of every "liberal society" as distinguished from feudal ones.[4]

In the same way, however, that conservatism ran afoul of the bewildering pace of events that transformed a feudal order into sprawling industrial societies, liberalism became the victim of its own origins. On the one hand, in the late Richard Crossman's words, both liberalism and socialism

tend to imagine that changes are morally or practically desirable simply because they are changes. Man reared in the doctrine of automatic progress cannot help feeling that everything that will be will be right. But most historical changes are morally neutral. It is difficult to maintain that the brotherhood of men is better realized in Eastern Europe than it was under the Austro-Hungarian Empire.[5]

On the other hand, liberalism was identified too narrowly with the claims and interests of the middle class, first as a fighting creed but subsequently as the justification of a new status quo that was threatened by too much government interference.

Liberalism, in its historical development, takes on a dual meaning. In its genesis as a defense of individual freedom, it was freedom interpreted in behalf of industrial and commercial groups. Consequently, in our own day, the original libertarian point of view has become the main bulwark for conserving the power of large enterprises and corporate groups. On the other side, the middle classes, having espoused liberalism's creed that justice depends upon freedom from outside restraint, have witnessed its application by others. As liberalism in the beginning served to justify protests by entrepreneurs against the restraints of government, newly emergent classes (labor, for example) seeking security and freedom themselves have called upon the state to redress the balance of power. The source and origin of restraints upon freedom for one segment of American life is powerful free enterprise, while for the other it continues to be the state. Thus, liberalism, having had its birth in the demands of society for freedom from restraint by the state, now in another version finds part of society calling on the state to become the protector of liberty, equality, and security against the overwhelming power of large industrial groups.

We should not be surprised that terms like liberalism take on different meanings if we recall Justice Holmes' well-known phrase: "A word is not a crystal, transparent and unchanged; it is the skin of a living thought and may vary greatly in color and content according to the circumstances and time in which it is used." The semantic problems of liberalism—arising from its dual meaning and its use simultaneously to justify the free play of the market in an uncontrolled economy and the centralization of power in the state as a means of arresting the concentration of power in the hands of a too-powerful industrial class—are not its most serious difficulty. Liberalism is steeped in the principles of the Enlightenment and in faith in man's essential goodness and his capacity to subdue nature. The articles of faith of the Enlightenment creed include the beliefs that civilization is becoming more rational and moral, that injustice is caused by ignorance and will yield to education and greater intelligence, that war is stupid and can be overcome through reason, that appeals to brotherhood are bound to be effective in the end, and that conflict is simply a matter of misunderstanding. Liberalism as a philosophy of life accepted the Enlightenment view of human progress and perfectibility. Democracy was a simple rational possibility. In Lord Bryce's words in the preface to Ostrogorski's *Democracy and the Organization of Political Parties* (1902):

In the ideal democracy every citizen is intelligent, patriotic, disinterested. His sole wish is to discover the right side in each contested issue, and to fix upon the best man among competing candidates. His common sense, aided by a knowledge of the constitution of his country, enables him to judge wisely between arguments submitted to him, while his own zeal is sufficient to carry him to the polling-booth.

One wonders why such a gross contrivance as a polling booth is necessary at all in the face of such an abundance of political virtue.

These ideas were basic to all the political miscalculations of the Enlightenment. It failed to take seriously the factors of interest and power, the rudiments of political order, the organic and historic character of political loyalties, and the necessity of coercion in forming the solidarity of a community. Indeed, the failures of liberalism have tended to inhere in a blindness to the perennial difference between human actions and aspirations, the perennial source of conflict between life and death, the inevitable tragedy of human existence, the irreducible irrationality of human behavior, and the tortuous character of human history.

The corrective to these liberal illusions in Western civilization has been conservatism. Conservatism speaks for the skeptical and cautious side of human nature that sees all about it too many examples of man's sinfulness, frailty, and caprice. It is full of grave doubts about the goodness and rationality of man, the sagacity of the majority, and the wisdom of reform. It seeks to put calipers on the possibilities of human attainment. It tends toward pessimism and displays a natural preference for stability over change, continuity over experiment, the past over the future. Two momentous events sparked its emergence: the French Revolution and the Industrial Revolution. Conservatism appeared as a reaction against the extravagant radicalism and utopianism of the former and the dismayingly rapid pace of social change brought about by the latter.

Moreover, the conservative tradition, while it is a worldwide phenomenon, has exerted its greatest impact in particular countries such as Great Britain. In France, the background of the *ancien régime* and an organic feudal order ought to have given conservatives an objective past to which to appeal. It would have done so but for one insoluble problem: French conservatives, imbued with an acute rationalism, were never able to agree among themselves as to just what it was they wished to preserve. Great Britain, by contrast, was able to absorb both the liberalism of John Locke and the conservatism of Edmund Burke. Its constitutional monarchy provides a fusion of the old and the new political philosophies. The conservative tradition grew up in reaction against the destructive forces released in the process of emancipation from aristocracy and feudalism. It was reasonable, therefore, that European, and in particular British, conservatives should sound the tocsin against Jacobinism and industrialism on behalf of the vestigial qualities worth preserving in a decaying feudal order.

In America, conservatism from the outset lacked a meaningful context in which it could raise its voice. The boundless opportunities of a new continent, the abundance of natural resources, and the spirit of freedom hardly provided the soil for its rapid growth and flowering. The industrialists, such as the railway builders and traders, who carved an empire out of this vast wilderness, were scarcely conservatives in the European sense. Their very successes made them easy prey for the liberal notions of progress and perfectibility. There have, of course, been conservative thinkers of distinction. Especially in the field of foreign policy, the Federalists left us a legacy of precept and example that seems partly valid even today. It was not that American soil was rocky ground from which conservatism could take no nourishment. Rather, in the revealing words of Clinton Rossiter, it was "a lush jungle in which a more adaptable group of principles—democracy, egalitarianism, individualism—sprouted in easy abundance and choked off conservatism except in isolated spots, like the pre-Civil War South."[6]

The points at which the qualities and convictions of American "conservatives" from the Civil War to the present coincide with those of traditional conservatism are not without consequence. Like their forebears abroad, American conservatives believe in the superiority of liberty over equality; accept as part of a concept of equal opportunity the fact of natural inequality; see the necessity for some form of aristocracy; are suspicious of most change except industrial expansion; and espouse laissez-faire. Yet the discrepancies are still greater than the identities. There is a tendency to substitute morale for morality, economics for ethics and politics, and the mood if not the method of the extreme Right for moderation. The essential role of expediency and mere politics is frequently obscured or derided; rugged individualism is glorified without an accompanying regard for its interrelationship with the community; instability rather than stability is fostered by harsh language and radical antistatism; and a fatuous optimism prevails in the leading views of man and human progress.

In a nutshell, American conservatism is more optimistic, materialistic, and individualistic than the Western conservative tradition. By ignoring the capacity for evil of men and states, the American conservative has provided no adequate means for dealing with it. By dismissing society—its nature, needs, and problems—conservatism has left unanswered and even unasked the eternal questions regarding the good society, the class structure we have and we want, the relationship between leadership by our "best members" (who are not necessarily all lawyers and businessmen) and our democratic precepts, the proper and necessary purposes of government in modern society, the prospects for a balanced individualism that is based on natural social and moral allegiances and is not a sand heap of separate particles of humanity, the requirements of statecraft beyond the simple proposition of "applying business methods to government," and the essentials of private and public morality.

The story is not easily brought up to date. Two strains in conservatism were manifested in the late 1960s and early 1970s. The one, exemplified by Watergate, brought to light the cynical and opportunistic strain that is found more often in American conservatism than in traditional conservatism. Secondly, and less obviously, conservative strains are evident in the "return to nature" movement among the young. The decline of the cities, intense competition and crowding, and a surfeit of materialism have all contributed to the revolt of the young. It may prove a supreme irony of the 1960s that a political movement whose members clustered on the radical left should have found the solution to their needs in a return to the land. Yet this conservative turn, which has no particular organic relation to the activist goals of the movement, merely illustrates the paradox of contemporary conservatism. A curious intermingling of conservative and radical impulses permeates present-day conservatism and the confusion is heightened by the lack of any organic relationship between the several elements which comprise it. And what can be said of conservatism can be said no less of present-day liberalism.

All these are issues that cry for attention, reflection, and exposition. On most of them, latter-day conservatives have chosen a posture of resounding silence. How can one account for this silence and for the glaring omissions of American conservatism seen in the light of an historic Western tradition? Perhaps the answer can be supplied in the form of a sweeping generalization: American conservatism is not the traditional conservatism of Western political history, which was rooted in the aristocratic tradition. American conservatism is rather a decayed form of nineteenth-century liberalism. American conservatism is the faith of the conservative sectors of the business community. It seeks to use government for the ends of business, not to remake it for its own emergent ends. At one point in Europe's history it was a revolutionary creed. It opposed the traditional restraints of a feudal society and sought to enlarge the liberties of the middle classes. Its claims of liberty, restricted admittedly to one class, were passionate, compelling, and urgent. But the odyssey of this original liberalism can be traced from John Stuart Mill's *On Liberty* to Herbert Hoover's *The Challenge of Liberty*. Liberalism turned conservative has in recent decades become less a rallying cry than an ideological facade. It has sought less to draw more men to its cause than to protect the economic power of those already under its shield. In domestic affairs its dynamic qualities have disappeared; in world affairs it has retained the worst illusions of traditional liberalism. In the aftermath of the turbulent disorders of the 1960s, conservatism has in the 1970s become stronger at American universities, but it is too early to know whether it can transcend the earlier forms.

The Western conservative tradition has dealt for generations with an endless succession of rivalries and combinations based on common fears, ancient sanctities, ethnic loyalties, and common goals. The conservative understands these forces because he has had to manipulate, persuade, coerce, resist, and accommodate them. However, American conservatism, because it has not been schooled in this tradition, lacks an understanding of the complexities of power.

Liberalism for its part has been far less sure of its ground in world affairs than in national affairs. Prior to World War II, the left in England and Scandinavia urged collective action against the aggressors at the same time as it was engaged in voting down appropriations for rearmament. The American labor movement has a history of isolationism. American liberals have tended consistently to exaggerate the influence of reason and moral force in the world. They have been endlessly tempted to espouse alternately an isolationist viewpoint, shielding liberals from the alien diseases of a decadent Old World, or an international approach that endeavors to refashion the remote and ancient societies of Europe and Asia. Indeed, among liberals isolationism and internationalism tend to be cut from the same cloth. Both are prone to underrate the resistance of external forces to the attainment of liberal goals and values. Liberal isolationists—from Jefferson, who urged that we cancel all our treaties, through Bryan, through those liberal revisionist historians who in the interwar period sought to show that America had only an insignificant stake in resisting the expansion of Imperial Germany or preserving some kind of equilibrium in Europe and Asia, to the cold war revisionists in our own day—have all been the victims of one illusion. They have erred by believing that a liberal society could remain free to achieve its national purposes, even though power was being concentrated in one nation or combination of nations bent on dominating Europe, or, in Hitler's case, the world. They overlooked the fact that, sooner or later, the marriage of overwhelming power and unlimited ambition anywhere in the world causes the United States to rally all its forces to resist tyranny and take recourse to a form of national organization that Harold Lasswell has aptly described as the "garrison state." Put to this test, liberal goals such as freedom are sacrificed to overriding demands of national security.

We have paid a high price for expressions of this particular liberal illusion. Spokesmen for the political-military strategy which prevailed at the end of World War II defended the withdrawal of American and British forces and the advance of Russian troops into the heart of Germany—a decision through which military strategy was divorced from political objectives. It was argued that whether Soviet influence was extended a few hundred miles west of

Prague was of little, if any, consequence for the shape of the postwar world. Without arguing whether this movement of Russian forces was inevitable, most competent observers today are agreed that these decisions by Allied leaders were among the most fateful of the war. Reacting to this, every policy for Europe since 1946 has been publicized as intending either to contain further Russian expansion or to roll back the Soviet Union from the line extending from Stettin to Trieste. Yet Republicans and Democrats have been equally cautious about overt support of rollbacks and liberation (e.g., Hungary).

The supreme tragedy of contemporary American thinking on foreign policy stems from the failure of either liberalism or conservatism to measure up to its task. Ironically, liberalism has been most successful when its spokesmen reflected some of the insights of the conservative tradition. President Franklin D. Roosevelt is the classic example of a liberal American President who felt at home in the troubled world of international politics, partly perhaps because he was a renegade Hudson Valley aristocrat. He wished to preserve the American system, and to this undertaking he brought all the skill and ingenuity of a conservatism whose exponents have seemed, as it were, to wield power by instinct and experience. Henry Steele Commager, in a review of Arthur Schlesinger's *The Crisis of the Old Order*, comments on Roosevelt's profoundly conservative character:

> He was conservative personally—born to wealth and tradition and *noblesse oblige;* trained at Groton and Harvard; deeply rooted in the land; a devout churchman. He was deeply conservative in politics . . . and—as events were to reveal—in foreign policy.[7]

In the same way, American conservatives who have contributed most in foreign policy have had a measure of liberalism in their approach. We can only note in passing that President Eisenhower, with his devotion to America's international responsibilities, was no less a classic example than President Roosevelt. For Mr. Eisenhower perceived both the limits of American power in the vast expanses of Asia and the necessity of confronting Russian power with firm countervailing power in the face of its expansion into the power vacuums of the world. He accepted compromises in Korea and Indochina because he recognized that, short of an endless struggle on the mainland of China, there was no alternative to the acceptance of a balance of power in Asia. At the same time, in Formosa and in the Middle East, he did not hesitate to assert American influence and power; he realized that to do otherwise might upset the world balance of power. His failures were a strange blending of the pacificism and rationalism of liberalism and the conservative illusion that smiles and goodwill would turn even the most stubborn foe into a friendly American.

In short, liberalism and conservatism have proved adequate to their tasks only when two conditions have prevailed. First, those liberal or conservative leaders whose foreign policies have been most successful can most accurately be termed realists. They have succeeded because their policies were founded on a realistic estimate of the given factors in the historical and political situation. Secondly, the shortcomings and failings of a liberalism that is too much the child of the Enlightenment and of a conservatism that tends uncritically to embrace a crusading nationalist point of view can be overcome only by a blending of the deeper insights of the two. Liberalism alone cannot save us unless it is freed from its worst illusions about human nature and politics. Conservatism—especially American conservatism—is bedeviled by its passionate attachment to each successive status quo and its tendency to see the advance of mankind through the narrow squint of upper middle class American life. England's political advance must be attributed at least partly to the creative interplay between its traditions of Lockean liberalism and Burkean conservatism. The one has a keen sense of justice; the other is more aware of all the inescapable aspects of community life that are organic in character.

Historic conservatism perceives that acknowledged rights and duties, acceptable standards of justice, and mutual interests are more often the result of slow and unconscious growth than of conscious political intervention. It likewise concedes that every political and social realm has its hierarchies of power and authority—the international realm not least. Finally it argues that it will not do to assume that peace, order, and a more stable community can be had through an effacing of these arrangements. The source of all conflict in the world is never solely the great powers or political parties. As often as not the weak tempt others to aggression; powerlessness is hardly an assurance of responsibility. One of the creative functions of conservatism is continually to remind liberals that, whether in field or factory, school or church, congress or the international society, there are hierarchies of leadership and an almost endless number of organic processes that hold the community together, give it whatever cohesiveness it enjoys, and regulate and integrate its life.

However, while conservatism in the West has seen the organic processes of each community in true perspective, American conservatism, which is chiefly the remnant of a once vital laissez-faire liberalism, has been blinded to these realities. It has clung to the errors and illusions, on the one hand, of Enlightenment liberalism, which saw an easy harmony of interests emerging from every conflict of interests, and, on the other hand, to a narrow conception of the hierarchies of leadership in America's national and international life, of the special privileges of the parochial segments of the business community or, internationally, of the nation as a law unto itself. Because the wisdom of traditional conservatism has been so imperfectly appropriated by American conservatives, it becomes the common property of all those groups, including liberals, who seek for greater realism in world affairs. Indeed liberalism stripped of its utopian errors appears at this point to offer the best hope, partly because liberal realists like George F. Kennan, Reinhold Niebuhr, and Hans J. Morgenthau have been the most diligent in seeking a coherent, relevant, and intelligible theory of international politics.

Yet, liberals in public life continue to utter the old clichés, to prate about principle and decry pragmatism, and to act imprudently in the face of harsh realities, as in proposals for unilateral arms reduction or the abdication of responsibility for a sound American foreign policy by leaving the initiative to the United Nations. Until the United States becomes the home of a realistic liberalism, especially in foreign affairs, the role of an enlightened conservatism and a responsible liberalism will continue to be essential. Whatever their limits, we have in their interplay and tension the best hope for America.

DOGMAS AND INTERNATIONAL REALITIES

Men never do evil so completely and cheerfully as when they do it from religious conviction.
                                                                Pascal

Men through the ages have seldom been free of reflection on right and wrong. Rationalists attribute this to man's ingrained capacity for right reason; religionists, to a spark of the divine. Explanations may be less important than the fact that for philosophers and churchmen, jurists and publicists, war has been a central ethical concern.

Two questions present themselves for us, as for those who have gone before. First, do people know what is right and wrong? Second, do the pressures of society prevent them from doing right? Are ethics for various countries the product of a dominant ideology? Where war is concerned, the answers are colored because we see the truth through prisms of nationalism. The literature of international relations is shot through with aphorisms concerning the pressures of national societies. Was it not Cavour who said, "If we had done for ourselves what we did for the State, what scoundrels we would have been." For many Italians, the invasion of Abyssinia was colored by Mussolini's view that "Sixty million Italians cannot be wrong."

The primacy given to national unity and security has had a profound effect on public morality. Personal and public morality have diverged not because all public leaders are venal, but because the demands of maintaining the unity of the state are paramount.

For a statesman, right and wrong must be measured in terms of the safety and well-being of present and future generations. His universe is the nation-state living in a half-organized and half-anarchic world. It is a world in which welfare and security are still nationally determined. As we have seen, at the heart of this problem is a moral dilemma. We cannot escape moral evaluations, but we are never as moral as we claim to be. This is no less true of the parent who disciplines the child for his own good, than of the powerful nation that works its will on less powerful and less virtuous states. Even when justice is the goal, it invariably becomes mixed with coercion, caprice, and injustice.

To be more specific about the context of contemporary international relations, what is the objective situation that determines the character of modern war? According to Raymond Aron in his important book *Peace and War* (1962), each nation in the world of sovereign and independent political units claims the right to take justice into its own hands and to be the sole arbiter of the decision to fight or not to fight. The threat of war hangs ominously over us. There has been no slackening of nationalism in our day. It is present in the new nations throughout Africa and Asia; it is evident in the relationships within the Soviet bloc and in the wider Communist world; it remains in Europe and the emerging European Community; it can be seen in the relationships between China, the Soviet Union, and North Vietnam.

The policies of strongly nationalist societies are still made in the shadow of war. The war-peace cycle is a fact of life. There has been almost a continuous alternation of the two with the world being free of war only for limited periods. For the last quarter-century we have lived in an age of "half-war, half-peace" which has depended more and more on a balance of terror.

The important fact is that war and peace throughout history have constituted a continuum. St. Augustine recognized this when he wrote: "The final object of war is peace. Peace is carved out in the shadow of war and war's only justification must be more stable conditions of peace." Morality or moral fervor about war must break into this circle. It must find ways of maximizing the chances that peace will emerge out of the stream of conflict.

Some see the new era as changing fundamentally the character of international life. Hiroshima and Nagasaki in August 1945 ushered in a new era of history. Writing in 1959 Aron could say: "Humanity has entered an unprecedented phase in which the great powers are, for the first time in history, preparing for a war they do not want to fight. How long can peace be preserved by the threat of a suicidal war?"[8] In charting reactions to his questions Aron separated the responses into those of optimists, pessimists, and realists. The optimists saw in the diabolical weapon the promise that this time war was going to end war, peace would reign at last, thanks to the progress in technology, not to a universal change of heart. The pessimists announced the approach of the Apocalypse, with the world carried away by a satanic impulse as punishment for defying the gods and refusing to recognize the limits of the human condition. The realists, rejecting both extremes, left the future open, reasoning that while contemporary international relations would be conducted within the shadow of war, options that might avert universal destruction were nevertheless open to the actors. War was more likely than the optimists predicted, and peace more possible than the pessimists believed.

There are lessons to be learned from a review of absolutes in present-day approaches to war. As we face the unique problems of a nuclear age, new theories are evolving to deal with the moral problem. The theories now dominant derive historically from searches for peace based on a single factor or an absolute. Thus, in the nineteenth century and to some extent in the eighteenth, men saw peace as achievable through reason, evolution, progress, and education. Other single-factor theories looked to peace through freeing the colonies, or through world law, or through the outlawing of war, or through world government—even though men should have known that government without community is unlikely to survive. Then there were the notions that nationalism or national self-determination would bring peace. (Writing of the French Revolution, Thomas Paine commented: "Monarchical sovereignty, the enemy of mankind and the source of misery, is abolished. Were this the case throughout Europe as it is in France, the cause of war would be taken away.")

All these theories have one thing in common. They root the solution to the problem of war in a single moral and political absolute. Today, the public debate centers around two simple dogmas. The first is the notion that peace can be achieved through its enforcement. We are called upon to be mindful of the lessons of the two World Wars. Both times we found that small aggressions, unchecked, spread until a worldwide confrontation occurred. Unless men are ready to resist at the first sign an effort aimed at upsetting the balance of power, peace will be the chief casualty. This view has been the dominant principle undergirding American policies through Asia and most of the world, and provided the major argument for the American intervention in Vietnam.

The other simple doctrine is the powerful peace philosophy which has attracted the loyalty of millions of people; it opts out of the question of relating force and peace. It bases a philosophy about the dilemmas of war on the successes of civil rights efforts.

Both of these approaches are not so much wrong as insufficient. They are lacking, not in possible justification, but in comprehensiveness. The belief that peace can be isolated as the ultimate and independent value in international society calls for critical discussion and examination.

In earlier times peace had been conceived as of dependent upon trends within and among states, upon political and social organization, upon eco-

nomic sufficiency, and upon the maintenance of a stable equilibrium of
power. Thus food supply, population growth, and national morale were
considered to be just as vital to peace as a single-minded devotion to the idea
of peace as the supreme value. In our day, peace is conceived of as an end in
itself to be approached frontally and directly, and less stress is placed on the
sources and conditions of peace rooted in social and economic life. Those
who are inspired by the peace philosophy are less inclined to see it in relation
to other values, more inclined to view it as unambiguously simple. The heart
of the problem is philosophical, even theological. But the religionist must
come to terms with the fact of good and evil. There is a need for the insight
that prompted a British commentator to write: "The doctrine of original sin
is the only empirically verifiable doctrine of Christian faith."

Man, carrying within him the spark of the divine, shares with all mankind a
deep and underlying solidarity. Yet it is no less a fact that evil persists,
despite continuous efforts throughout history to rid the world of it. Liberal
theories of progress and utopian movements like world communism herald
the end of greed, exploitation, and self-interest, when men will throw off the
shackles of obsolescent social and economic creeds. But history has overwhelmingly challenged this optimism. Indeed the evidence seems clear that it
is easier to talk of abolishing tyranny and war once and for all than to work
with modest success at limiting, containing, and controlling it. Perhaps, for
this reason, skeptics and pragmatists have often done more than the overtly
religious in bringing some measure of justice into the management of the
social order.

Significantly, most of those who see peace as an absolute have practised
pragmatism in their own societies. They labor faithfully through programs of
social reform to reduce poverty and suffering, realizing these can never be
eliminated. They accept the necessity of charity, even within blatantly
oppressive and unjust social systems whose purposes they ultimately condemn. If they are right in striving to bring aid and comfort to victims of an
unjust political order, even at the risk of strengthening that order, how does
one explain their austere rejection of ethical pragmatism in confronting, for
example, the armaments problem. Surely limited war is morally superior to
total war, and the cold war is to be preferred to a shooting war. Yet moral
relativists who see some justice in the most tyrannical regimes become moral
absolutists in the claim "that there is no other course for the Church but the
final rejection of war as an instrument of achieving justice."

Students of religion and international relations have recently undertaken
to consider the problem of war in a setting beset by the strident clash of two
strains of thought. The first view is a bold recognition that the context of
international affairs gives a special role to morality and religion. Woodrow
Wilson, for all his towering idealism, was aware of this when he wrote,

"Morality is a great deal bigger than law." Individual morality involves one man's sense of right and wrong. Social morality must strike an average, and this is where reformers make their tragic mistake. There can be no compromise in individual morality, but there must be a compromise in social morality. There is indeed an element of morality in every social compromise.

It would seem then, following Wilson, that the beginning of wisdom in the study of political ethics is a recognition of the endless complexity and uncertainty of much of social life. Morality in such a setting can seldom be applied by rote. For example, we deceive ourselves by assuming that others are as we are and that the perplexities of world politics can be solved by affirming national values and standards as if they comprise the law of mankind.[9] Professor Herbert Butterfield of Cambridge University has wisely counselled: "What society needs is every possible variation and extension of the art of putting oneself—and actually feeling oneself—in the other person's place."[10]

The task of the statesman, as of the moral philosopher, is not to pronounce the law of love and then in a fit of moral irresponsibility leave the world to tyrants. To do this would be to conclude that because we represent democracy and the Communists or Nazis totalitarianism, we have a special obligation to turn the other cheek and leave the world to them. Surely, something less than the purest love, but more than the law of the most powerful, is the goal we seek. The pathway to a more dependable and less uncertain international order lies not in moral pronouncements, but in an unending succession of hard choices between right and wrong, not in the dictionary sense, but in the spirit and anguish of great statesmen like Lincoln. How few of our contemporary moralists have had much to say about the tragic sense of life, yet this is the heart and essence of international politics and of politics in general. Decisions are tentative, the alternatives imperfect, and choices unsatisfactory, not only from a practical, political viewpoint but also from an ethical and religious standpoint.

NOTES

1. Richard Crossman et al., The New Fabian Essays (New York: Praeger, 1952), p. 162.

2. Quoted in Clinton Rossiter, Conservatism in America (New York: Alfred A. Knopf, 1955), p. 41.

3. Quoted in Crossman, p. 162.

4. Reinhold Niebuhr, "Liberalism: Illusions and Realities," New Republic, July 4, 1955, p. 11.

5. Crossman, p. 169.

6. Rossiter, p. 223.

7. *New York Times Book Review,* March 3, 1957, p. 3.

8. Raymond Aron, *On War* (New York: Doubleday, 1959) Preface.

9. A classic example here is the collision between the Jesuit missionaries and the Apaches. In traditional Apache society, theft under certain circumstances is a positive virtue. They literally could not comprehend, therefore, the Ten Commandments—nor could the Jesuits understand the Apache code.

10. Herbert Butterfield, "Morality and Historical Process in International Affairs," unpublished manuscript for June 12, 1956 meeting of Columbia University Seminar on Theory of International Politics, pp. 8-9.

Part Three:

Politics and International Politics:

The Search

for a Theoretical Framework

I have come across men of letters who have written history without taking part in public affairs, and politicians who have concerned themselves with producing events without thinking about them. I have observed that the first are always inclined to find general causes, whereas the second, living in the midst of disconnected daily facts, are prone to imagine that everything is attributable to particular incidents, and that the wires they pull are the same as those that move the world. It is to be presumed that both are equally deceived.

Alexis de Tocqueville

9: PHILOSOPHERS, POLITICS, AND POLICY-MAKERS

The world is made up of thinkers and doers.
Anonymous

One perennial issue that troubles every society and divides its citizens is the relationship between intellectuals and policy-makers. By definition, each plays out a role in keeping with his mission, talents, and calling. Intellectuals are conceptualizers who look for underlying causes, interrelationships, and meanings. Policy-makers are practitioners, doers, actors, operators. Their strength is in working within a problem-oriented context seeking short-run solutions. In theory, the relationship between philosophers and practitioners ought to be complementary. In the real world, there is a tendency for them to drift farther and farther apart. Philosophers, who should be viewed as a valuable resource to policy-makers, have come to be seen as troublesome critics. President John F. Kennedy, when asked why he had recruited a certain professor, is said to have replied, "It's worth $25,000 to me not to have him firing broadsides from the Charles River." The story may be apocryphal, but the principle illustrates the separation that, seemingly, inescapably grows up between intellectuals and policy-makers, even intellectual policy-makers.

In few areas are the possibilities for division as great as in international relations, where forces conspire to drive men of thought and action apart. For the philosopher, a primary goal is to abstract from reality general principles that will illuminate the present and point the way to a better future. The older and more "scientific" a field of study, the more specialized and precise its focus and concern. Policy-makers, on the other hand, are daily confronted with problems that are both larger and smaller than this. With cables pouring in from every corner of the globe, there is little time for testing hypotheses or settling on first principles. All this and more leads to irritation and frustration even for those who would have it otherwise. Add to this that neither are amused by ripostes that question their very *raison d'être,* and the conflict is complete.

137

The present state of international studies has added to the conflict. For those whose first end is professional advancement, the test is not communicating with policy-makers but model building, not imaginative designs for new policy initiatives but abstract schemes for more rational decision-making, not simple guides for action but more sophisticated research designs for handling a larger number of variables. The schools of thought which currently have the greatest scholarly acclaim are calculated to widen, not narrow, the gulf and to perpetuate the divorce. It is not by accident that policy-makers have turned increasingly to physical scientists capable of helping with discrete technical problems, rather than to the philosophers.

Nevertheless, a handful of philosophers and scholars have kept themselves considerably closer to the real world with which policy-makers must deal. Taken as a group, their intellectual interests are varied and diverse. I have selected for discussion, as the archetype of this relation, an American theologian, partly because I am familiar with his work and partly because he represents a counterforce to the divorce between thought and action. Throughout his career, he moved back and forth between philosophers and policy-makers. He was until the end a social critic, but he knew the thinking and the predicament of the policy-maker. Scholars when they differed with him called him a mere preacher; practitioners when he threatened their complacency said they could not understand him. Both in the end paid him homage for his many-sided contributions. It may illuminate the problem of theory and practice to trace the origins and development of his thought on politics and international relations.

POLITICAL PHILOSOPHY AND THE NATION-STATE
REINHOLD NIEBUHR'S CONTRIBUTION

*Only humble men who recognize the mystery and
majesty of life are able to face it . . . without exulting
over its beauty or becoming crushed by its terror.*
                                                        Niebuhr

Until the late 1940s, few students of international affairs were concerned with the theoretical aspects of their field. This is especially true to the extent that theory is distinguished from history, law, and science. Historians have sought to uncover the facts and recite them with the most fastidious regard for the circumstances of time and place. Lawyers have tried to detect in the case law of international agreements and treaties the normative structure of international society. Political scientists have increasingly turned to new scientific methods and statistical techniques designed to measure public opinion and its influence on foreign policy. But few scholars have concerned themselves with the fundamental characteristics of international society or of good or bad foreign policy. In this intellectual environment any explicit, systematic theory of international relations has had to await a threefold development. It has required a broader conception of the proper methods for studying international affairs, a clearer identification of basic concepts and "laws," and a more serious discussion of fundamental theoretical problems.

More recently it has become obvious that the study of international relations since 1946 has witnessed impressive attacks on all three of these problems. The intellectual resources of government and scholarship have, at least in a limited way, been mobilized to build a new framework or rediscover the older structure of a theoretical approach to international politics. The extraordinary group who in its earliest years made up the Policy Planning Staff in the Department of State found that without the tools of theory it was impossible to proceed in a rational manner. Insofar as their efforts were informed by a desire to separate consideration of the national interest from consideration of the probable domestic consequences of a particular course of action, they contributed in a most significant way to theory. It is obvious that the lectures by George F. Kennan contained in *American Diplomacy, 1900-1950,* coupled with his Stafford Little Lectures at Princeton, serve this end. So do the books on foreign policy by Louis Halle, C. B. Marshall, and Dorothy Fosdick. In more systematic terms, scholars like E. H. Carr and Herbert Butterfield in England, and Hans J. Morgenthau in the United States have added to our conception of theory. It is not without significance that these authorities admittedly owe an important intellectual debt to Protestant theologian Reinhold Niebuhr, who as early as 1932, in *Moral Man and Immoral Society,* elaborated a realistic theory of international politics. Not long ago Kennan, in surveying the growth of interest among the small group of responsible theorists, identified Niebuhr as the precursor of the realists or, in Kennan's words, "the father of all of us." Morgenthau's first volume, *Scientific Man vs. Power Politics,* which remains in some ways more fundamental to his philosophy than all his subsequent writings, bears the imprint of Niebuhr's influence more than that of any other American scholar. Marshall, Halle, and Fosdick have not been hesitant in acknowledging their debt to Niebuhr.

Influence of this magnitude would indicate that Niebuhr's approach to the study of politics among nations might profitably be analyzed and systematically appraised. His writings, which extend over nearly a quarter of a century in nearly a dozen published treatises and numerous major articles, provide a rich background for discussion. In this connection the political essays which appear in the two journals he edited, *Christianity and Crisis* and *Christianity and Society,* are often overlooked. The scholar who turns to the sources of Niebuhr's writings will discover that his contribution to international politics bears the closest relationship to the preconditions of growth for a legitimate theory of international relations. For as theory itself has required a broader conception of method, the identification of basic concepts, and the illumination of resulting theoretical problems, Niebuhr's philosophy has been focused on the real issues foreshadowed in this enumeration of the threefold development of theory.

The Proper Study of Politics

Most contemporary thought has assumed that the proper methods for the study of politics are those which have been so extraordinarily successful in the natural or physical world. It has been widely assumed that all that separates the physical and social sciences is an unfortunate cultural lag resulting from the use of archaic and imprecise methods by backward and unsophisticated social scientists. The technique of social science "lags far behind that of natural or laboratory sciences" and prominent research scholars proclaim that concentrated efforts will have to be made if the old classical methodology of social science is to be broken down.

For Niebuhr there is an alternative to the scientific method—political philosophy. The political philosopher observing the pattern of history is obliged to articulate the basis on which he interprets its meaning. At some point he must make explicit his theory of human nature. The practice of rooting political theory in political institutions and processes rather than in human nature belongs mainly to the last few decades. Niebuhr, by contrast, explicitly assumed that an understanding of political phenomena, whether international or domestic, is inseparable from a clear picture of human nature. The Gifford Lectures, begun at the University of Edinburgh in the spring of 1939 as warclouds hovered over Europe and completed in the autumn as the threat became a dreadful reality, represent their author's most systematic attempt to demonstrate the need for and broad outlines of a realistic theory of human nature. The lectures begin: "Man has always been his most vexing problem. How shall he think of himself?"[1] Any affirmation he makes involves him in contradictions. If he stresses man's unique and rational qualities, then man's greed, lust for power, and brute nature betray him. If he holds that men everywhere are the product of nature and unable to rise above circumstances, he tells us nothing of man the creature who dreams of God and of making himself God, and of man whose sympathy knows no bounds. If he believes man is essentially good and attributes all evil to concrete historical and social causes, he merely begs the question, for these causes are revealed, on closer scrutiny, to be the consequences of the evil inherent in man. If he finds man bereft of all virtue, his capacity for reaching such a judgment refutes the terms of his judgment. Such baffling paradoxes of human self-knowledge point up the vexing problem of doing justice at one and the same time to the uniqueness of man and to his affinities with nature. Only a theory inspired by a knowledge of both qualities can be adequate. In Reinhold Niebuhr's words:

> The obvious fact is that man is a child of nature, subject to its vicissitudes, compelled by its necessities, driven by its impulses, and confined within the brevity of the years which nature permits its varied organic forms, allowing them some, but not too much, latitude. The other less obvious fact is that man is a spirit who stands outside of nature, life, himself, his reason and the world.[2]

Modern views of man which stress exclusively his dignity or his misery are fatuous and irrelevant chiefly because they fail to understand the dualism of man's nature.

The paradox of man's existence arises from the fact that he is suspended perilously between freedom and finiteness, spirit and nature. Through spirit he is enabled to survey the whole, but in so doing he is betrayed into imagining himself the whole. While enabled through freedom to use the forces and processes of nature creatively, he comes to ignore his own creatureliness. His ambiguous and contradictory position at the juncture of freedom and finiteness produces in him a condition of anxiety which is fundamental to understanding political behavior. Man is anxious because he is conscious of the imperialism of others while secretly aware of his own limitations. Yet as finite reason, he can never be sure of the limits of his possibilities and so endlessly seeks security in the pretense that he has overcome his finiteness and human limitations.

For our purposes, the most important observable expression of human anxiety politically is in the will to power. Man shares with animals their natural appetites and desires and the impulse for survival. Yet being both nature and spirit, his requirements are qualitatively heightened; they are raised irretrievably to the level of spirit where they become limitless and insatiable. In Niebuhr's words:

> Man being more than a natural creature, is not interested merely in physical survival but in prestige and social approval. Having the intelligence to anticipate the perils in which he stands in nature and history, he invariably seeks to gain security against these perils by enhancing his power, individually and collectively.[3]

To overcome social anxiety, man seeks power over his fellows, endeavoring to subdue them lest they come to dominate him. The struggle for political power is merely an example of the rivalry which goes on at every level of human life.

However, the human predicament has its roots primarily, in what may be called the security-power dilemma. Weak men and weak nations assume that if they had more power they would be more secure. Yet the more power an individual or a nation has, the more of its life impinges upon other life and the more wisdom is required to bring it into some decent harmony with other life. In the political arena, groups are motivated much as individuals to seek dominion over one another. In 1944, Niebuhr answered the criticism that labor was jeopardizing the common interest by pressing its cause when he said: "It is silly to talk of the danger of pressure groups. Labor has merely fashioned its own political power inside the Democratic party." The various groups or corporate entities in society compete for power in the manner of the individuals who compose them. Their success is dependent on their unity and vitality, for in politics as in warfare, numbers count for nothing without cohesion and organization.

Power is the organization of factors and forces which are impotent without organization. Some group or coalition emerges as the holder of a preponderance of power. It assumes to itself the responsibility for government or the administration of the system wherein the power struggle continues. This group, in turn, is supplanted by another and the endless and inescapable conflict goes on. Effective limits on the struggle, especially among larger groups, are usually far more modest than is generally understood.

> In the field of collective behavior the force of egoistic passion is so strong that the only harmonies possible are those which manage to neutralize this force through balance of power, through mutual defenses against its inordinate expression, and through techniques for harnessing its energy to social ends.[4]

For Niebuhr the limits of human imagination, the easy subservience of reason to the passions, and the persistence of collective irrationalism and egoism make social conflict inevitable in human history, probably to its very end.

Moreover, the possibility of force or resort to coercion is present in all social conflict. The threat of force, whether by the official and governmental representatives or by the parties to a dispute in a community, is a potent instrument in all communal relations. Coercion is inevitable and universal in even the most intimate community, the family. Political power represents a special form of coercion, for it rests on the ability to use and manipulate other forms of social, economic, and religious power for the purpose of organizing and dominating the community.

Furthermore, Niebuhr noted the ferocity and intensity of the struggle among groups when compared to the rivalry of individuals, stemming from the tendency of collectivities to express both the virtue and selfishness of their members. Social unity is built on the virtuous as well as the selfish side of man's nature; the twin elements of collective strength become self-sacrificial loyalty and frustrated aggressions. From this it follows that politics, whether in organized political groups or in large organizations, is the more contentious and ruthless because of the unselfish loyalty of the members of the groups, which become laws unto themselves, unrestrained by their obedient and worshipful members. Group pride is in fact the corruption of individual loyalty and group consciousness; contempt for another group is the pathetic form which respect for our own frequently takes. The tender emotions which bind the family together sometimes are expressed in indifference for the welfare of other families. Niebuhr's ultimate conclusion is that in international society a nation made up of men of the greatest religious goodwill would be less than loving toward other nations, for its virtue would be channeled into loyalty to itself, thus increasing its selfishness. The consequence for Niebuhr's political theory is his conclusion that

> society ... merely cumulates the egoism of individuals and transmutes their individual altruism into collective egoism so that the egoism of the group has a double force. For this reason no group acts from purely unselfish or even mutual intent and politics is therefore bound to be a contest of power.[5]

Relations among such groups must always be essentially political before they are ethical and the study of political science becomes the study of the objective distribution of power.

Keys to a Theory of World Politics

It should be obvious from what has already been said that Niebuhr founded his theory of world politics on a general conception of human nature. His theory was essentially architectonic. Man, in a condition of social anxiety, seeks security in power only to find it escaping him. Nations as massive collections of individuals have recourse to much the same quest for prestige and influence, heightened for them by the unabridged loyalties and contemporary frustrations of their members. In international society what nations claim they seek is some measure of attainment of national interest. Niebuhr was willing to concede that the concept of national interest is central to the study of world politics. He observed that nations are, on the whole, not generous. A wise self-interest is usually the limit of their moral achievement. The demands of self-interest and national self-protection inspire actions that appear to override all accepted moral impulses. For example, the decision to build the hydrogen bomb gave offense to many sincere people. However, Niebuhr more than once cautioned humanitarian critics of American foreign policy against assuming that the limits of choice for a nation are broader than they are. Of the bomb he observed in 1950: "No nation will fail to take even the most hazardous adventure into the future, if the alternative of not taking the step means the risk of being subjugated." Every nation is guided by self-interest and does not support values which transcend its life, if the defense of these values imperils its existence. A statesman who sought to follow such a course would be accused of treason.

This conception of the primacy of national interest broadly conceived has not been popularly acceptable or congenial in our liberal democratic age. Idealists and adherents of scientific humanism have maintained that concern for the safety, integrity, and preservation of the nation-state belonged to an older authoritarian age. Some observers have looked to international organization as one substitute for the national interest. Its more ebullient protagonists have implored men to abandon selfish national and parochial attachments for more universal loyalties. In contrast, Niebuhr conceived of international organization as essentially another framework within which historic and emergent national purposes might be pursued and adjusted. For him they never symbolized the demise of national interests. Instead, action by an international organization has been associated with the vital interests of one or more major powers.

There is another popular approach to the displacement of the national interest deriving from the view that unresolved conflicts among nations would quickly be resolved once taken out of the hands of statesmen and assigned to men of science and culture. Niebuhr associated this view with some of the work that has gone on at UNESCO. He questioned the

> belief that the difficulties which statesmen face in guiding their nations are due, not so much to their responsible relation to their several nations, as to their intellectual inferiority in comparison with cultural leaders. This misses the whole point in the encounter of nations with each other. Such an encounter is a power-political one, in which statesmen distinguish themselves from philosophers and scientists, not by their smaller degree of intelligence but by their higher degree of responsibility to their respective communities.[6]

Sectarian Christianity and other modern religions, in particular, have sometimes promised release from the hard demands of the national interest through a religious renaissance whereby partial loyalties would be swallowed up in universal faith. In February, 1941, Niebuhr founded his journal, *Christianity and Crisis,* with the primary goal of reexamining the Protestant and secular solutions to the complex problems of the political and economic order. But in contrast to those modern Christians who seek at almost every point to commend their faith as the source of the qualities and disciplines required to save the world from disaster, Niebuhr as Christian remained self-critical, judicious, and reserved. For example, some Christian leaders have maintained, in opposition to their secular critics, that democracy is the product of the spiritual resources of religious faith. In their view, democracy is the direct outgrowth of Christian faith. However, this sweeping proposition was unacceptable to Niebuhr since, as a matter of history, *both* Christian and secular forces were involved in establishing the political institutions of democracy. Moreover, there are traditional nondemocratic Christian cultures which prove that the Christian faith does not inevitably yield democratic fruits. A fairer appraisal is that modern free societies are a fortunate product of the confluence of Christian and secular forces. More specifically, in this country Christianity and Judaism provide a view of man incompatible with his subordination to any political system, while secular and some other forms of religious thought combine to assure critical judgments of human ends and ambitions, social forces, and political powers, in order that the false idolatries of modern tyrannies may be avoided. Christianity provides insights through which the chances for democracy are improved, as with the Christian concept of human dignity, making all efforts to fit man into any political program, even in the name of social engineering, morally ambiguous or offensive. Moreover, individual freedom is encouraged by the assumption of a source of authority from which the individual can defy the authorities of this world. (We must obey God rather than Man.)

The biblical insistence that the same radical freedom which makes man creative also makes him potentially dangerous and destructive leads to the requirements of restraints or balance of power and the equilibrium of social forces upon which effective democracy in action generally rests. Beyond this, however, there is another part of the story, involving the hazards of the relationship between Christianity and democracy and the positive contributions of secular thought. On the one hand, there are grave historical and psychological perils in associating ultimate religious truths with immediate and proximate causes.

> Christians cannot deny that the religious theory of divine right of kings has been a powerful force in traditional societies; nor must they obscure the fact that even a true religion frequently generates false identifications of some human interest with God's will.[7]

On the other hand, the ascribing of secular content to nonsacred objects and ends of society has endowed a multitude of lesser activities with a practical moral respectability and at the same time discouraged the premature sanctities in which both traditional societies and modern collectivism abound. It should be noted that an explicit secularism, disavowing reverence for the ultimate, may itself generate new idolatries, such as the worship of efficiency or of the self-sufficient individual. Compared with the noxious idolatries of modern secular totalitarianism they are comparatively harmless, but they prove that an explicit denial of the ultimate may be the basis for a secular religion with excessive pretensions and sanctities of its own.

On the international scene, religion can be the means of inspiring patience, humility, and forbearance among states, but the evidence of its transforming qualities is more modest than is frequently claimed. We repeatedly hear requests for greater emphasis on spiritual values, as contrasted with material or national interests. Spiritual values are considered abstractly, as if they were something that could be added to or subtracted from what a nation already had. Our problems, however, involve persistent questions like freedom and order, or peace and power, and it can be said that "we do not solve them simply by devotion to abstractly conceived spiritual values." Moreover, these problems are nicely symbolized by the fact that the atomic weapons, which give an immediate security by deterring the aggressor, can easily become the means of a civilization's material and moral destruction. "A Christian faith which declares that all of these horrible ambiguities would not exist if only we loved each other is on exactly the same level as a secular idealism which insists that we could easily escape our predicament if only we organized a world government." Moralists maintain that if Christians were only sufficiently unselfish to be willing to sacrifice "their" civilization as faith has prepared them to sacrifice "their" life we would quickly solve the problem of war. It is fair to ask how an individual responsible for the interests of his group is to justify the sacrifice of interests other than his own. Moreover, "in such terms, Christian unselfishness requires that we capitulate to tyranny because democracy happens to be 'ours' and tyranny is 'theirs.' Thus disloyalty and irresponsibility toward the treasures of an historic civilization become equated with Christian love."[8]

But modernist religion is as often irrelevant because it fosters a hard as well as a soft utopianism. A hard utopianism is best characterized by a crusading moralistic approach, wherein every moral scruple is suppressed because a nation assumes it is fighting for God and a Christian civilization against atheism. It is ironic that we should so endlessly appeal to the moral supremacy of our cause at the moment when communism, as distinct from fascism, is claiming to embody the absolute objective moral law. On reflection, we can observe that communists are so uncompromising primarily because they are idolators—not atheists—who in their fierce moral idealism are willing to sacrifice every decency and scruple to one value: the classless society. Democracies, by claiming too much for their moral cause, whether by design or through ignorance of its partial and fragmentary character, run a somewhat similar risk. In describing the problems of postwar American foreign policy, especially in maintaining allies, Niebuhr explained: "Our difficulty is significantly that we claim moral superiority over them too easily, not recognizing that each man and nation erects a pyramid of moral preferences on the basis of a minimum moral law." Because of the pluralistic character of national values, this law is most universal when it states obligations in minimum and negative terms—as "thou shalt not steal."

But the moral issue in international relations, even with these restrictions, remains the fundamental problem. If in international organization men of culture and modern religion are unsuccessful in supplying the instruments by which national interest can be transcended, Niebuhr was nevertheless persuaded that men and states cannot follow their self-interest without claiming to do so in obedience to some general scheme of values. Two very grave moral and practical questions continued to trouble him and led him to make a series of distinctions regarding the national interest. First, he asked whether a consistent emphasis upon the national interest is not as self-defeating in national, as it is in individual, life. Or put in other terms, does not a nation concerned too much with its own interests define those interests so narrowly and so immediately (as for instance in terms of military security) that these very interests and securities, which depend upon common devotion to principles of justice and upon established mutualities in a community of nations, are sacrificed? Secondly, nations which insist on the one hand that they cannot act beyond their interest claim, as soon as they act, that they have acted not out of self-interest but in obedience to higher objectives like "civilization" or "justice."

In the conduct of contemporary American foreign relations, we claim more for the benevolence of our policies than they deserve and arouse the resentment of peoples already inclined to envy our power and wealth. Thus national interest is imperiled at one time by the hazard of moral cynicism and at another time by moral pretension and hypocrisy. In his earlier writings on the subject Niebuhr dealt more with moral cynicism and later with pretension and hypocrisy. In the evolution of his thinking, moreover, he came to view them as parts of a single problem. The problem involves our continued ambivalence toward the moral issue, claiming at one moment that nations have no obligations beyond their interests and at the next moment that they are engaged in a high moral crusade without regard for interests.

Moral cynicism arises from the identification of the brutal facts with the normative aspects of international politics. Interest, which is the lowest common denominator of political behavior, is made the highest practical standard. It is, of course, obvious that the ultimate norms of religion are almost never the effective ethical standards of politics, which is generally marked by some form of coercion, force, or resistance.

Pacifists and perfectionists who undertake to translate the law of love of the Kingdom of God directly into the language of politics provide at best a protest and at worst a wholly unrealistic and harmful alternative to a more cynical approach. As Niebuhr saw it, they try to make a success story out of the story of the Cross. There is one form of pacifism, pragmatic in character, which accepts the world as it is with interest set against interest and seeks through political imagination and intelligence to adjust, harmonize, and mitigate the conflict on the assumption that overt violence is a great social evil. For the most part, however, the purest standards of love and generosity are not directly relevant to the life of nations. But neither are they wholly irrelevant as final norms, for while love is never fully realizable in history, it never loses its significance as an ultimate moral norm. It inspires ethical conduct at a more proximate level and provides a standard against which social ethics may be evaluated and judged.

If the standard of love is to be made useful and relevant, however, it must be translated into relative and proximate terms more appropriate to the realities of politics. Justice, for Niebuhr, satisfies this demand as the most significant approximation of the ideal of love in politics. But justice involving the compromise of love with the darker elements of politics is also its contradiction. It should be explained that Niebuhr in his analysis of the international scene proceeded simultaneously at two levels. As we have seen, he constructed a rational theory of the behavior of states based on the primacy of their interests, and here he traveled the same road as other contemporary realists. Beyond national interest, however, he was concerned to establish a normative theory in order to avert what he called the abyss of moral cynicism inherent in a merely rational theory. The decisive problem with his theory arises precisely at this point. For in attempting to transcend the harsh realities that emerge from a realistic description of international politics, he was confronted with at least three crucial unsolved problems which must trouble and confuse any scholar who walks the lonely path of normative thought, especially as related to the anarchy of international relations.

First, he sought to distinguish what is possible for governments from what is possible for nations. He maintained that while governments in their policies cannot transcend the national interest, the people, by loyalties transcending the nation, can prevent the national interest from being conceived in too narrow and self-defeating terms. Most present-day realists would maintain that the continuum of national interest is more limited and precise than this statement seems to imply. They would say that the issue in practical state-craft is not between a narrow and broad interpretation but between an intelligent and rational and an irrational view of the national interest. For example, once the stalemate had been reached in Korea, the issue was not whether American policy-makers should take a broad or narrow view but whether our interest in Korea, as contrasted with our interests elsewhere, measured against our antagonist's interests in holding the line—conceived in terms of relative power—called for a policy of armistice or stalemate, of withdrawal or of extension of the conflict. Popular loyalty to ends transcending the national interest, say to a military crusade against world communism heedless of the limits of our power, might have led to a policy directly at odds with the rational choice of those who served as the guardians of national security at the time. It is possible that in some crucial decisions for a democracy the chief obstacle to popular support of a rational foreign policy is exactly loyalty to principles transcending the national interest.

Secondly, Niebuhr conceived of justice in social and political ethics as involving "the harmony of the whole which does not destroy the vitality of the parts." The criterion of moral value becomes the freedom of each unique part to assert its vitality; equality and liberty are the informing and regulative principles of justice. In all communities, however, and in particular the international community, order sometimes demands the subordination of one member to another. Coercion and power introduce ambiguity into political morality, and equality and liberty are never simple possibilities. Self-interest is so powerful on the international scene that a nation cannot espouse a more universal value at the expense of its selfish interests. Hence Niebuhr's critics can legitimately ask what role is played by justice or equality or liberty if the highest morality possible for nations is not a sacrifice of its interests to maintain other nations, but an effort to find the point of concurrence between its interests and those of others. If justice demands not conformity to some abstract formula but a tolerable harmony between competing forces, who are to be the contrivers of this harmony if not statesmen acting in response to their national interests?

However, Niebuhr questioned whether statesmen acting solely from self-interest are capable of discovering mutual interests unless they are motivated by a spirit of justice or a sense of obligation to a wider community. Against this it can be argued that among nations which share common moral values, as in NATO, a spirit of justice may be discovered, but peace between foes or rivals for power is little more than a forlorn hope if it awaits the development of a shared sense of justice. The discrimination of compatible national interests is a more modest, equally essential, if more cynical enterprise, in which prudence and judgment are more significant than justice. Soviet-American relations symbolize this problem, for while an uneasy armistice, based on a negotiated territorial settlement the violation of which would constitute a *casus belli,* can be established, a commonly accepted system of justice among the parties is inconceivable.

Thirdly, Niebuhr, who was the father of the realist approach to international relations in this country, sought as do all men to reconcile realism with idealism as one aspect of a normative theory. In this effort, however, he left to others the more precise formulation of the boundaries of political realism. Most students in the field recognize idealist approaches as those which look for conditions and solutions which are supposed to overcome and eliminate the selfish instincts of man. Realism, on the contrary, takes self-interest for granted and seeks in the improvement of society to work with men and political forces as it finds them. The test of a scientific theory is its capacity for bringing order and meaning to a mass of data which would otherwise remain unrelated. It is legitimate to ask whether the concepts of idealism or realism as formulated and applied by Niebuhr contribute more to this end than the definitions of other political scientists who conceive of politics, as distinct from economics or aesthetics, as the pursuit of interest defined in terms of power.

It must be said that Niebuhr's formulation, while more satisfying from an ethical standpoint, leaves numerous questions. Realism for him is the disposition to take into account all factors in a social and political situation which offer resistance to established norms. The vital question concerns the meaning, application, and content of these norms. Is it not true that norms, like equality, become in the political arena objects of endless contention, rationalization, and self-deception? What, for instance, does the norm justice, which Niebuhr construed as requiring that each man be given his due, mean in practical terms? What are the standards by which to determine what "is due" labor and management, or the United States and Russia, in a concrete situation? Is it possible in politics, especially at the international level where the first standard of values is usually success, that the continuous transfusion of morals into politics which still remains politics is the most we can ask? Can moral principles serve as standards of politics unless derived from political practice or filtered through circumstances of time and place?

It must be said that Niebuhr's most serious political errors arose from a confusion of normative principles with the possibilities inherent in a given political context. For instance, he judged the New Deal against the background of its achievement of normative goals such as equality and justice, thus obscuring its character as a moderately progressive, pragmatic political movement. In 1945 he confused the abstract principles of British socialism with the realities of foreign policy when he proclaimed that Labour's victory:

> puts a stop to Churchill's abortive efforts to keep discredited monarchs on the throne in Greece and Italy. . . . It will most probably contribute to the invention of a *modus vivendi* between Russia and the Western world and thus reduce the peril of a third world war.[9]

His failure to perceive the clash of historic Russian interests with Europe's interests led him to predict in the Winter 1944 issue of *Christianity and Society* that geographic propinquity and common sympathy for revolutionary ferment would encourage Russo-European relations more intimate in character than Europe's relations with the United States. It can be argued that these errors, which Niebuhr was the first to identify, stem largely from an analysis which has subordinated interests to abstract norms.

Fundamental Problems of Theory and Practice

Edmund Burke, who is probably the greatest of English-speaking political philosophers, bequeathed to the West a concept which Niebuhr appropriated in the final stage of his thinking. Theorists, and more particularly scientists of society, as we have seen, have often yielded to the inclination to believe that the historical realm was analogous to the realm of nature and that the proper scientific or theoretical techniques would assure men mastery over their historical fate. Yet there is no more perplexing problem than that of the relation of political theory to the practice of statesmen, despite the illusions most characteristically expressed in the influence of Auguste Comte upon our social thought. Most of our scientific studies have been largely irrelevant to the practice of statecraft in a day when the watchword must be "sufficient unto the day is the evil thereof." The dimensions peculiar to history and politics have often been ignored or obscured. For Burke the problem of the relation of theory and practice is bound up in the concept of prudence. For him, prudence, not justice, is first in the rank of political virtues; it is the director, the standard, and the regulator. Metaphysics cannot live without definition, but prudence is cautious how it defines, for it has learned to live with ever-changing reality.

Niebuhr, as he moved in the direction of a pragmatic view of world politics, dealt with increasing emphasis upon the limits of a rational as well as a normative theory in practice. He was ever more impressed with the practical wisdom of a statesman like Churchill, who in his estimate of the present found his way through the dogmatic predictions about history to the real unpredictabilities. While men can learn from the past, they would do well not to make any past event into an analogy for unique present perplexities. Even the proximate moral norms of politics are seldom realized in practice; and statesmen must settle more often than not for a series of infertile and uncertain compromises. Thus while normative theory can be made relevant in a remote regulative way, the opposite dimension from love, which is the dimension of interest and power, sets limits to the meaning of theory. Love, expressed in abstract principles of justice as an absolute natural law, is still unrealized in a relative natural law in which abstract principles are compromised by interest and power. Historical or civil law may embody the proximate principles of a more relative natural law, as for example with our Higher Law, but international affairs for the most part lie beyond mere legal enactments. In the irrational realm which remains, the struggle is so intense and perennial that the only possible peace is gained through armistice and the only order through a tentative balance among the various forces.

Niebuhr therefore returned to the sphere he early identified. His concern with theology and normative theory in a way sometimes drew him above and beyond national interest and left to his followers the systematic study of the "laws" of interest and politics. Yet if Niebuhr failed to transcend the tragic paradoxes of politics, he clarified and illuminated the problem as no other present-day political philosopher has done. If, by accepting the brutal facts of the international scene, Niebuhr limited the relevance of normative standards, he invited for the people and their statesmen a kind of cosmic humility regarding the moral qualities of their action. Moral pretension which derives from policies of self-righteousness and generates conflicts and war is made the basis for Niebuhr's final conclusion that it is as necessary to moderate the moral pretensions of each contestant as to make moral distinctions regarding the national interest. Theory and practice in international politics are enveloped in the ambiguity which derives from the importance of rational and normative theory limited by its relevance for practice.

PURPOSE, PROCESS, AND PROBLEMS
IN AMERICAN FOREIGN POLICY

Maybe only a Republican President could have gone to Peking.

                                                    Dean Rusk

The problem with which Niebuhr struggled was essentially the relation of purpose to politics. He increasingly saw that a discussion of norms out of their context was of little value. Americans, in the period between the two World Wars, were often exhorted to seek world peace through international law and world institutions. Many loyal and responsible persons in the aftermath of World War I felt a deep sense of shame and guilt since, although Woodrow Wilson had been the prophet of world law and order, the Senate had repudiated the League of Nations following his return from the Paris Peace Conference. The generation which comprised the intellectual leaders of that era, and included such men as Nicholas Murray Butler, President of Columbia University, and James Shotwell, President of the Carnegie Endowment, called for rededication to world organization and effective world law. Their resolve and conviction, along with that of many others, paved the way for American sponsorship of the United Nations and a new International Court.

Perhaps because these international goals were so largely realized postwar leaders have concentrated increasingly on another aspect of America's responsibility in the world. Recent history makes it abundantly clear that new and more orderly forms of international relationships have not altered an ancient requirement in world politics—that a nation that aspires to world leadership must achieve a clear image of its role in the world, the purposes for which it stands, and the policies its security and traditions require. A great power that calls on the world to embrace international values must first enunciate its own national values and trace out their points of contact and consistency with universal and worldwide values. Nor will it do to simply affirm that the rest of the world should pursue our goals, worthy as they may be. The needs of men are too variegated, and there are many mansions in the present international society.

In the eyes of the rest of the world, the United States is frequently less successful in articulating narrow, working national purposes than in listing broad international goals. Even our friendly critics abroad point to the gap between what we do and what we say. The annals of interstate relations clearly attest that other world leaders, from the time of the Roman Empire to the British Commonwealth, share with us the dubious privilege of being objects of widespread criticism. However, their shortcomings and the apparent inevitability of attacks cannot excuse us from the task of marking out the ethical guide lines for America's conduct in the world.

Superficially, American thought has always been sensitive and alert to the ethical challenges of the day. As President Calvin Coolidge found that his clergyman was "against sin," most Americans are "for virtue," or "for values." Almost every private and public national commission pays tribute to the central importance of ethical purpose. Nearly every President invokes God's help. By contrast, countries like Germany and Italy in the 1930s were imperiled by excessive moral cynicism. In those years whole societies and peoples were seized by a prevailing belief that "might makes right." This seldom has been an American affliction although during the cold war "negotiating from strength" and therefore the building of strength to this end was recognized as a necessity. We tend to pursue national goals, even overwhelmingly materialistic ones, in a spirit of religious fervor.

Moreover, when we do make statements of ethical purpose they are incomplete or premature. They neglect the means by which goals can be pursued; sometimes they turn means into ends. Partial and fragmentary acts of justice are cast in the frame of universal justice partly because self-serving individual and collective aspirations are served thereby.

The problem is nowhere more acute than in Western society in the last half of the twentieth century. The doctrines of religious philosophers, such as Albert Schweitzer, may have less relevance for this society than they have for a more primitive society. The political writings of theologians like Reinhold Niebuhr, historians and philosophers like Herbert Butterfield and Jacques Maritain, and jurists like Professor Charles de Visscher may be more attuned to the present. Chester I. Barnard, former President of the Rockefeller Foundation, has pointed out that theologians are wont to speak of "a nomadic and simple agricultural life—of sheep and lambs, of shepherds—in an industrial age in which the majority have no experience of rural life." The present-day world bears almost no resemblance to the ancient world of saints and prophets. Its hallmark is human behavior in the aggregate; it suffers from the clash of great collectivities, each a law and morality unto itself. Big industries, big unions, and big government dominate the national scene. The nation-state is the prevailing organization in the international arena. Individuals who are robbed of self-fulfillment by the fragmentary nature of rewards that most vocations provide turn to Leviathan.

The precariousness of man's existence, his limited satisfactions, and his unquenchable will to power and prestige lead him to seek recognition where he can. More often than not, he finds it vicariously as his nation or his corporation achieves greatness. Unfulfilled aspirations channeled into national ambitions generate the fierce enthusiasm and crusading zeal of today's nationalism. The more intense the alienation of individuals, the more extravagant their national fervor. Insecure and uncertain persons, because they can realize themselves only in the group, lose their identity and with it their critical faculties. They accept unquestioningly the group's moral judgments because ambition and self-respect require it; they reinforce the spirit of national self-righteousness. In the end, they help make collectives morally autonomous communities.

The Process of Foreign Policy

The belief in "my nation right or wrong," which is a corruption of Carl Schurz's far wiser statement: "Our country right or wrong. When right to be kept right; when wrong, to be put right," illuminates only one illusion men may have in the search for moral purpose. It is an illusion that singles out one aspect of moral judgment; it concludes prematurely that inevitably my nation is morally righteous. But this viewpoint is not suffcient because the observer who tries to demarcate national purpose must face the stubborn realities inherent in the situations within which national purpose must be formulated. He must come to terms with the ethical problems raised by the nature of foreign policy. What are some of these realities touching the process, problems, and the dimensions of foreign policy? The incredible complexity of the process by which present-day foreign policy is formulated is the first datum deserving consideration. In the eighteenth and nineteenth centuries, peace required the agreement of a handful of rulers whose judgments and opinions were tantamount to decisions. They shared a common moral universe and were at home with one another's political discourse. They were not any more or less virtuous than other men, but their virtues and objectives were mutually perceived and comprehended. They understood one another and were able to settle disputes without the involvement of the wider public.

In democracies, the anatomy of a foreign policy decision is infinitely more complicated. Our allies and friends abroad are continually bewildered in their search for a point of decision within our sprawling political system. They ask where we stand on NATO, or Vietnam, or thousands of other policies. Where in the machinery of government is an issue at any given time? Who is responsible? The Executive, the Legislature, or the Judiciary? Where does one find the source of a policy when it may be in any one of a dozen places: the ideas of a statesman or Senator, a letter from a friendly ambassador, a file for the United Nations agenda, or a paper for the National Security Council? With whom ought the representatives of foreign countries to consult: the President, the Secretary of State, the National Security Advisor, or an ambassador? How reconcile conflicting policy statements? Who coordinates and who decides? The Secretary of State is responsible, historically, for marshalling and ordering the business of foreign policy. With the multiplication of nonpolitical agencies for economic, cultural, and propaganda purposes a far-reaching and often bewildering diffusion of responsibility and decision-making has resulted. Policies are continually being reformulated and renegotiated, and key officers like the Secretary and the President must, through their representatives, round up support for each new program. Like sheep dogs they rally their followers and bring them into line behind a continually changing policy. Beyond external pressures, hundreds of factors leave their imprint on policy: tides of public opinion, dominant personalities, the President's or Secretary's concept of his office, and the scope of legislative bipartisanship. The relative influence of each of these forces makes firm political and moral judgments hard to come by.

The point of this recital of the complexities of the foreign policy process is that collective morality is invariably less simple and unambiguous than personal ethics. Individual morality commonly involves the relations between two persons. Each bears obligations and responsibilities to the other. In democratic foreign policy, obligations are diffused and obscured. Burke's dictum has relevance, both for the nation and for the individual, for it remains true that no one has found a way to indict a whole people nor in the case of most decisions can we point the finger to a single individual who is accountable. Every day somewhere in the world some American official attending an international conference is expected to state United States policy. But who is ultimately responsible: the representative or those who have drawn up his instructions, the President, the Congress, the State Department, or one of the myriad agencies in the government with international interests? And what of those conferences for which instructions are incomplete and officials on the spot are compelled to improvise a policy?

Officials representing the United States are in attendance daily at approximately a dozen international conferences; Secretary Dulles during the early months of his term in office met with committees or subcommittees of

Congress nearly twice a week and Secretary Rusk only slightly less frequently. The cable volume of the Department of State exceeds that of the
Associated Press and United Press International combined. High officials,
particularly in recent years, are asked to approve policies contained in
position papers for which only a tiny fraction of the supporting evidence is
put forward. The Secretary no longer sees or signs the bulk of departmental
communications which go out over his name. During Secretary Rusk's eight
years in office, he sent out 2.1 million cables and of these personally saw and
signed no more than an average of ten a day—the President one a day. Can
responsibility be fixed at the level of top officials—the chiefs—or does it also
rest with the so-called Indians at the working level? If so, how are we to
divide responsibility in some appropriate fraction among those who recom-
mend and those who decide, when the latter do not share all the evidence and
the former are not constitutionally responsible? The issue of the U-2 plane,
overflying Russia on the eve of the abortive Eisenhower-Khrushchev summit
meeting, is only one of the most dramatic examples of the problem. Who in
the vast network of intelligence operations made the decision regarding that
particular overflight of Soviet territory, and who carries responsibility for the
unhappy and tragic turn of events? In this case President Eisenhower publicly
assumed responsibility although privately he had struggled to establish relations with Premier Khrushchev, whose downfall began with this event. The
irony of the President's publicly announcing his responsibility was that
Khrushchev, who could have lived with the knowledge that the President
knew of but did not acknowledge the overflying of Russia, had no alternative,
given the alignment of forces with the Politburo, but to break off preparations for the Summit Conference.

Foreign Policy Problems

The complexity of moral judgment is not solely the result of the diffusion of
decision-making within democratic political systems. It also inheres in the
nature and scope of the problems themselves and the pace at which they must
be resolved. Outsiders often see foreign policy problems as clear-cut moral
issues: peace or war, negotiations or conflict, support of the United Nations
or selfish nationalism. However, the form of contemporary problems is
almost never so simple. Before there can be a decision on policy, someone
must frame the question. The vast majority of questions are practical,
specific, even narrow in scope. Should a visa be granted? Ought trade
arrangements be modified? What are the grounds for negotiating a treaty? Is
now the time for a visit by the chief executive of a neutral country? Such
questions are practical issues in which the moral problem is several stages

removed. Having in mind the preponderance of decisions of this kind, a State Department official observed that in thirty years of foreign service he could not recall a single case in which issues had been weighed primarily in ethical terms.

Once valid questions are formulated, some of course answer themselves. Others may not be susceptible to answers and still other problems deteriorate before any answer is possible. Some questions are resolved by obsolescence and others must be reformulated before officials can deal effectively with them. And sometimes the validity of the question itself is questioned. As an Assistant Secretary of State, Dean Rusk relates that each year he kept a personal list of the sixty or seventy most urgent problems that appeared on his agenda for action. Coming back to the list a year later, the Secretary was · astounded at the number of problems that time had resolved or that had over time been translated into other issues. Doing nothing may be a policy no less than taking decisive action. Yet the public often sees in inaction a sign of weakness or immorality or both. It is a peculiarly American view that "It is always better to do something than to do nothing." This ignores the fact that in diplomacy doing nothing may sometimes be the best policy.

In fact, the private citizen, and particularly the moralist, does no one a service by merely exhorting from the sidelines. He who persistently calls for a new policy for this area or that problem misunderstands the nature of foreign policy. His voice is like that of a man calling from the platform to a friend caught in the subway rush. For the friend crushed and hemmed in by surging humanity the outsider can hardly be of much help. The milieus in which the two men must act are so utterly different that insistent demands to do this or that can only be confusing. The most recurrent example of the relationship between men living in two worlds is that of the scientist and policy-maker. When a philosopher such as Bertrand Russell viewed foreign policy problems through the "squint" of the natural scientist, he was counselling action with little or no immediate relevance for viable programs of action. Almost every rational and predictable pattern familiar to the scientist is missing from the political realm.

The New Dimensions of Foreign Policy

Further, the pace and magnitude of international problems and their dimensions conspire to complicate moral judgment. From the days of the first Secretary for Foreign Affairs, John Jay, the office and its duties have radically changed. Some of the early Secretaries succeeded in combining part-time legal practice with diplomatic duties. Secretary Jay's office numbered an assistant and two or three secretaries, barely enough to enable someone to remain in the office while colleagues were at lunch. Today the department has more than twenty thousand employees and some form of representation for approximately 135 countries. On every important issue the United States is expected to have a policy—not in due course but immedi-ately. News of events in Europe and the Middle East reaches the department in the early morning hours, and before the day has passed the United States is expected to announce its policy. Multiply this by a thousand and you have a rough picture of the decision-making problem.

Until World War II, it was probably sufficient for the United States to have viable policies in Europe, Latin America, and a few scattered outposts in Asia. Today the United States has become increasingly involved in all parts of the world. To meet these new obligations, the President and the Secretary of State have become two of the world's most constant travelers. In the jet age, finding time for serious reflection on all the facts has become more and more difficult. One casualty of modern technology has been having time in which world leaders could search their consciences as did Lincoln, McKinley, and Wilson in earlier periods of American history. In other words, the expansion of the international system has further complicated the moral problem.

The Rediscovery of Purpose

In the face of these massive and far-reaching changes in the anatomy of foreign policy, the observer asks himself whether moral purpose is obsolete in foreign policy. Are ethics in world politics like a living organism that in a changing environment loses its earlier function? Or can we point to areas in which men and states can rediscover a sense of national purpose compatible with the goals of others?

There are at least four spheres in which ethics and values have a central role to play. The first is the domain of the individual, and of one man's attitude toward another. The second is the domain of national life and the values men share as citizens in search of the good life in a more tolerable society. The third is the domain of a national approach and attitude toward the harsh realities of international politics. Finally, the fourth is the domain of the broader international community, the kind of world in which we live, and the sense of our destiny under God.

The first domain is often obscured by complexities and uncertainties. In the same way that personality is extinguished by the pressures bearing in on the organization man, human qualities of honesty, judgment, and responsibil-ity often fall victim to demands for national conformity. "A diplomat is a man sent abroad to lie and deceive in the interests of his country," wrote an early diplomatic observer. The British historian Harold Nicolson has amended the statement by adding "but he must return to negotiate another day." The qualities by which men measure their friends are therefore not wholly irrelevant for diplomacy. A strong, trustworthy, and responsible diplomat is more likely to build up the intangible nexus of solid human relations from which understanding can grow. One can point to a complex of personal qualities memorialized by writers in phrases and aphorisms that have endured. They include a set of virtues not exclusively in the realm of personal ethics, but political qualities nonetheless, by which the extraordinary individual is measured. One such virtue is courage: "In politics courage is the master virtue and without it there can be no others." Another is the capacity for leadership: "There is this to be said for a strong and scrupulous man; when he gives his word he can keep it." Professionalism in the broadest sense is a hallmark of responsible politics: "The worst blunders of practitioners are less dangerous than the sciolism of the amateur." Our procedures for selecting representatives abroad, particularly at the level of ambassador, risk obscuring the importance of professionalism. If the public were made more keenly aware of the prospects of morally responsible conduct by the best of professionals, the republic would be better equipped to fulfill its purpose in the world. Summitry, open diplomacy, and spectacular exposés in congressional hearings—all stem from a lack of confidence and respect for professional public servants. A government with vast commitments around the world can scarcely afford this viewpoint, any more than it can accept denials of standards of excellence in its cultural life. Resourcefulness coupled with a sense of a Providence transcending all fragmentary human virtues is the quality well exemplified by Lincoln and Washington: "Act as if everything depended on you while knowing that all depends on God." Taken together these qualities are capable in the best of men of making for firmness free of arrogance, idealism devoid of hypocrisy, and justice uncontaminated by claims of absolute justice. In this way, personal ethics, which so frequently seem alien in the clash of great collective groupings, reappear in the association of their representatives and leaders.

The second domain touches the values men cherish most as they reflect on the social and political order within which they live and move. What is the good society? What is the current state of national life and what ought it to be? Moralists need to remember that religious and ethical values are never the sole support for a more tolerable collective order. History offers too many examples of monarchical states on the "right" which have exploited religion for their purposes in suppressing rights and making tyranny legitimate. As we saw earlier, American democracy is the product of a happy confluence of Judeo-Christian precepts and liberal humanitarian values. The "higher law" that englobes the American Constitution provides the framework within which sharp but acceptable debates are pursued on the methods of achieving justice. In Paul H. Nitze's well-chosen words: "Over and beyond the values of any particular array . . . of human beings there exists an ethical framework which has objective validity, of which men can aspire to have some degree of understanding—not perfect, but approximate—and which can give a measure of insight and of guidance to those who seek it."[10]

A third domain concerns the ethical principles that carry meaning for the harsh realities of international politics: power struggles, armaments races, and self-interest in national security. Moralists and international lawyers, out of genuine concern for the predicaments that confound the participants in world politics, often contrive rules and standards meant to reduce international conflict. However, when external standards run athwart their natural aims and drives, men and states find ways of abridging or destroying them. If standards and limitations can be made to serve the purposes of states, they will be honored and observed for long periods of time. One significant example stands out in the law of treaties. Nations, like individuals, keep their international commitments when it is in their mutual self-interest to do so. The Rush-Bagot agreement settling the Canadian-American boundary dispute has been long-lived because the parties have found it serves their national interests. Other agreements, particularly in the armaments field, have been scrapped when their terms conflicted with national interests. Disarmament negotiators face the task of discovering standards that will be self-enforcing because on balance they will serve all sides.

Beyond this, however, the observer can point to general moral concerns that have meaning in the interstate system. One is the concept of forgiveness and another the principle of charity. Following every international war, the victors have essentially two alternatives as guides in the drafting of the peace. The one is to approach this task in a spirit of *revanche* and vindictiveness, to "wipe from the earth the evil force responsible for the conflict." Unlimited war-aims and unconditional surrender tend to drive men in this direction, although there are exceptions. (The treatment of Germany after World War I illustrates this tendency while that of Germany and Japan after World War II reflected the determination of Britain and the Unites States to avoid this.) The trouble with such conceptions is that, almost inevitably, they sow the seeds of the next conflict. The destruction of one great power creates a political vacuum into which another state must extend influence and control. Not only does the laying waste of a nation assure that the reestablishment of internal order will be more difficult, a situation that extremist political groups will exploit; at the same time it constitutes a standing invitation for power from the outside to flow into the vacuum.

Forgiveness in world politics presumes that most international struggles take the form of a tragic predicament. Although one nation's cause may be more just than another's, neither side is wholly right and neither is totally at fault. They conflict and dispute, break off diplomatic relations and take up arms when neither can afford to yield great moral points at issue. They find themselves after long contention at a point of no return. Once at war they abandon the tentativeness of the political process for full-scale moral and military crusades, and when they approach the peace table in this same spirit the chances for conditions of lasting peace are remote. By contrast, forgiveness has been combined with political realism in certain peace settlements. At the Congress of Vienna, France was reinstated almost immediately to the councils of state, partly on moral grounds, but also because the order of Europe required it. Realists such as Metternich, Castlereagh, and Talleyrand recognized the rising threat of czarist Russia and the states of Germany. To stem the threat, the peace was drawn with an eye as much on the new danger as on the ancient foe now vanquished in defeat.

Charity is another moral purpose that on its face seems too compassionate, gentle, and civilized for the brutalities of international life. Yet the rise of new nations crying out for aid and respect may well become the dominant problem of the last decades of our century. In sheer self-interest, but no less from moral impulses, the wealthy nations have perceived their responsibility to aid impoverished states. Walter Lippmann may be stretching a point when he draws an analogy from American life where the rich through taxes and gifts now plainly bear responsibility for helping the poor. Yet his comparison is sufficiently close to the mark to point up a lesson. The "have-not" states ask and receive technical assistance from the "haves" because in this era of rising expectations the powerful must aid the weak if they would maintain any form of international peace and order. One challenge confronting a maturing democracy like our own is to learn to discriminate in word and deed between short-run self-interest—that should be interpreted as such—and longer-run charity and magnanimity. We can no longer afford to call one the other, for while concealing self-interest is hypocrisy, we need not shrink from the proper explanation of acts of charity in relief, reconstruction, and foreign aid. From case to case, we are often more selfish or generous than we are credited with being, either in our own words or in those which describe our motives.

The fourth and last domain is the international community itself. This community comprises subcommunities that hold values deserving respect. Writing of the American Secretary of State, Paul H. Nitze observes:

> The Secretary has a primary obligation . . . to the interests of the United States as a nation-state. . . . The Secretary, in representing the coalition system and alliance systems of which the U.S. is a leading member, has obligations . . . to a much wider . . . group. . . . If the thesis . . . is accepted . . . that a principal task of U.S. foreign policy is today the construction and defense of a world system of order to replace that shattered in two

world wars, then the values to be pursued by the Secretary of State include those associated with a ... group virtually coterminous with mankind as a whole.[11]

Nitze points to layers of responsibility which taken together make for an international order. In part, the building of an international system is a public and governmental act. Underlying this, private groups and individuals build up networks of common interests. Church groups, voluntary agencies, universities, foundations lay more solid groundwork at deeper levels of reality. The growth of a regional system such as the British Commonwealth resulted from an infinite number of individual acts, some of which were sufficiently sound so that on independence states such as India and Ghana continued to embrace many inherited values. The growth of an international order may equally depend on a succession of small actions taken by men who sense and seek to build a more stable international system in which their own humane values have a fair chance of survival.

Through all this, the importance of the relation between initiative and moral purpose looms large. Moral purpose in foreign policy is realistic when cloaked in flesh-and-blood programs. It rises above the limits that restrict morality in foreign policy when expressed in concrete programs for action. Failing this, moral purpose is no more than pious moralism because it touches no one directly and plants seeds of doubt that moral purpose can ever be brought within reach. The link between morality and political realism is political initiative that gives form to concrete hopes. The less said and the more done about moral purpose through specific measures and programs, the more likely our friends abroad, who now condemn us, will praise us for the realism of our national purpose.

NOTES

1. Reinhold Niebuhr, *The Nature and Destiny of Man: A Christian Interpretation,* 2 vols (New York: Scribner's: 1943), 1:1.

2. Ibid., p. 3.

3. *The Children of Light and The Children of Darkness* (New York: Scribner's, 1944), p. 20.

4. *An Interpretation of Christian Ethics* (New York: Harper & Brothers, 1935), p. 140.

5. "Human Nature and Social Change," *Christian Century* 50 (1953), 363.

6. *Christianity and Crisis* 9, no. 17 (October 17, 1949), 132.

7. Ibid. 12, no. 3 (March 2, 1953), 20.

8. Ibid. 40, no. 1 (February 5, 1951), 3.

9. *Christianity and Society* 10, no. 4 (Autumn 1945).

10. Paul H. Nitze, *The Recovery of Ethics* (New York: Council on Religion and International Affairs, 1960), p. 24.

11. Ibid., p. 25.

10: THE PROSPECTS FOR THEORY
IN INTERNATIONAL RELATIONS

As no event and no shape is entirely like another, so also is there none entirely different from another: an ingenious mixture on the part of Nature. If there were no similarity in our faces, we could not distinguish man from beast; if there were no dissimilarity we could not distinguish one man from another. *All things hold together by some similarity; every example is halting, and the comparison that is derived from experience is always defective and imperfect. And yet one links up the comparisons at some corner. And so do laws become serviceable and adapt themselves to every one of our affairs by some wrested, forced, and biased interpretation.*

Michel de Montaigne

Statesmen and scholars, religious and secular spokesmen proclaim with one voice the need for "an applicable body of theory" and for general principles of international relations. At the same time, many question the relevance of existing theories and some even speak with scorn of scientists, seers, and saints "who have remarkably little to offer." This juxtaposition of enthusiasm in principle and skepticism in fact symbolizes the state of theory today. Whether the theory concerned is normative theory or the theory of international politics, the limitations are similar in kind. Walter Lippmann, writing of the normative realm, observes:

> The deposit of wisdom in the Bible and in the classic books does not contain a systematic and comprehensive statement of moral principles from which it is possible to deduce with clarity and certainty specific answers to concrete questions.

He might equally well have made comparable statements about other forms of theory, and indeed he and his contemporaries have done precisely this in other ways.

The problem that arises in translating ideas from one modality to another is a perennial one. Religion, like philosophy, assumes that objective and ultimate truths are absolute in character. Yet as we have seen, absolutes in

163

domestic or international politics are singularly inappropriate. This ought not
to suggest that the ultimate and general have no contact with the real but
rather that someone must mediate between the ultimate and the concrete.
Who can speak but with contempt of what John Milton called that "fugitive
and cloistered virtue, unexercised and unbreathed, that never sallies out and
sees her adversary, but slinks out of the race where that immortal garland is
to be run for, not without dust and heat." But who in turn would suppose
that general principles in most social fields give concrete guides to action.

It is useful to explore the place of theory across a broad and varied front,
and these are the themes discussed in the pages that follow. Such discourse
illustrates the problems and limitations of theory, but also the true long-range
prospects.

ORIGINS, USES, AND PROBLEMS OF THEORY

Philosophy triumphs easily over past evils and future
evils; but present evils triumph over it.
                        François, Duc de la Rochefoucauld

Three general issues arise as one considers the role of theory in international
relations: what are the origins of the present interest in theory; what are the
uses or possible uses of theory; and what are the problems that confront the
theorist as he goes about his task?

The origins of interest in the theory of international relations can best be
traced by describing the dominant trends and problems of three major
approaches to international studies. The foundation of theory is inherent in
the nature and limitations of these approaches. Each contributes elements to
the structure of international studies, and each illustrates the fundamental
problem of theory.

This fundamental problem arises from the inescapable predicament of the
theorist. On one hand, he stands within a historical and social context which,
if his theory is to have signficance, must in a meaningful and continuous way
have influence on his writings and research. In the same way that the medical
researcher can never afford to be too far from the patient in the sickbed, the
theorist must never be far removed from the realities of international life. On
the other hand, the theorist, if he is to have a significant role, must transcend
the historical contingencies and contemporary experience of which he speaks.
In other words, he must do more than simply reflect reality. His conception
must be future-directed, much as the hunter leads the bird in flight lest he get
only tail feathers for his pains, or the astronaut aims not at the moon but
where the moon will be when he gets there.

The dual role of the theorist in both reflecting the conceptual framework and reality of the present and anticipating one that may exist in the future is illustrated by considering the very large issues that confront students of foreign relations. We may ask of past and present theories, "How well have they understood the present and how have they illuminated the future? How lasting have been their contributions?" One thinks of what theorists have had to say—political theorists and legal theorists—about the role of the citizen, of groups, and of individuals in foreign relations. For example, consider the widespread conception, nurtured primarily by liberal democratic philosophers, that the whole citizenry must be equally concerned with issues of foreign relations. The conclusion that foreign policy, to make sense, must be democratic is based fundamentally upon a theoretical assumption about government and foreign policy. In part, it reflects the experiences of national policy and in part is meant to correct the sense of helplessness that seizes many citizens in thinking about foreign policy. And yet I would suggest that the dominant view which prevailed, particularly in this country, in the 1930s and 1940s, and was reasserted in the 1960s, whereby good foreign policy was equated with action based on a kind of continuous referendum, may have misled more than it helped us. We may have forgotten that the individual is not responsible for the United States but only for his part in it. Any individual starts from where he is, and not everyone is or can be an expert. Everyone cannot be the Secretary of State. And much of the impetus of popular movements and even university-directed programs that led people to believe they could may well have been misguided.

I think it is noteworthy that during the period of the severest criticism of Secretary of State Dean Acheson and the foreign policy of the Truman Administration, only twenty-three percent of those people questioned could identify the Secretary by name. In 1974, a Gallup Poll found that eighty-five percent of those it questioned had a positive view of Secretary Henry Kissinger. Does this immense gulf between the known position of the one and the lesser public standing of the other prove that Acheson was unsuccessful as Secretary of State? Or indicate that public interest in and awareness of one figure and ignorance of the other mean that the one foreign policy is good and the other bad? As the future theorist formulates his views on the role of the individual, he should strive not to talk down interest in foreign relations, but rather to talk up peoples' interest in building good schools, shaping the community in which they live, fighting social abuses—all of which may lie within their power to control. All through the nation there are attitudes which pull against our relations with other nations. And these are as much an aspect of the total fabric of American foreign relations as are those issues to which people address themselves in public resolutions or study groups.

It is tempting to suggest that the theory of total participation in foreign policy is informed by frustrated professors or publicists who themselves yearn for mass followings. This would miss the point, however, that a concept of foreign policy by referendum misconceives the nature of the foreign policy process and its problems. The proper and necessary role of the people is to set broad directives and outlines of policy which responsible officials in turn must test out and apply in awesome and private moments of decision. These constitutionally recognized leaders are not free to act without restraint, for they are part of a system of representative government. But neither should they be tossed about by waves of popular reaction to crises that call for expertness and careful thought.

In the whole broad area of the organization of the government for the conduct of foreign policy, better and more solid political theory and analysis is needed. Problems of responsibility and power have long been a concern of political theorists. Certainly, this is the central issue in relationships between the President, the Secretary of State, and Congress. The erosion of authority in a particular department or institution is a subject on which a political scientist ought to have something to say. What are the connections between responsibility and power? If the President is the custodian of the residual initiative of the United States government, then where does his responsibility begin and end? What are the inherent limitations of delegation? Where does executive privilege begin and end? Throughout the history of government, students have debated merits of the division of authority or its preservation as an indivisible whole. Any discussion of authority and power plunges the theorist into this treacherous and complex area.

I mention these rather concrete examples at the start of an excursion into theories of international relations because they illustrate great contemporary issues worth discussing in terms of underlying assumptions. We are obliged to ask: "How effectively have earlier approaches dealt with major current issues? To what extent are their contributions relevant to the immediate present and to the future? What questions are asked? What are the limits of inclusiveness and exclusiveness? What are the appraisals of foreign policy? What have been the greatest sources of error with regard to these approaches?"

The Origins of Theory in Major Approaches

There are three major approaches that one can identify in the study of international relations in the Western world and in particular in the United States which have been alluded to directly or indirectly in earlier pages of this book. If one excludes the discipline of history, then the legal approach is undoubtedly the first great effort to come to terms with both problems of American government and problems of international affairs. This point of view dominated the early stages of thinking on foreign relations in virtually every developed country (witness Japan today), and its sources of influence are obvious. As we compare national and international life, the one missing element on the international scene appears to be the absence of law and government. And the implicit theory of most international lawyers has been that only by substituting law for lawlessness could the unhappy circumstances of international life be rectified.

Lawyers have often served as innovators by stepping in to fill the vacuum when others were ignoring current problems. In the study of American government the first comprehensive framework for studying current problems was a legal framework. This viewpoint has been dominant as well in the foreign relations field. For in a rather alien, ambiguous, and disillusioning sector the moral impulses of the American people made this particular approach congenial. There was a long and respected heritage (the subject of a brilliant analysis written for discussion by the British Committee on Theories of International Relations by the late Professor Martin Wight of Sussex University) of international lawyers in the seventeenth and eighteenth centuries who contributed to a more ordered and rational world outlook.

In viewing the legal approach, one is struck by a prevailing oversimplification at three broad stages in its development. In the 1930s, the predominant interest of lawyers was in legislating against war. The Pact of Paris and the instructions of Andrew Carnegie to the trustees of the Carnegie Endowment (suggesting they first address themselves to eliminating the problem of war and only when this had been accomplished turn to other social problems) symbolize the predominant attitudes and viewpoints. Beginning in the 1930s and 1940s, law was merged with an interest in organization and the League of Nations. Scholars with excellent minds were preoccupied with these issues. A sense of guilt coupled with a liberal humanitarian outlook led people to turn to such questions as why the United States had failed to throw its weight behind the new international institution.

Since World War II, international law studies have shifted from an interest in broad theoretical problems to increasing concern with *ad hoc* issues, although exceptions include the writings of men like Charles de Visscher and Julius Stone. A growing interest has been manifested in what law could contribute to the resolution of daily problems of industry, finance, and agriculture as their activities span national boundaries. The acquisition, use, and disposal of property and its legal aspects became a concern of the law. Such specific problems as why, when no guarantees were given for private investment, investment nevertheless flowed to some countries; and why, in other instances, when explicit guarantees were given or discussed, investment had not developed, became a preoccupation of those who studied international legal issues across traditional disciplinary lines. Since World War II, the multiplication of international organizations and institutions with recognized international legal personality has led to the creation of a new branch of international law.

The great contribution of the legal approach is its effect on a more orderly way of thinking about international problems. It also serves to carry men beyond the status quo through anticipating and regulating those disturbing tensions that lead to war.

Yet international law has failed in the quest for a theory, partly because its own theoretical presuppositions have so little relevance to many of the more urgent and tragic problems of international society as a whole. Where it succeeded, it has tended to deal with areas peripheral to war and peace—for example, the Universal Postal Union—and it has failed almost completely in its many attempts to regulate and control armaments. It has paid too little attention to the intimate relation between political objectives or national interests and the willingness of nations to abide by principles and rules of law. It has been seen as a Western product, leading to its rejection by nations emerging from a status where legal principles allegedly worked against them.

Another major approach, originating chiefly in the post-World War II period, has been the political approach. Here one finds students of international relations searching for a point of focus and finding it in the ready-made basic discipline of political science. The political approach is an attempt to discover a core or center for the subjects that make up the totality of international relations. It reflects an effort to order and relate the elements of international society to some overarching set of concepts, problems, and questions. In terms of field theory, what questions does one ask of primary concern and interest as one considers the varied and changing play of forces within a given system? This fundamental issue must be faced in every attempt to construct a theory. The questions that can be asked, while in theory unlimited, reflect the needs and problems of the day. The overall interest in the political approach stems in part from the orientation of students after World War II. The postwar generation was one which had been schooled in a given way of looking at international problems, had experienced the pathos of World War II, and had found earlier ways of facing the world insufficient.

Treatises by Professors Hans J. Morgenthau, William T. R. Fox, and Frederick S. Schuman had as their objective the regrouping and clarification of those aspects of international studies they saw as most relevant to contemporary needs and requiring more rational and systematic treatment. They placed stress on the analysis of the relationship between power and policy, diplomacy and military strength, statecraft and popular support for policy. A whole clustering of issues not commonly dealt with by those with primarily legal concerns prompted attention to political and sociological problems and led to the political approach.

The stages in the development of this approach are readily identified. The initial stage was one in which survey courses laid the groundwork for subsequent works and when the great enabling documents were issued in the form of original and creative texts. For this field, as for the study of economics where the writings of Paul Samuelson and others were formative, texts have had the effect of ordering the data and reorienting the thinking of serious students and observers, including some not fully aware of the shift in their viewpoint.

A second phase came with the merging of the interests of a wide variety of people. It involved a marriage of interests between political philosophers, theorists, policy planners, columnists, and observers who addressed themselves to basic issues of international politics.

A subsequent development, less amenable to simple generalization, was the growth and proliferation of specialized and fractionalized interests within this wider approach. Research institutes sprang up—dealing with military problems, civil-military relations and defense policy, behavioral studies and the role of the actor and decision-maker in foreign policy, political philosophy and its implications for theory, and game theory and conflict resolution—at centers such as Harvard and the University of Michigan.

There are now signs that scholars and practitioners are turning to the application of general principles to specific emergent problems in foreign relations, to the analysis of modes and forms of diplomacy, and to the testing and use of overall theories. This way of looking at foreign relations can be a means of injecting greater realism into foreign policy analysis and of helping man to understand the dilemmas and problems of those who daily work at the tangled skein of foreign relations. Ironically, it has also served to knit contemporary foreign relations studies more closely to the past, because if one assumes that the world is not utterly new, he thereby perceives the value of a study, say, of Castlereagh or Canning grappling with living problems in an earlier historical era.

An organized body of knowledge has evolved from interest in international politics: this focus has served to reunite policy-makers and scholars. But there are certain grave uncertainties inherent in this approach, for hidden from view is the risk of making norms out of past and current practice. It is tempting to argue that what is must always be.

Beyond this is the problem of adapting any theory to researchable problems or giving content to broad categories that set boundaries to the field but do not necessarily help in asking the specific questions that are crucial at the working center. Economists may have had an easier time, for example, working within a cost-benefit frame of thought or in using the idea of economizing as a theoretical framework to move to the consideration of data amenable to statistical and quantitative analysis. Therefore, economists and their "trade" have become more "operationally relevant" to consumers of this function. The data of international relations is too intractable for this, it would seem.

A third overall approach to international relations is through the international institutions. Here the data are the multiplication of international institutions and the evolution of more regularized patterns of discussion in international affairs, beginning with the Hague Conferences in 1899 and 1907, if not with the Congress of Vienna. The rise of representative national governments and their preference for the familiar institutions and processes of domestic governments have spurred the scholar and citizen alike to support this approach. The impact of the United Nations idea coupled with the desire of new nations to be numbered among those who participate in the community of nations has given additional impetus and force to this perspective. For the great powers, it provided opportunities for marshalling support. For the smaller states, there is evidence that the cancelling out of disparities of power and influence is more likely within than outside an international institution.

The institutional approach has moved from the 1920s and 1930s, when scholars were heavily preoccupied with building their own models of an ideal international community, to emphasizing institutional description and analysis, and assessing the role of the League of Nations Secretariat, changing concepts of the Secretary-General, the unique structure of the International Labour Organization (ILO), and similar questions.

Later, beginning in the late 1930s and 1940s, political science entered the field more aggressively, with studies by Arnold Wolfers, Hans J. Morgenthau, Walter Schiffer, and Rupert Emerson of the relation between foreign policy and international organization. These inquiries dealt with the structure and functioning of institutions, but also tried to relate them to the great forces and motivations that influenced states within and outside the organization to act as they did.

In the 1950s and 1960s, growing attention was paid to the techniques and methods of parliamentary and multilateral diplomacy. These investigations strove to impose on the study of international institutions some of the time-honored interests and questions with which scholars of international politics have for decades been concerned, but to do so within an institutional framework.

A companion interest was the rising concern for wider theoretical formulations of the principles of international organization. This reflected an effort to impose some kind of orderly framework on the study of international organization. In this same general category are studies that call attention to the relation between responsibility and representation within international agencies. It has been estimated that, at most, 10 to 20 percent of the positions taken on issues and resolutions in the United Nations are taken on the basis of instructions to delegates by home governments. For some of the new nations the size of their delegations to the United Nations exceeds the number of people in the foreign ministries they represent, so the uninstructed are uninstructed because there is no one to instruct them. Moreover, many of these delegates have had no particular experience or training in foreign affairs. In these terms, conventional concepts of responsibility for policy within an international body become complex and even meaningless.

The contribution of the institutional approach has been to focus on a very vital and significant trend. It has spurred reflection on evolutionary developments in world institutions. It has provided rough guides for practioners and offered clues on the relations between continuity and change. The Trusteeship Council and other bodies in the United Nations have often mirrored and sometimes magnified the great social revolutionary movements in Africa and Asia. In this respect, what was happening in the United Nations has kept scholarly attention on the main target.

However, as with other approaches, this outlook has bred its own problems. A too-passionate dedication to the object of study has sometimes misled and confused the scholar. The very proliferation of material has made research difficult. The tendency to settle for organizational realities rather than dealing with realities both inside and outside has forced discussion into sterile and formalistic molds. And finally, the lack of a clear and accepted point of focus contained in an ordering theory has limited the enduring value of some research and writing.

What one can say as he surveys these varied approaches is that implicit theories can be extracted in almost every instance. Perhaps it is fair to say that in order of concern with theory the political approach ranks first, partly because it has been the most self-conscious about its interest. The legal and institutional approaches follow in that order. This ranking may be debated, especially by some of the emerging theorists of international institutions, but the evidence seems persuasive, at least at this juncture.

The Uses of Theory

If we turn to the question of the uses of theory, one of the complicated problems involves the relationship between notions of rationality as present in the various social sciences and the implications these have for social theory—and, in this case, international theory. Underlying Western thought from Plato to the present there has been a belief in the fundamental rationality of man and of the political order, writ large in concepts of rules of reason and the idea of the reasonable man. This tradition found its way into American constitutionalism and the practice of American law. In a neighbor-

ing field, the construct of economic man provides a roughly similar conception of man responding rationally to the predominant forces influencing the
economic actor and shaping choices in the economic area. In economics and
constitutional law, the major stress is on man responding within an identifiable sphere to the most persistent of a set of distinguishable forces conditioning if not determining action. However irrational from an ethical or philosophical standpoint responses in terms of marginality, utility, or maximiza-
tion of profits might be, these concepts have nonetheless given a crude and
rough guide for measuring and sometimes predicting action within the realm
of economic behavior. As more has been learned, more refined tools have of
course supplanted earlier formulations. But the object of study is man's
actual economic behavior, not behavior as society might wish it to be. This
has been a focal point for research and study in economics. And if one asks
why economics is operationally relevant today, it is in large part due to this
fact.

If then we ask about the uses of international relations theory, the issue of
rationality has again played a prominent role in determining the relevance, or
lack of it, of theory today. For rationality in international politics—and
particularly in international relations more broadly construed—has been conceived of in substantially different terms than in other disciplines. Here, the
starting point has been the overarching desire for peace in international
society. According to this assumption, the behavior of nations in earlier
epochs was marred by self-interest and rivalry. The pressures, demands, and
necessity for peace were such that a new motive power had been introduced
that would reintegrate and reorder international conduct around a more
rational and civilized goal. If in fact some states were laggard, the responsibility could be placed on those which everyone would agree were the delin-
quents and troublemakers. Only a small handful of states or an occasional
troublemaker stood athwart the pathway to peace and order.

Viewed in this context, for the overwhelming majority of states peace was
construed as the one end that they kept unceasingly in mind. Reason and
peace were equated, and no reasonable and responsible state could be expected to place another goal ahead of peace. Law was the instrument of peace
and reason, and scholars such as Quincy Wright argued in his lectures that
"No human society has ever discovered an ordered substitute for violence
save through the use of law and legal institutions."

This stress on peace as the object of states and of law as its instrument was
consistent with dominant nineteenth-century consciousness of mankind that
progress, more and more heralded as inevitable, rested on the twin supports
of reason and law. National achievements, in particular within Western
democracies, confirmed the belief that law and government assured internal

peace. The application of this principle to the international scene was a short and logical extension of an established political truth. It is argued that the Hague Conferences, especially that of 1907, had succeeded in codifying the law governing the conduct of hostilities and the rights and duties of neutrals. They bred confidence that even war would not interrupt the rule of law. They established rules of arbitral procedures, set up panels that today nominate judges, and anticipated Article 33 of the United Nations Charter. No one concerned for the welfare of mankind can but be touched by the clear and unequivocal call to rationality inherent in this approach.

Yet at the same time, no constructive purpose is served by claiming that men have reached an ordered world when the evidence around us daily attests that motivations of states are more varied and conflicting than the rationalists and legalists claim. International waterways systems, exchange of diplomatic and consular missions, and protection through mutually accepted privileges and immunities represent areas of effective international law and suggest the forces and practical needs that prompt states to transfer authority and responsibility to international bodies. Judge Philip C. Jessup was unquestionably right when he declared that it would be a major error to think of international law solely in terms of those relationships which are subjected to the greatest strain but for which it is most needed.

Yet the political scientist must account for the persistent reluctance of states to trust their national destinies to legal judgments. International lawyers frequently deplore the frame of mind that so often exists in foreign offices which seems to consider it a distinctly unfriendly act for another government to bring an international dispute before some tribunal which may have jurisdiction. They say that submission to impartial adjudication is an amicable and noble proceeding. But in many states there is a profound distaste for being cast either in the role of defendant or respondent.

Many have resolved the problem of observance and nonobservance of law by distinguishing between lawful and lawless states, peace-loving and aggressor nations. This point of view dominates much of the current debate within international bodies. However, those concerned with international theory would say that such problems have far deeper roots. They suggest that the United States, while sponsoring the United Nations and the International Court of Justice, nevertheless felt called upon to hedge its commitment to the compulsory jurisdiction of the International Court by the so-called Connally Resolution, which said, in effect, that it reserved the right to submit or not submit justiciable issues to the Court. Britain and France, with strong traditions of international law, chose military action instead of adjudication when they considered that their vital interests were in danger at the time of the Suez crisis. Italy had done the same in Ethiopia, causing Edwin Borchard of

Yale to say of Mussolini: "The fellow is right but the fellow is late." Before World War I such actions were accepted procedures in colonial areas. Indian and Pakistan preferred, in their dispute over Kashmir, to trust the workings of time and diplomacy rather than the clearcut arbitrament of international justice. And on and on the examples multiply. As is well known, the International Court has had few disputes on its agenda these past two decades, and many of those were put there for political reasons, not because a workable decision was expected (e.g., Namibia).

Indeed it must be said that the rejection by states of arbitration in most cases throws doubt on any too-simple classification of lawful and lawless states. The scope of international arbitration is necessarily limited because tribunals as a rule decide the dispute on the basis of the existing status quo and the relevant rules of international law. Thus problems connected with change seldom, if ever, can be solved through international arbitration. Peaceful change could be implemented more properly by international legislation but the world is very far from the establishment of an international parliament. This problem requires that the political observer reconsider motivations, behavior, and national conduct in world affairs—a conduct determined by vital interests geographically defined within national boundaries and expressed in action calculated to defend and advance national security and interest.

Initially, scholars dealt with the conditioning factors of national interest affecting policy, calling attention to geographic forces in historical roles, relations with neighboring and distant powers, national objectives, goals, and purposes, and other discussions too well known to require enumeration. An example is Great Britain and its role as an island state, the discussion of its historic policies, expressions of interrelationships of interests—as in the debate over whether to draw nearer to Europe or preserve ties within the British Commonwealth—or in the powerful British impulse to play the honest broker in bringing East and West together, even at the risk of sacrificing principle. Such tendencies, attitudes, and interests have made up the relatively permanent features of British foreign policy, and even with Britain's membership in the European Community, these historic interests continue to play a role. In much the way that benefits and costs provide an ordering framework for study by the economist, the political scientist can profitably explore the underlying interests and objectives of a state before he seeks to answer the question, "Will it observe international law, and, if so, under what circumstances is this most likely?" By posing the issue in these terms, he may avoid careless use of the great simplifying slogans, such as "lawful" or "lawless" states or "aggressor" and "peace-loving" states. By treating the problem "politically," he is more likely to consider elements that yield to orderly and systematic discussion.

The Problems of Theory

It is perfectly obvious that most of these notions are central to recent theoretical writings, and one might quote from treatises which elaborate and extend them in a significant way. But what problems arise in connection with this approach to theory? The most persistent problem and the one which the theorist can never overlook is the essential limit to the contribution an international theorist can make. More specifically, how is the theorist to encompass in any kind of a theory the role of accident in history, the impact of particular personal relationships, the function of a dominant and over-powering ideology that leads states to act, not rationally within an essentially irrational ideological framework, but irrationally within an irrational framework? Consider the heedless irrationality, whether from the standpoint of ideology or of interest, of Hitler's Germany in conducting major warfare on two fronts simultaneously. Or reflect on the apparently irrational anticoloni-alism of some of the new states, heedless of the greater present threat of Soviet or Chinese imperialism.

There is a further problem. How can the theorist put forth principles that are operationally relevant, when principles often conflict and continually compete with one another? With Cuba, we base our policies ultimately on the Monroe Doctrine, but we also are bound by a network of treaties of nonintervention within the Western Hemisphere. We believe in the health and vitality of the North Atlantic Community, but we have been no less dedicated to the support of the colonial nations in their rise to independence. How are we to sort out the relationships between competing principles?

The fundamental dilemma of the international relations theorist is that, in contrast to economics, the policy-maker is confronted with a galaxy of complicated factors to be sorted out in a political system that frames policy not on dictate but on consent, not in terms of a single calculus, as with the price mechanism, but in multiple factors. And all the while the Secretary or the President must make his decisions with the hounds of time snapping at his heels. The nub of the problem may lie in the distinction between a "conclu-sion" and a "decision." Consider the contrast between the luxury of a scholar, deferring a "conclusion" until all evidence is in and even then returning to revise, reformulate, and adapt to new facts, with the perennial problem of the decision-maker, who not only must act instantaneously but must live with the consequences of his actions. This basic distinction suggests a range of considerations and a set of problems for which theory, if it has any relevance, has relevance that is circumscribed and limited.

All our principles confront us at some point with exceptions. One princi-ple which most of us have found persuasive as we view the drama of institutional life in America, or of mankind generally, is the inevitability of the struggle for power among those holding office. Yet some would argue that this struggle, for those who make foreign policy, is true only in a formal bureaucratic sense. There is also, they argue, a struggle to diffuse responsibility. They observe a flow of power to those who are prepared to use it, and by contrast, even among men of ambition, the trend toward a jungle of committees, a reluctance to accept personal responsibility, the substitution of a committee for a mind, delay for action, and the introduction of the lowest common denominator of thinking for an initiative. It is said this reflects the limits of a principle which, by and large, one can test and observe all around him in the behavior and the actions of men.

These examples are advanced as warning signs, much as historians react to the invoking of sweeping historical principles based on limited examples. The fact should never be obscured that international relations is not a realm in which the data are readily at hand, easily subjected to tests and measurements, but one in which the wisdom and insight of a statesman must mediate and order broad principles which have significance only in the most general terms. Thus, while the theorist addresses himself to the role of theory and calls upon others to direct their attention to the great task of formulating general principles within the international studies field, he is also obliged to invite attention to this utterly complicated fabric that makes up the warp and woof of international politics.

As history makes shipwrecks of all philosophies of history, so the problems of foreign relations complicate the application of principles evolved and in process of evolution. This need not deter those of extraordinary intellectual power from grappling with the formulation of a more orderly framework, nor should they, or their students, be discouraged if the immediate achievement of an operationally relevant formulation awaits further inquiry and processes of history not yet observable by man.

A Reappraisal of the Role of Theory

No more egregious error could be made, therefore, than to assume that the development of a theory of international relations is a simple and modest task. No one can commission or order the elaboration of intellectual work of lasting significance. Throughout history, theory and philosophy stem from the application of intelligence of the highest order to problems of greatest urgency and moment. No mechanical or administrative contrivance can assure that these two ingredients are brought together in a single intellectual act. One of the consequences of universal education and of the stress on equal educational rights for all has been to obscure the essential mystery of the rise and impact of creative scholarship or thought in a given field. The sobering lesson of most of intellectual history is that formal academic attacks on problems have more often served to consolidate existing knowledge than to push forward the frontiers of understanding. Professor Norman Jacobson of the University of California has distinguished between teachers of political theory and political theorists, and has put forth the view that the great political philosophers of the past tended to be creative writers or observers who appeared on the intellectual scene without apparent warning and with few, if any, formal credentials. Someone has asked whether agencies concerned with economic or political theory would have identified Karl Marx, at work in the British Museum Library on the development of his scheme of economic development and political economy, or John Locke, Adam Smith, David Hume. It is significant that theorists who have had the greatest impact in recent times—men such as Walter Lippmann, Reinhold Niebuhr, and George Kennan—have not been teachers of political theory as such.

It would also be pretentious for those who have developed theories in other dimensions of social life to propose that their concepts or theorems are readily transferable to the realm of international society. The problem of transference is a stubborn and intractable one. Economics, which has been in the forefront of theory-building among the social sciences, may well have lessons for the theory of international relations. However, the efforts thus far to adapt and apply leading concepts from economics to international politics are not convincing. Thus input-output analysis, where the data can be quantitatively measured and where a laboratory situation more nearly applies, has been formulated with reference to political questions in broad and general terms, without as yet proving its usefulness to the crucial problems with which statesmen and scholars must contend. The same can be said of game theory, although relatively simple experiments at the Massachusetts Institute of Technology have been illuminating regarding the usefulness of certain precepts. The basic problem remains, however, of shifting from one subject matter to another, for the burden of proof falls heavily on those who would argue that the social experiment is so universal that scholars can adapt with little difficulty concepts and ideas which have demonstrated utility in one limited sector.

A further problem arises from the urgency of the international problem. One grave difficulty for social science, as distinguished from natural science, is the nearly irresistible pressure exerted on theorists to solve vital and sometimes life-and-death problems before their body of theory is adequate to the task. Everyone is concerned with the problem of cancer, but most understand that scientists can solve the problem only when *all* the facts are known, not simply on the basis of present discoveries. However, those who are appalled by problems of peace and war can not avoid calling, sometimes in strident tones, upon the theorist to solve these great and overarching issues.

Perhaps this is a matter of scale, perhaps a flaw in our system of education, but in consequence the theorist vacillates between a preoccupation with broader and more universally applicable principles and the demands placed upon him as a trouble shooter. He moves back and forth from his office to a position on the firing line, and it is tempting both for him and for society to judge him as a theorist by the success of his recommendations for policy. In one sense, this may provide a happy corrective to an ingrained tendency of some social scientists to abstract formulations excessively. But it also frequently leads to confusion and misunderstanding.

At the other extreme, the argument that theory need bear no relationship to the great and pressing problems of the day is equally calculated to mislead. It can be shown that John Stuart Mill or Niccolo Machiavelli were not unmindful of the crucial and far-reaching constitutional and political issues of their day. In regarding their writings, one is again and again impressed with an essential contemporaneity. Thus Mill brought his views on liberty, freedom, and equality or justice, law, and social order to bear on the most vital problems of his day. He frequently referred to a judicial opinion that had been rendered within the week in which he wrote or in the very recent past. This reminds us that no theory worth its salt can be kept stored away in an ivory tower. Somehow, it must be made to fit the needs and circumstances of the everyday world. It does not stand or fall with these tests, but neither can it be held aloof from them. A theory which deals only with some bygone problem or evolves with reference to some purely mythical or imaginary issue is not likely to be of use.

The theorist must therefore possess a resoluteness and moral courage that few if any intellectuals in any age are likely to possess. He must not become the handmaid of those who decide upon great public issues nor must he pretend that these issues do not exist. His value to the policy-makers depends to a significant degree on his standing both within the setting of the needs and perplexities of the day, and above and outside them. Perhaps for this reason the contributors to philosophy or theory in any age are likely to be numbered on the fingers of the hand.

Nor is it helpful for those who undertake the great task of stating broader and more enduring truths to be told that they should do so without reference to past wisdom. Those who are unqualifiedly critical of the efforts of students of international law, international organization, and diplomacy over the past century to contribute to a theory perform no lasting service. The problems and pitfalls which have confronted past scholars and observers tend to become obscured. The perennial problems of all philosophers who must deal in a world where elements both of uniqueness and of continuity exist are likely to be forgotten. What the theorist says in one era about one type of political phenomenon may well be overtaken by a new era and new political phenomena. If he recognizes this peril, he will be more likely to frame his philosophy in the light of a permanent limitation confronting all theorists.

The phrase "merely descriptive" may also divert men from an intrinsically valuable and respected intellectual enterprise. Before the theorist can begin his work, he must have a grasp, through his work or that of others, of the essential facts with which he must deal. This, incidentally, is one of the problems about theorizing on the problems of the new nations. We lack the basic data on the political societies of Africa, Asia, Latin America, and the Middle East to put forward generalizations which have the same relevance that earlier theories concerned with Western Europe or the United States might have had. If descriptive analysis and historical writing are confined to a second-class status, this will retard rather than advance knowledge and understanding. The qualities of mind and character which support the one type of endeavor are often at odds with those required for the other, and to enlist men competent in one sphere to undertake work in the other merely leads to confusion, frustration, and disillusionment.

Nevertheless, the willingness and the desire of serious and responsible scholars to address themselves to the problems of a philosophy of international relations also carries promise for the future. It focuses the spotlight on one of the major neglected areas in international studies, and redresses a balance which had placed the overwhelming weight upon other modes of thought and study. It liberates the mind from attention to the "trees" in any given set of problems and redirects attention to the "forest." It also challenges the trend of thought, induced by modern Western technology and science, that would limit serious and significant work to highly specialized activities. Knowledge in the twentieth century must be to a certain extent compartmentalized. Progress in any field depends upon intensive study of identifiable and manageable problems. Yet those who suppose that when these specialized studies are completed the day's work is over are at least as much in error as those who imagine that careful, painstaking, and patient study of more limited problems has no validity. This is particularly true of the field of international studies, where the most vital issues overlap and merge with one another. Every problem is in some way interlaced with every other one. If study is confined to a host of discrete and separate problems, the understanding for which men and societies are waiting is unlikely to be realized.

If some become discouraged by the magnitude of the problem of international theory, this may also be a blessing, for the world is filled with writers and private citizens who see the issues of world politics in far simpler terms than they perceive their own needs and problems. Thus the businessman who recognizes the ongoing character of the questions with which he is forced to grapple day after day is often inclined to lecture students and practitioners of international affairs. He reserves for the international sphere a simplicity and clarity he would never express or defend in his own field of professional competence. Some of the acumen which goes into an understanding of the difficulty and the uncertainty of ordinary workaday problems is needed for the even more difficult area of international relations.

The literature of recent international studies suggests that superior minds are not unmindful of this range and order of problems. There is immense intellectual vitality and ability continually being released in the discussions and the study of international problems. There is a growing awareness that most of these problems call for professional competence. There are sharp reactions against the oversimplifications of the past. One would hope there might also be a willingness to test out and patiently explore the relevance of abstractions and intellectual simplifications that may yield understanding for the future. For the task of theory is to an important degree one of abstracting from the total reality some part which may permit the study and examination of living problems. This abstraction removes one aspect of international relations from its total context, whether it be power, interest, or community. There is merit in this approach, at the same time that it runs the risk of all abstraction. A vigorous debate on the issues of theory may serve the purpose of separating meaningless abstractions from those that have usefulness.

The most severe and demanding jury is that of events and circumstances against which concepts and principles must be judged and tested. While this jury in turn can find its judgments overturned by the course of events, it also provides a body of experience against which the theorist can be judged. All history is in one sense past politics, and the knowledge of international politics of earlier generations or centuries is not irrelevant. Although the winds of change are at work affecting the relations of states, they remain, at least into the mid-twentieth century, sovereign societies who behave in ways that show points of similarity with past sovereign states. Nationalism may be superseded by higher loyalties, and the signs of the shift of popular loyalties to higher political and social organizations can be traced, but this shift has not wiped out loyalty to the nation-state, as the experiences of the new nations make abundantly clear. If costs and profits provide data for the study of economics, the behavior of nation-states and transnational corporations is data for international studies. The form and character of nationalism may change, but in a crude and general way it reveals characteristics reminiscent of the past. Higher loyalties depend on an awareness of the stubborn and intractable character of the lower loyalties in any social situation. Studies of the family or of local or tribal interests illustrate this fact in other areas of study.

But if the theorist were to limit himself to the nation-state, he would also be remiss in his wider responsibility. He must keep in mind a growing sense of identification with larger units. He must also recognize that security, which for centuries could be assured either by the city-state or the nation-state, rests upon wider systems, such as the United Nations. For this reason, the emergent efforts at building a theory of international organization comprise a vital part of the task of the theorist. This is also true of the efforts to generalize about the role of law in international society. If diplomatic historians could overlook international law or international organization in the past—although those whose contributions have endured appear not to have done so—they will hardly be able to do so in the future. The parish of the theorist is the whole of international relationships and no one should presume to dictate the theorist's findings to him in advance, any more than those who would contribute can come to theorizing empty-handed.

The organized body of facts and knowledge upon which the theorist must depend spans the limits of human knowledge. The efforts of the social psychologist on contemporary problems may therefore be as important as those of the lawyer or political scientist. There are signs that this truth has not escaped those who labor in the field. The needs are so vital and pressing that the best efforts of many approaches are required. This suggests that an attack on a broad front holds out more promise than a limitation of the discussion to a few specialists concerned solely, for example, with problems of contemporary diplomacy. The nonlegal or nonpolitical contributions will have greatest value, however, if they are advanced by students fully acquainted with the nature of the fundamental legal and political problems. This is not to disparage past work by political scientists or international lawyers but to suggest, with William Langer, who challenged historians more than a decade ago to look to other disciplines in his presidential address to the American Historical Association, that more must be done if theories of international relations are to have the broad intellectual foundations required.

THEORY AND INTERNATIONAL STUDIES
IN THE COLD WAR

I pass with relief from the tossing sea of Cause and Theory to the firm ground of Result and Fact.
Winston S. Churchill

Men have ideas; ideas have consequences.
Max Lerner

Raymond Aron begins his monumental work *Peace and War* with the words, "Troubled times encourage meditation." Legend has it that Minerva's owl flies at twilight. Turbulent eras have been rich in philosophical inquiry. Aron, like Toynbee, Morgenthau, and Niebuhr, reminds us that Plato's *Republic* and Aristotle's *Politics* coincided with crises of the Greek city-state. Hobbes, Spinoza, Locke, Rousseau, Marx—all wrote in times of revolution, crisis, and turbulence. The "golden age" of American political thought was generated at the end of the colonial era.

The winds of change that transformed international society following World War II, in Arnold Toynbee's words, ushered in a new "time of troubles." World power gravitated to a pair of nation-states, the United States and the Soviet Union, whose authority had formerly been exercised on the margins of the European state system. Not since the Roman Empire had the West witnessed a similar concentration of power. Pundits will debate and historians will long consider whether this new and far-reaching involvement of the United States foreshadowed a brave new world or the passing of a simpler, more civilized age. Was it the twilight of the multistate system that went back to the Treaty of Westphalia or the dawn of a new world order? Was it the first phase in the emergence of a fledgling international system in which universal membership in a worldwide body was joined with great power responsibility? And if so, how would power and responsibility be joined with a proper respect for equality of states, including those with few if any vestiges of sovereignty?

The unfolding of new patterns of international relationships prompted a dramatic advance in international studies following World War II. Returning servicemen and women turned in increasing numbers from preparation for national to international careers. Bold designs for research and training were advanced, and not since World War I had interest been as flourishing. Universities not celebrated for their internationalism entered the field, new courses were designed, graduate enrollment mushroomed. A generation of postwar M.A.'s and Ph.D.'s emerged into newly created positions in teaching, research, journalism and mass communication, government and foreign service, and business. Public and private support reached its height, and pressing problems (such as armaments control) introduced a sense of urgency normally reserved for wartime endeavors.

Yet something was missing from the sudden surge of interest—the ferment and philosophical interest of which Aron spoke. The last quarter century has not been particularly rich in writings on the overall theory of international relations. Instead, we have had an abundance of textbooks and teaching materials, monographs and articles, simulations and games on specific problems of both policy and theory, and some attention to piecemeal theorizing on particular segments of the international scene. The cold war has not witnessed anything like a proliferation of philosophical and theoretical works, even though it is not difficult to point to specific writings that have exerted widespread influence. These include texts that are far more than introductory surveys, the most notable of which is Hans J. Morgenthau's landmark text, *Politics Among Nations* (1948, 4th ed. 1967). This work and a handful of others have played a formative role and generated sharp controversy and debate in which numerous scholars have become involved. They represent, at least at this stage, the limits of theory in international relations.

The crucial point that bears emphasis is that different viewpoints and approaches have characterized the field. No single work in theory has dominated discussion, nor has there been a rigorous and full outpouring in theory.

It should, of course, be self-evident that there is no single route to understanding. The history of thought offers abundant proof that great minds are capable of substituting clarity for confusion, order for disorder, and direction for aimless commentary on the day's happenings through a variety of approaches. Indeed, when we search for the lasting contributions to international thinking, we are confronted with one inescapable conclusion. The contributors have been pundits and philosophers, theologians and historians, political scientists and social scientists. No single perspective holds any monopoly on wisdom; the quality of insight of the observer and his intellectual power outweigh the merits of a particular social theory or methodology. If this is heresy for modern social science, it is orthodoxy in the long history of social thought. For any other conclusion would obscure the timeless importance of Thucydides, Machiavelli, Marx, and Burke, and leave unexamined contemporary writings as diverse as Spykman, de Visscher, Aron, Butterfield, Lauterpacht, Jenks, Halle, Wight, Niebuhr, Morgenthau, and Toynbee.

The point to be made is that theory has not flourished in the cold war to the same extent as a broad interest in emerging world areas, the foreign policy of a particular nation, or a problem like that of military deterrence. There has been no Keynesian-anti-Keynesian debate nor schools of thought as thoroughgoing and far-reaching as these traditions. Notwithstanding, the field has progressed partly because of the immense generalized interest in world affairs and partly because of the modest advances that have been made in limited areas of empirical, normative, and theoretical work. We may usefully explore these advances to gain insight into these areas.

An important stage in the unfolding of any scholarly or intellectual discipline is the quest for empirical reality, and the history of social sciences reflects an early stress on rigorous empiricism, antedating the cold war. In the interwar period, the inquiries of political scientists at the University of Chicago, under the leadership of Professor Charles Merriam, addressed themselves to the firsthand problems of local government, ramifying in turn to interrelated questions of metropolitan, state, and national government, seeking firsthand knowledge. The Public Administration Clearing House was founded to meet the need of drawing together the best available knowledge and expertise on the demanding problems of organizing and managing governmental programs. The inner workings of governmental enterprise at every level were subjected to detailed scrutiny. Men such as Louis Brownlow,

Herbert Emmerich, Leonard D. White, and Don Price ranged across a broad spectrum of governmental problems calling for practical knowledge and a keen sense of reality. They trained a generation of specialists willing and able to grapple with the minutiae as well as the policy problems of administration in the public sector. Many from this group were called to staff departments of government, regulatory agencies, and public enterprises like TVA. Concurrently, text writers like Frederic A. Ogg and P. Orman Ray directed attention to the varieties of institutions and practices that make up American government. The numerous editions of their volumes on American government reflect a patient attention to detail and a passion for reporting changing constitutional and institutional arrangements at every level of government. Early studies of political leadership, including the political boss, political parties, and pressure groups, are further examples of the empirical approach.

Empirical Studies

International studies from the first phase of development were dominated by an empirical emphasis. Historians were in the ascendancy and in their studies expressed devotion to the tenets of historical sciences. Diplomatic history was a respected and established branch of history in general. It had evolved its own time-tested methodology. Since international relations throughout the eighteenth and nineteenth centuries were primarily if not exclusively inter-state relations, diplomatic history embraced the greater part of relevant international behavior. Studies of major diplomatic conferences by historians such as Charles Webster and Harold Nicolson sought to tell the story with all its richness of interplay between personalities and nations in historic diplomatic encounters. Later historians of the Congress of Vienna and the Concert of Europe hark back to these interpretations of historical facts. William Langer, Bernadotte Schmitt, and Sidney Fay were engaged in comparable studies of the diplomacy leading up to World War I. Taken together, the rigorous scholarship and painstaking research that undergirded this laid an empirical foundation for international relations.

Less rigorous but more continuous in preparing the way for an empirical approach to international studies was the daily reporting and commentary of newspaper and periodical coverage of the international scene. International events are, potentially at least, matters of life and death. The threat of war hangs over the participants. A diplomatic miscalculation in a far-off land or marching troops in a remote corner of Asia may spark a worldwide conflagration. With the shrinking of the globe and greater interdependence, more and more ordinary men and women are caught up in international business. Is it any wonder that national newspapers and journals offer a steady stream of facts intended to explain all about world affairs? Readers are tempted to believe they know more about international affairs than about the village hall or the statehouse. Laymen who would not claim to be authorities on other subjects outside their professional fields grow in confidence that since they are bombarded by empirical facts, they are indeed authorities on world affairs.

Grayson Kirk, in *The Study of International Relations,* observes that in the 1920s and 1930s the *New York Times* was an essential feature in the classroom. The job of the professor was to review and discuss the latest dispatch from abroad, or to lecture on the remarks of his favorite diplomatic columnist. What students learned in the "ivory tower" they could relate to the world around them. An atmosphere of contemporary relevance reigned within the lecture hall. While this method of study led to spirited debate and intense conversation, it did not help the field of international relations to move in the direction of cumulative knowledge, nor did it aid in the construction of a coordinated set of principles and ideas. This approach demanded little more from the teacher than it did from his counterpart in the mass media, for each in his own way analyzed the flow of news and attempted to draw conclusions from it.

Representatives of a third school of thought advanced arguments for throwing the spotlight on public policy. In 1916, the Institute of Government Research (which later became the Brookings Institution) was established to encourage responsible and serious analysis of the problems that face public servants. Its goal was to bring together the best minds from the field of scholarship and the field of government. In their classes, professors threw out the challenge, "What would you advise the President to do if such and such a crisis occurred?"

The young observer introduced in this way to international realities was less tempted to oversimplify solutions. He was less inclined to bring to speedy resolution issues that had vexed the minds of experienced scholars for years. Exposure to the complexities facing the decision-maker at least has the virtue of tempering the self-righteousness into which people are apt to fall when others, not themselves, must carry the terrible weight of responsibility of governing a nation.

Nonetheless, the thoroughgoing empiricism and self-proclaimed devotion to facts of the public policy approach was illusory from one standpoint. Unanswered if not unanswerable was the question, "What are the 'facts'?" It was difficult in any given crisis to identify the real issues between adversaries or allies. If the primary issues were clear, the secondary ones were more obscure. Problems had a way of ramifying out from the immediate to the contingent; the primary determinants for policy-makers were infrequently on the surface.

Even for democracies, the conduct of foreign policy necessarily involved private deliberations. The public, including scholars researching for publication in the public domain, is seldom privy to the counsels of government. The daily business of executives, cabinets, security agencies, and staff officers carrying out their sensitive and unpredictable tasks must by definition be free from continuous public criticism and scrutiny. What is true in the governance of every organization—voluntary civic groups, churches and religious bodies, or local and national governments—is even more strongly the case in international affairs. Public discussions are at best a troublesome and awkward procedure. Where national prestige is at stake, governments, totalitarian or democratic, cannot afford to negotiate in public. They cannot run the risk of losing favor with national constituencies by yielding up points at issue.

The structure of diplomacy today makes the study of policy an extremely difficult operation. The observer simply cannot get on the inside track of a government if he is not part of a given administration. How can a researcher speak with authority on policy when he must remain remote from the vortex of decision-making? These are the questions which have brought policy studies diminishing prestige in recent years. Even today, policy research is at best viewed with skepticism by policy-makers, who consider they have the means of carrying on their own policy studies within the structure of government. And even when they profess interest and respect for outside research and study, most of them give little evidence of encouraging it. There are exceptions, of course, as with studies by Rand, the Department of Defense, CIA, and the State Department, which have greater influence and scope than policy studies in other countries. But even here, security regulations often prevent much public discussion of facts thus learned.

Normative Studies

One criticism of policy research has been that it was primarily value-free research. Scholars assumed a degree of detachment denied the hard-pressed decision-maker. Observers enjoyed a greater measure of freedom and broader range of options than policy-makers. Choices that are conceivable to observers are often unthinkable for those whom the public hold accountable as guardians of the national interest. Since scholars and policy-makers perform different functions, this is inevitable and wrong only if the gulf is so wide that all forms of communication break down. National values comprise the framework for rational decision-making; standards for judging good and bad foreign policy are fixed by evolving conceptions of the national interest. The norms of a foreign office, however vaulting the values its spokesman affirms, must in the end be tested by their responsiveness to national security and interest.

The normative emphasis in international studies in the post-World War I period derived from another source and reflected another perspective. The beginnings of international relations as a separate field of study were reformist in outlook and set out to remedy international anarchy. The failure of the American Senate to support the creation of the League of Nations was taken as an object lesson; it spurred American scholars to devote themselves to the task of laying the foundations for the building of an effective international organization. The purposes of the first chairs of international study were described in these terms. Occupants were to assist in the creation of a climate of opinion favorable to new international institutions. The directives of scholars were therefore not primarily scientific. They had a mission to ensure that what had occurred with the repudiation of the League would not happen again. If scholarly writings often took on a moralistic and legalistic flavor, this was the underlying reason. International relations had a purpose and a norm defined fairly simply and unequivocally as building a commonwealth of nations. What contributed to this goal was viewed as positive and good; what detracted from it was judged as negative and antagonistic.

This version of a normative approach had certain undeniable strengths and virtues. It gave to an early phase of international studies a definite and rather uncomplicated point of focus. It assisted university leaders in making clear-cut judgments on the requirements for filling new academic posts in an emerging field of study. Indeed, in the interwar period the overwhelming majority of professors in the field were authorities in one of two closely interrelated "disciplines." Either their major concern was with international organization or with international law. Their chairs were so designated and their writings and research reflected this emphasis. They undertook both to teach and to prepare the way, successfully as it turned out, for a new system of international institutions.

While the normative view of international relations has been sustained and continued into the present, interpreters and scholars have chosen to deal with more complex and less malleable realities. If the objective of the early stages of normative thinking was straightforward and simple, it grew more sophisticated and pragmatic in later phases. This can be made clear through stating the objectives of the two periods. Early the objective was "peace through organization;" later it became "peace and justice through the convergence of interests, organization, and power."

Normative thinkers in recent times have felt constrained to look at international realities through bifocal lenses. On one hand, international trends and development are, as earlier thinkers had proclaimed, indispensable to national survival. On the other hand, nationalism is possibly the most stubbornly persistent reality of our times. It acts as the channel and, sometimes, transforming agent for worldwide ideological movements. It reshapes communism to fit Russian, Chinese, and Yugoslav patterns. It may sometimes be disruptive, disorienting, and evil. It can also be constructive, integrating, and unifying. The once simple dichotomy of bad nationalism and good internationalism that prevailed in the early stage of normative writings has had to be revised to correspond with the facts. Communism is a worldwide internationalist movement seeking to remake the world in its image. How does the normative interpreter evaluate this form of internationalism along-side, say, the process of nation-building in newly independent states? Isn't it too simple to define the world in black and white categories of good and evil when most developments fall in an area of grays?

Moreover, recent contributions in normative thought have set out to demonstrate that values and norms, like men and states, are plural and not single. Norms for groups and nations, as norms for individuals, are multiple and interrelated. The route to clarity and the beginnings of wisdom are not necessarily achieved through simplicity. This comes through in any evaluation of the policies of a given state. The United States since World War II has proclaimed its dedication to "peace through international organization." It also espouses the goal of justice in the world, but who defines the meaning of justice in specific cases? How are the goals of peace and justice to be maintained? What resolution is possible if they conflict? What if these norms, that are clear as general directives, point to conflicting policies in practice? When is the norm of peace to be pursued at all costs and at the expense of justice, and when is justice to be the paramount goal in guiding the conduct of the United States? Is it true that international order and justice which were supreme as the norm in a prenuclear era must be sacrificed to the pursuit of peace in the nuclear era?

There are other issues that arise for the normative thinker. What influence does the stage of development of a nation-state have on the legitimate goals it holds and defends? Is isolationism or neutralism defensible for colonial America and newly independent India but indefensible for Britain or the United States today? How do we distinguish between guiding principles for rich and poor nations? Can we draw a line between, say, the use of force that runs counter to the principles of the United Nations Charter and its employ-ment in maintaining the unity of a threatened nation-state?

In short, students and observers who have written about norms in interna-tional society since World War II have placed far greater emphasis on circum-stances and situations. They have tried to relate norms to context, and have put greater stress on the preconditions for viable rules and effective institu-tions than was true in the work of their precursors following World War I. They reflect, therefore, greater concern with the link between ethics and context; they are children of the trend of thought called "situational ethics."

International law as an expression of normative thinking reflects a similar point of emphasis. It looks at international obligations through spectacles that relate the conduct and behavior of states to forces and circumstances. Today's lawyers are more likely to ask, "What are the circumstances under which treaties and commitments are most likely to be observed? When will these obligations be set aside or bypassed and when will they be transferred to larger international bodies?" Charles de Visscher, Wilfred Jenks, and Philip Jessup all provide examples of this approach. So do participants in some of the larger projects financed by the Ford Foundation that sought to establish links between the legal superstructure and the economic and political infrastructure in various societies. (The concept of "living law" in contrast with "promulgated law" was formulated early this century by an Austrian scholar who studied the effects and application of rules of law formulated by the Parliament in Vienna on life in Bukovina. *Plus ça change, plus c'est la même chose.*)

Thus, normative thinking is still an important feature of international studies. It has lost none of its significance nor is it any less central to the purpose and direction in which states and the world are moving. The temper and purpose have been altered, however, and the spirit is more likely to be analytical and critical than crusading. Fortunately, able minds have been at work in each period of the developing study of international norms. Thus, contributions in this area have helped to clarify the nature, structure, and framework of the working of an international system.

Theoretical Foundations

The norms of international society and the facts of international life have not exhausted the subject matter of international studies. Growing emphasis has also been placed on discovering viable theories of international relations. It is a sign of the times that the same differences of approach that mark other branches of learning are evident here. There are differences between the classical and behavioral theorist, historical and quantitative outlooks, legal and philosophical perspectives, and political and sociological viewpoints. It is difficult at this stage to measure the contributions of any single approach. The usefulness of each will depend on intellectual trends and changes in international society. The important conclusion to be drawn from current thinking is the state of ferment and activity that manifests itself and the lively interest in many quarters in moving in the direction of meaningful theorizing on international problems.

The origins of interest in theoretical approaches go back to the contributions of a few pioneering scholars who were minority voices in the dominant reformist-legalist school of thought during the interwar period. Foremost among this group was Professor Nicholas Spykman of Yale University who, beginning in his early writing on Simmel, sought to introduce an organizing framework into the study of international relations. His introduction of classical sociology and European social thought into the study of international relations was of twofold importance. First, it demonstrated that a fundamental discipline in the physical sciences or social sciences had relevance, through its organizing concepts, for international studies. Secondly, the attempt to examine international problems in broad societal terms had the effect of placing national and international communities within a broadly social context. It set in motion a trend of thought which began to break down the *either/or* viewpoint of the reformist outlook. After Spykman, there was less excuse for speaking of good internationalism or bad nationalism; each fell in place as part of a larger social whole.

Another reason for the quest for theory was the growing awareness that international relations lacked both a center or core and a body of general principles. Given the scope and magnitude of international events, it needed governing concepts or rules for determining what should be included or excluded. Every major commentator discoursing on the state of international relations was constrained to say that from algae to zoology every national enterprise had been internationalized. It was not so much that a single definitive theory was necessary or possible. It was rather that some means must be found for organizing data and drawing conclusions from patterns of behavior. Scholars reasoned that it should be possible to organize separate and disparate data under some type of subordinating concepts. Treaties, armaments, or diplomatic conferences could be studied in terms, say, of underlying interests and power. International society could be appraised in relation to concepts of society and community. The important consideration was to search out organizing concepts that might bring meaning into the study of the vast and amorphous data of international relations.

Since the pioneering work of these early scholars in the field of theory-building, it has become increasingly clear that the formulation of organizing concepts in international studies is a difficult assignment. The theorist faces severe requirements, and it is significant that few scholars have taken up the task. In the early 1960s the Rockefeller Foundation announced that it would consider individual study grants in three broad areas: emergent problems of international relations, diplomatic history and diplomatic analysis, and theories of international relations. The first two categories attracted the overwhelming majority of candidates. Only a small handful applied under the third category. Perhaps this reflects the fact that theorizing is an extremely exacting intellectual effort. Perhaps it shows that international studies are still in the early stages of development. Or perhaps the invitation was not formulated so as to catch the imagination. Whatever the explanation, international relations theory has occupied a less prominent and well-defined place in its field than, for instance, theory in the field of economics.

This is not to say that progress has not been made. Much space has been devoted to international theory in journals such as the *Review of Politics, International Studies Quarterly,* and *World Politics.* The *Journal of International Affairs* has been dealing systematically with problems and trends in theory, as has *Political Studies Quarterly.* As a result of these and other activities, theory has gained a permanent place and the possibility of important progress in the future has been assured.

The Future of Theorizing

The future of theorizing will depend both on the developing and refining of broad generalized approaches to reality and the construction of rational theories for important segments of international reality. This approach seems more congenial to the present stage of theorizing and more attuned to the urgent priorities of the cold war. Foreign aid, arms control, and emerging international institutions all deserve appropriate attention and discussion. At the same time, theories must be derived that are more inclusive than has been possible in, say, economics. The isolating of tiny fractions of reality so fruitfully practiced in macro- and micro-economics may not be sufficient where every choice is influenced if not controlled by an underlay of political, psychological, economic, and social forces. It may be, as some have argued, that we will have to settle for simple and limited theories. Karl Popper remarks that there is probably no natural sequence of three events which can be explained by a single natural law. A physicist would be unable to predict with any precision what will happen in each stage during which a house burns down. But what if the house is the world and the threat is thermonuclear destruction? Can he sit back and say a theory of arms control is too broad for any kind of useful theory? Difficult as these more general concepts must be, there is need to take up the task.

A starting point in a theory of foreign aid, to cite one instance, might be to probe the operational motivation both of the donor and recipient states. We need to know more about the factors that play a role in shaping the will and determination of states to help others, not alone in the public sector but in the private sector as well. To test out assumptions of community-mindedness or respect for the general welfare alongside those policies attuned to the national interest that can be sustained over long periods might be one hopeful area of exploration. Gerald Garvey's review article in *World Politics* (July 1966) set forth lines of thought and investigation that need further attention and elaboration. Professor Hans J. Morgenthau has offered the most searching and penetrating discussion of theories and categories of foreign aid in his celebrated *American Political Science Review* article (June 1962).

The challenge of international relations theory is not too difficult to define. It cannot, at the risk of becoming a kind of intellectual grab bag, approach the world's problems without some sort of ordering and disciplining set of concepts. To gain those organizing principles we must turn to the working ideas of separate scholarly disciplines. Thus sociology (Spykman), political science (Morgenthau), philosophy (Aron and Niebuhr), and law (de Visscher, Ross, and Wright) have contributed to the beginnings of a theory of international relations. We have today what order and rigor we have because students have approached international politics and society through the ordering channels of sociology and political theory. Yet more is needed. The realities are too complex and varied; the variables too difficult to comprehend and control. The pressures are too strong to permit easy simplification, and the data often resist these efforts.

For some future agenda a worthwhile approach would be to examine the several fronts along which theory can move ahead in international study. Certainly one area is a continuation of bold general theories, ever more refined and developed to fit changing patterns of international reality. Significantly, in all the debates about realism and idealism and about the centering of international relations in notions of politics or law or order or authority, these broad generalizing notions have had an unmistakable usefulness, even for particular studies. It is worth looking at the Garvey piece in this connection. While it is a review article of an economic study, Garvey finds that the hope for some kind of developing theory of foreign aid may well rest with the testing out of broad generalized theories in specific areas like aid, where they either apply or do not apply.

This suggests a second order of theorizing. In other words, there are independent and separate orders of national and international behavior having to do with armaments, foreign aid, and so on. Is there any justification for testing broad theories, much as our friends in the agricultural sciences have developed certain basic principles of plant development, and then gone on to test them in new varieties adapted to a given climate and culture? Thus, for example, the so-called Miracle Rice IR-8, which yields three or four times the output of other rices, has been developed at the International Rice Research Institute. Agricultural scientists there did not rest content with the development of a single variety. Their scientific colleagues tested it in Thailand and India and Burma, used it alongside other varieties, and worked on hybrids combining it with local varieties of high quality rice. In Indonesia scientists adapted it to cultural preferences for a more polished rice or alternately, a rougher, more chalky rice. Since 1965, when IR-8 was released, nineteen other varieties have been released, each with its own virtues and weaknesses, each adapted to a particular situation. And then in each given culture the respective national scientists try to develop what is most appropriate for moving ahead with rice production for the area. Is this analogy at all conceivable for international relations theory as one looks out on a terribly complex and difficult world?

I remember a comment by Reinhold Niebuhr directed at the relating of broad moral principles to different cultural situations. He addressed himself to the problems that arise in applying certain Judeo-Christian principles in modernizing societies with a high accent on competition and on the struggle for recognition. Then he made the comment to an audience which included a good many Asian, Latin American, and African students, that he did not know firsthand about the notions of political ethics as they related to each culture, but he thought it would be extraordinarily helpful if someone could examine the prospects for relevant political norms in societies where the cultural setting and the religious undergirdings of the ethical system were altogether different from our own.

A third area in international theory worthy of exploration is the whole realm of narrow testable theories and propositions of the sort that have proven so fruitful and useful in economics. This is an area beyond the competence of most of us because it reflects a degree of specialization that few achieve. It is important to ask if there are sectors of international relations comparable, say, to the firm in the business world in which such theorists ought to work? Are there other aspects for which similar concepts to those used in price theory can be derived and worked out? The same issue of *World Politics* (July 1966) that contains the Garvey review contains a piece by Hayward Alker, which strives to meet the criticism that efforts to quantify international realities are bound to be too narrow and hence self-defeating.

There is a fourth area in which the usefulness in historical policy areas of careful and critical examination of theoretical assumptions and viewpoints can be applied. The importance in history of examining working assumptions is obvious. Historians today would probably agree that there is no such thing as a historian dipping into the stream of reality without applying a set of questions to which he seeks answers. A former colleague, Warren Weaver, used to say that nature never speaks to man in the sciences. Man speaks to nature by framing problems for study and inquiry as it provides the data required in scientific inquiries. In the same way, historical experience undoubtedly speaks to the historian only to the extent that he brings to his study of this vast and endless stream of events, episodes, and crises a set of questions to which he seeks answers. Even the early empirical studies, particularly those by Webster and Nicolson, involved an attempt to apply specific questions and propositions to the historical experience surrounding the Concert of Europe and the Congress of Vienna, and later studies by Henry Kissinger, Roland Stromberg, Stephen Kertesz, and Stanley Hoffman have continued this mode of thought.

Possibly the theorists can be most helpful over the course of time to the historian by sharing with him some as yet only partially tested propositions about behavior in the international field; the historian can use and apply these in a given research experiment. In the same way, authorities in given disciplines—for example, in psychology, sociology, and political science—may, through the introduction of historical or contemporary theoretical methods and propositions, be helpful to historians looking for new perspectives on reality. Nor have historians been averse to this, if one examines efforts such as Benson's study of the elections in the United States in the 1860s in which he employed propositions of political scientists such as the late V. O. Key.

Finally, there is another area even more central and more urgent. Nothing is more determinative of the foreign policy of this nation or of any nation than the assumptions, convictions, and beliefs its leaders bring to the formulation and execution of policy.

The story is told concerning the decision to intervene in Korea. This was the decision announced at midnight which mobilized the energies and efforts of the United States and of the United Nations. It broke on the world suddenly, with a shattering immediacy and surprise. Earlier statements by Secretary of State Dean Acheson had seemingly ruled out such action. Those who participated report that the men who met in Blair House to make the decision represented a wide range of thought and opinion. They were men from various parts of the country, with differing amounts of formal education and with greater or lesser experience in foreign relations. They saw the facts in different terms and from different professional perspectives. But more than one of them has said that the unifying factor in the policy discussion centered around lessons learned from the interwar period and the events leading up to World War II. That is to say, they had gleaned from pre-World War II history one overarching conclusion: aggression that was not resisted at its source was bound to spread, grow, and expand to a point where only a general world war of momentous proportion could turn it back. In other words, the underlying notion of resistance to aggression, of collective resistance where possible and national resistance where necessary, was the main working assumption, the theory, by which these men approached international reality. Read the *Memoirs* of Harry Truman, the biography of General Marshall, or the personal testimony of other leaders who took part in this decision, and the theme of resistance to aggression recurs in all that they write and say, and similar considerations of course prevailed in the course of the American decision to intervene in Vietnam.

The question worth considering is whether this working theory was then sufficient for the conduct of foreign relations and whether it is adequate for the years ahead. Is it a viable theory of foreign policy which has proven its worth? When it has been missing have the results inescapably been evil consequences such as those which occurred in the months and days leading up to World War II? What are the lessons of Vietnam and Korea, Egypt and Cyprus, Israel and the Arab states? When, how, and where has the theory been tested and what is the evidence to support its universal applicability? Scholars who have something to contribute, theorists who have bodies of experience and knowledge on which they can draw, must bring this knowledge to bear firmly and clearly so that those who carry the enormous burdens of responsibility can at least know that there are confirming or conflicting lessons of history against which they can measure their own responses. No one would underestimate the difficulty of differences in outlook, perceptions, and generations leading men to draw different conclusions from the same events. There are forms of theory that, in the international relations field as in other fields, will not have immediate application but are nonetheless useful. Beyond this, there are also forms of theorizing that can conceivably have early and far-reaching application fraught with consequences for the survival of the human race. In addition to the other types of theory I have explored, this last kind of international relations theory is worthy of exploration particularly in this era—and whatever epoch is to follow.

THE SOCIAL-PSYCHOLOGICAL APPROACH: OVERVIEW OR SINGLE VIEW?

Our understandings are always liable to error. Nature and certainty are very hard to come at and infallibility is mere vanity and pretence.
                                        Marcus Aurelius

Some of our ablest scholars, representative of the dominant behavioral approach to international problems, have written forcefully on the social-psychological view of international politics. At first glance this overview seems to meet the requirements of a scientific approach to social problems. A more careful review of its perceptions raises issues and questions that at least throw a shadow over its immediate applicability and relevance. In reviewing this work, I intend to raise certain issues, primarily for discussion, of behaviorism in general.

Such scholars quite properly describe international relations (quoting Charles McClelland) as an "unruly flock of activities." There is variety in the field and great diversity. They are also right in stressing that any one of us "will emphasize some members of the flock and tend to ignore others." They seem to be saying that what is decisive in this matter of emphasis is the scholarly discipline represented.

The problem cuts deeper than this, however, for the division of interest and of communication among political scientists reflects the profound schism which lies at the heart of political science. One school represents the social-psychological approach to international political problems. Their heroes are those who have "borrowed from psychology, social psychology, sociology, organization theory, communications, and the philosophy of science." Their personal devils, among others, are those associated with "realism," which tends, in the end, to "idealize military power and to offer it as a single explanatory factor." Their categories are decision-making, systems analysis, integration, simulation, military strategy, disarmament, and peace research. The first four are inextricably bound up with the social-psychological approach, and the others have found their most notable expressions in representatives of the psychological school of thought.

The irony of this definition of the field is not its preference for certain writings but the belief that they represent the sum total of the field of international studies. This leads to skepticism about the claim that "we have come a long way . . . in the last twenty years." One compares the inclusiveness of Quincy Wright's view of international studies with the exclusiveness of the present-day behaviorist outlook. For Wright, there were many mansions for international studies; for the behaviorist there tends to be one strong and prevailing dominant international view.

Despite the vaunted empiricism of the social-psychological outlook, one of its major weaknesses is the gulf between assertions and evidence. Thus, in speaking of decision-making and systems analysis, the view is put forward that work on decision-making and systems analysis has led scholars away from unsupported assertion to practical application. In reviewing research trends, however, spokesmen give few, if any, examples of specific research which has been completed testing the usefulness of analytic tools for assessing the links between work on the gross characteristics of nations—population, gross national product, military hardware—and the behavior of individuals acting for nations. Fifteen years ago, proponents of this mode of study protested that more time was needed before the new methodologies could be put to work on specific research problems. The years have come and gone, however, and still instances of significant completed research, tested against the raw stuff of history and made accessible to those who would employ it, seem few and far between. One has only to contrast the usefulness of economic theory and research, and the manner in which its practitioners have been employed, with the scant use which is made of decision-making or systems analysis in order to see the difference between the two areas of study. The Secretary of State rarely calls on the newest and most sophisticated disciple of peace research before setting out for peace negotiations in Paris or Geneva. The Secretary of the Treasury or the head of the Federal Reserve Bank, in contrast, is seldom if ever without his equivalent of a "council of economic advisers."

If the social-psychological approach is insufficient in accounting for the variety of approaches existing for international studies, it is also narrowly parochial in its definition of processes like data-collection. Data-collection involves the utilization of laboratory techniques in international relations research. The important point in asserting this preference is whether those who are psychologically oriented have solved their own methodological problems. Have they, for instance, found ways of testing in meaningful terms "how the success of alliances is affected by adding national benefits, in contrast to strictly collective benefits?" It could well be that a Secretary of State, weighing the prospect of a successful alliance, would find a "controlled experimental intervention" and "rigorous analysis of results" useful sources of guidance in his decision-making. At this writing, there is no evidence that such exist.

But even were this evidence to be at hand, and even if the superiority of this approach to assessing the value of alliances by the time-tested methods which diplomats and historians have known through the years were clear, any "overview of international studies" which implied that one brand of data-collection exhausted the field would not be complete. In other words, the historian viewing his problems, or the international organization researcher his, or the international lawyer a problem in treaty observance, is just as likely to collect data systematically, it would seem, as those engaged in "systematic data-collection." The two may not be the same, and conceivably one may be more rigorous than the other, but to preempt the realm of data-collecting for a certain breed of scholars is as wrongheaded as to preempt international studies as a whole for the social-psychologically oriented students of international affairs.

Furthermore, I find it difficult to agree that the best or only way of arriving at operational definitions in a field is through the use of quantitative techniques. One harks back to the earlier arguments concerning the nature of international relations as measured by the volume of mail flowing back and forth between two countries. It is interesting to know that x percentage of Frenchmen correspond with y percentage of Germans, but can this really tell us much about the state of international political relations between the two countries at any given moment? Would it have helped us understand, say, the policies of de Gaulle and Kiesinger or of Wilson and Brandt on the Common Market or the growing tensions between the leadership of two states? Is it enough to know that Singer and Small found that they had to decide how many men had to be killed before they would include an outbreak of violence in their operational definition of war? How does this relate to the defense put forth by international organizations which stress the peace-enforcement functions or policing operations of such bodies as against old-fashioned national warfare? Does not the context and situation affect the operational definition of war, including who does what to whom and under what mandate, as much as the number of men who are casualties? Are there not qualitative distinctions with at least as much importance as quantitative ones for arriving at operational definitions?

The question may be raised whether there is in effect a social-psychological approach to the problems of war and peace and to international studies. Is there not as much diversity here as there is uniformity of viewpoint? Or is there a common code for the approach? One scrap of evidence which suggests that this latter is true is the prevalence of those who are so oriented in the pages of social-psychological journals. Another is the fact that in the Singer volume it is demonstrated that even those selected political scientists and historians invited to contribute cite sociology and psychology journals more frequently than they cite political science journals, and cite interdisciplinary social science journals most frequently of all. My proposition is that those political scientists who tend to be the largest components of the interdisciplinary social science community for international research represent a clear-cut and readily definable body of thought and, to some extent, represent (and are probably the numerically largest group struggling with) the "flock of activities that make up international relations today." But do they represent the sum total of the field? The behaviorists' overview notwithstanding, I doubt that they do.

What is sobering about this is the relative modesty of the contributions that such men have made to practical international relations down through the years. The concern of psychologists and sociologists with international relations began at least as early as the 1930s when associates of L. I. Thurstone at the University of Chicago studied attitudes toward war and related matters. Following the war, men like Gardner Murphy and Otto Klineberg, with impetus from UNESCO, continued and extended the emphasis on social-psychological study. All of this work, and much which followed, has illuminated various facets of human behavior. It has clarified our understanding of groups in relationship across social-psychological barriers.

But the single most important question that cries for an answer is: "What have been the results thus far?" What is the product resulting in an operationally relevant scheme of analysis for problems of international relationships? To what extent have the social-psychologists gravitated toward the international relations equivalent of a council of economic advisers? While there is evidence of projects of cooperation between the State Department and modern social scientists, there is less evidence of how helpful they have been to policy-makers. In what way has their success in describing, if not predicting, the behavior of states required that they be drawn in, rapidly and effectively, to share the responsibility of statesmen? To what extent has their research on the international aspects of development or international education or public health as expressed in foreign assistance programs required that they be called upon by those who practice or make policy in these areas? And if their usefulness is limited, have they shared with others, in some way, the preparation of materials which could be meaningful for those carrying the burdens of decision? Is there a risk that creating new concepts, new terminology, and a variety of methods for systems analysis may create a Tower of Babel? If the end result of borrowing technical terms from other disciplines is special jargons understood only by the initated, won't it become more and more difficult for the policy-makers to understand what the specialists are talking about? Have they been able to speak through mediating voices to those who make policy, as the natural scientist has done? If the answer is "no," could part of the cause be the mutually exclusive character of the social-psychological and the historical and political approaches to international problems? Is there too little recognition that, in fact, none of several approaches exhausts the field? Would it be better to understand this before, rather than after, reviewing "trends in international relations research?"

The heart of the problem may be that no single approach can solve our understanding of "conflict and its adjustment among groups of people who acknowledge no common supreme authority." And if this is the case, then an overview should, in fact, incorporate, with some inclusiveness, the contributions to disarmament, development, and the formulation of foreign policy which come from various points of the compass. Otherwise, the result is not an overview, but a single view.

II: THE MORAL ISSUE

The only admissible moral theory ... is that the Principle of Good cannot at once and altogether subdue the powers of evil, either physical or moral.
                                                            John Stuart Mill

Albert Camus observed that the seventeenth century was the century of mathematics, the eighteenth century that of the physical sciences, and the nineteenth the century of biology. The twentieth, he said, was the century of fear.

> The most striking feature of the world we live in is that most of its inhabitants ... are cut off from the future. Life has no validity unless it can project itself toward the future, can ripen and progress. Living against a wall is a dog's life.[1]

Camus relentlessly pursued these themes and elucidated them in terms of the moral issue. Without values and faith in himself and humanity, man "lives against a wall." Always in the past when the future appeared closed men found a way to transcend it by appealing to new or recasting ancient values. Today old values are shattered and new ones have not taken their place. History appears in the grip of blind and deaf forces. Men have lost faith in the transforming role of words and goals; the experiences of the twentieth century have killed something in man.

> We have seen men lie, degrade, kill, deport, torture—and each time it was not possible to persuade them not to do these things because they were sure of themselves and because one cannot appeal to an abstraction; *i.e.*, the representative of an ideology.[2]

Persuasion and reason were unable to break through the crust of political self-righteousness which justified every sordid deed.

Camus found a simple and elemental answer to the moral issue. He accepted the fact that, in their quest for power and domination, modern nations were driven by powerful forces that the solitary individual could neither further nor obstruct. The individual can ask, what if their fierce and murderous competition winds up in a dead end?

> What if, despite two or three world wars, despite the sacrifice of several generations and a whole system of values, our grandchildren—supposing they survive—find themselves no closer to a world society?[3]

This led Camus to define the moral issue in terms of the answers given to two questions: "Do you or do you not, directly or indirectly, want to kill or assault?" and "Do you or do you not, directly or indirectly, want to be killed or assaulted?" Anyone who says "yes" falls on one side of a "terrible dividing line" and must accept the consequences of being a murderer or an accomplice of a murderer. He who says "no" and refuses with all his force and being falls on the other side. The world's fear is rooted in the prevalence and legitimacy of murder and violence. It can be removed only when men reflect on murder and make a choice. Whatever the odds, "the only honorable course will be to stake everything on a formidable gamble: that words are more powerful than munitions."[4] The moral issue and moral choice is to reject murder and violence and a world where respect for human life is trifling.

Choice or rejection of murder and violence is indeed a noble vocation for the individual. Even for individuals, however, it is vital to recall that the forms and varieties of murder are legion. Society and individuals do violence to people or to one another as often through neglect, mental cruelty, or indifference as through the use of overt force. On the world stage, the problem is thrice compounded. First, the exercise of authority and coercion internationally involves undisguised violence and force. In a world of sovereign states with no organized and legitimized center of authority, coercive measures are decentralized and lurk on the periphery of every national choice. Second, the great historic attempts to outlaw violence and warfare constitute an uninterrupted procession of conspicuous and glaring failures, the most notable being the Kellogg-Briand Pact of 1928 outlawing war. Indeed these noble endeavors have by their failures served to "tempt thieves" and invite aggression. Third, those in our day who have rejected murder and violence in one sector of life seem destined to pursue it in another, as the annals of the peace and civil rights movements make plain. Devotion to the outlawry of violence framed in absolute and unequivocal terms stirs within the breasts of the faithful the same moral fervor that has always characterized morally self-righteous movements. Not Camus but the followers of his "truths," including the truth that "domestic policy is in itself a secondary matter" have practiced violence in the name of their own utopia, a nonviolent world. Robert Pickus, a lifelong champion of peace, who sees Camus as misunderstood by the Vietnam antiwar movement, discovers "an incredible admixture of good and evil" in it with "justification of hatred and violence against America, replacing official justification of violence by America."[5]

Perhaps the highest price a peace movement which condemns all violence but practices forms of violence that serve its cause must pay is the absence of its spokesmen from council tables where the reduction of violence is being attempted. The United States, in successive conferences beginning at the turn of the century and ending with the nuclear test ban treaty and the arms control agreements, has been on the side of those who have fought politically and diplomatically, admittedly with lapses, for the control and limitation of the means of violence. Yet the results of some of the strategems pursued by certain peace movements would be to withdraw American power from world politics. What they overlook is the fact that the decisive choices affecting the means of violence are incremental choices. If no violence is better than limited violence, limited violence, particularly in an epoch when world-destroying thermonuclear power is a reality, is better than total violence. Yet by withdrawing from the arena of world politics with all its ambiguities and contradictions, the champions of nonviolence would leave the field to less peaceful leaders.

The plain fact is that on every past or present index of state behavior, we can count on the existence of violence, privilege, and exploitation; and the statesman's task is to limit and control them, even while he dreams of their eradication. He does so in an endless series of proximate moral and political choices, not in one blinding, final burst of absolute moral choice. Living statesmen must contend with the fact of evil and try within narrow limits to make the world more peaceful and less violent. One day the choice may be a bold gamble in favor of a treaty establishing controls in outer space or over the seas far beyond those achieved on *terra firma*. The next the choice may be the localizing of a conflict, drawing a ring around the combatants and seeking to prevent the spread of the conflagration.

The moral issue, in a nutshell, is to act with moral discrimination and judgment in an essentially immoral world. Moral choices are made in an atmosphere of trial and error, never once and for all. Moral decisions, as the great moralists have proclaimed, are made not in the abstract but in context, measuring the endlessly complex array of forces that are part of every moral choice. For those who would see the issue resolved once and for all, there is a kind of emotional catharsis in outlawing violence and war. Yet even within national borders, order, which is a precondition of justice, requires not the end of violence but a monopoly of the means of violence in the hands of constitutionally established authorities. In the half-anarchic, half-organized international order, violence is limited through changing equilibria of power. The moral issue in international relations is the final and still most baffling issue with which a philosophy of international politics must grapple.

NORMS AND REALITIES IN INTERNATIONAL RELATIONS

*Ideals are like stars; you will not succeed in touching
them with your hand, but like the seafaring man on
the desert of waters, you choose them as your guides.*
                                                    Carl Schurz

In United States foreign policy since World War II, public opinion has engaged in a succession of great debates on foreign policy. Yet significantly, no discussion of policy has been free of reference to moral issues.

If Vietnam, for example, had been a simple clash either of military systems or of political ideologies, we could have argued the issues with greater understanding and clarity. The problem of arriving at valid and acceptable policies is at root the problem of defining the nature of the crisis. The uncertainty we feel about policies is basically an uncertainty about the crisis.

The dialogue between those who supported and those who opposed American policy in Vietnam floundered on conflicting moral assumptions. The acceptance of one or another premise lead inescapably to mutually irreconcilable moral and political conclusions.

One trend of thought has drawn on historical and legal arguments that justify the defense of South Vietnam in the name of the commitments of four American presidents. A nation's word is its bond, and our promise to come to the aid of a Southeast Asian country whose independence is threatened must be observed. Otherwise aggression will spread and lead to a general conflagration.

Those who supported President Johnson's and President Nixon's policies argued that whether we liked it or not, we were engaged in what became a $130 billion effort to resist the military and political invasion of South Vietnam by North Vietnam. Whatever the elements of the struggle may have been at the outset, the movement of men and materiel from North Vietnam into South Vietnam had become a reality.

The other trend of thinking on Vietnam placed the stress on the civil war characteristics of the struggle. It condemned American policy-makers for intervening in an internal struggle, arguing that the major conflict was between local factions organized around the National Liberation Front and the government of South Vietnam.

Senator Fulbright, the leading critic of the Johnson administration's pol icy, felt that the world had passed from a cold war to a post-cold war era. The core of the crisis was no longer the clash between Soviet and American power centered at the heart of Europe. The threat to world peace was no longer Soviet imperialism as a carrier of international communism. Rather, the real issue was what form and shape the developing countries would take and how and in what directions they would move. At the heart of Fulbright's position was a deep concern that American commitments were tending to outrun American power: that we were seeing ourselves as "God's avenging angels, whose sacred duty is to combat evil philosophies." A spirit of national self-righteousness had taken hold of policy-makers, and the Senator feared that we would come to grief as did the Athenians in their fateful attack on Syracuse, and Napoleon and Hitler in their invasions of Russia. To critics who challenged comparisons with Hitler, the Senator replied that deep currents of American tradition and outlook feed our sense of universal mission and exaggerate our notion of world responsibility. Puritanism causes us to transform every war into a crusade, "to see principles where there are only interests, and conspiracy where there is only misfortune."

I do not propose to discuss the rights or wrongs of the two opposing views toward American policy in Vietnam. They serve only as a point of departure for a discussion of the profound nature of the moral problem in international politics.

In the United States, philosophers and churchmen, internationalists and isolationists, congressmen and diplomats, journalists and scholars have tried to answer this problem for the better part of the last half-century. Their answers comprise a capsule history of Western thought, and while they resist any convincing system of classification, there are broadly speaking four types of answers.

The Cynical View

Cynicism is one answer, although few consistently maintain that political action can remain permanently bereft of moral content. Hitler presumably set aside all benevolence or loyalty to goals beyond race and state. Stalin's consistent deprecation of the influence of non-Communist ideals and his willingness to sacrifice the human lives of deviationists or kulaks if it served Soviet political purposes was blatantly cynical. The cynic tends to argue, if he justifies himself at all, that politics and ethics are not cut from the same cloth. Politics are means and ethics are ends, he says, and while the means employed may seem evil, good ends can make them good. The simple formula of the end justifying the means has brought about resolution of the problem.

Yet for men and for nations, the universal practice is to justify every evil measure by claiming it serves an ethical goal, as for Stalin the gross brutality of liquidating the kulaks found justifications as an inevitable step in the history-fulfilling Communist design. Since nations in the present anarchic world society tend to be repositories of their own morality, the end-means formula has often prevailed as an answer to the moral dilemma, for undeniably it is a concealed but essential truth that nations tend to create their own morality.

In its extreme form, however, this development has found nations accepting as ethical whatever redounded to their own material advantage and judging whatever was detrimental to their purposes as immoral and evil. Yet it inheres in the nature of man and politics that statesmen and nations never wholly escape the judgment of elementary ethical standards. The history of politics discloses that no people have completely divorced politics from ethics, but, however grudgingly, have come to see that men are required to conform to standards more objective than those of success.

Hypocritical Attitude

There is another answer—whether it be called hypocrisy or national moralizing. Every person and every nation shares to some extent in this response. For whenever men or nations act, they make larger claims for their morality than can be warranted. If this is deception, it is apparently an almost inevitable form of self-deception since nations, no less than individuals, must persuade themselves that their deeds are legitimate because consistent with some larger frame of value. (The powerful nation never goes to war except in "the interests of peace and justice.") The problem about these actions is not that they are all devoid of some residual justice, nor that claims of goodness never serve to lift men and groups above the selfish and the mundane. Rather, morality falls short of rhetoric.

The Reformist View

A third answer is reformist and apocalyptic in nature. It concedes that at present there may be conflict between eternal principles and the imperatives of statecraft. At present, men and states pursue selfish and parochial ends but, in Woodrow Wilson's phrase, "national purposes have fallen more and more into the background so that the common purpose of enlightened mankind has taken their place." The point on which liberal and conservative utopians agree is that politics in which there are conflicts of interest is but a passing and ephemeral phase of an earlier inferior aristocratic era.

For the liberal, new world institutions and world law can transform man. For the conservative, more businessmen with the homely virtues of private life—honesty, simplicity, charm, and geniality—can bridge the gulf between ultimate and political morality. This last philosophy virtually destroys the well-known tension between the private and public spheres or between man as man and man as citizen. It excuses a political leader for failure, irresolution, imprudence, and for ignorance of the demands of politics if only he is honest, well-meaning, and a good fellow.

The reformer cannot believe that in international relations situations arise where justice for one nation means injustice for another; where one nation's security and its requirements mean another nation's insecurity; where armaments, defense preparations, and alliances organized in self-defense can appear as threats to security when viewed through other eyes.

Faced with these realities, the reformist maintains that at present men may indeed pursue a double standard of conduct in their private and public lives. Privately man is honest and ethical; publicly he covers his acts with a tissue of lies and deception. His virtue in private affairs is seen as the conquest of culture over barbarism, of a rational age over an irrational one. Once, in an earlier stage in man's evolution, his private conduct was marred by brutality and violence, but education, a legal order, and free institutions transformed him. In the same way, the reformist claims, the cultural lag from which nations have suffered in international relations is being erased. The forward march of history is carrying nations from a retarded condition into a new and enlightened era when private standards will become public international rules. Those who doubt that all this is true are denounced as foes of progress and men of little faith.

Yet this simple rationalism pays little heed to the depth of the problem. In its zeal it ignores the distance between private and public standards. Religious ethics call self-interest into question (man must lose himself in order to find himself). As soon as we move into the level of organized communities, the problem of legitimate self-interest arises, for political ethics take self-interest for granted. A political leader cannot constantly ask his people to sacrifice themselves. His first duty is to preserve the Constitution, and he owes allegiance to the safety and well-being of the nation and of its generations yet unborn.

Reinhold Niebuhr distinguished between moral man and immoral society, and while he subsequently modified the sharp lines of his dichotomy, he would have held, I believe, to the "hidden truth" which this distinction lays bare. Accordingly, those virtues of gentleness, magnanimity, love, and trust which enrich the dimensions of our family life at its best and are possible in our more intimate communities, must be viewed with circumspection, reserve, and uncertainty on the world stage where states press their claims and counterclaims.

A More Realistic View

The fourth answer to the problem is the one Meinecke gave.

Every authentic tragedy is a shattering demonstration that moral life cannot be regulated like clockwork and that even the purest strivings for good can be forced into the most painful choices. . . . In relations between states, moreover, clashes between private morality and state interest are plainly inevitable and as old as world history itself.[6]

What sets this outlook apart is its clear recognition of the tension between morality and politics or foreign policy. It alone among the viewpoints of cynicism, hypocrisy, and reformism points up the need for humility. This position accepts at the start the persistence of self-interest in all political communities and the impossibility of persuading any community to sacrifice itself. The assumption is made that the best the nations can do is to find the point of concurrence between their interests and purposes and the interests of others. There is reluctance to claim universal validity for national policies and hesitance to proclaim that what is good for me is good for everyone, or that what one group or nation views as in its interest is in the interest of the whole world. Moral crusades and national self-righteousness are as feared as are outright denial of moral principles.

Churchill, Lincoln, John Quincy Adams, and some of the great religious leaders epitomize this view. Inescapably it has a place for the tragic element in life, for it leaves for another better world the utopias and final justice that men and states so often claim for themselves.

The nature of the moral problem has played havoc with every attempt to explain foreign policy in too-simple terms. It is ironic that while the United States has almost consistently stated its policy in unqualified and unblushing moral terms, this country is everywhere suspected of cynicism and hypocrisy. Perhaps this is the inevitable price of world leadership; it seems clear that some of the moral burdens the United States carries are not of its own making. For example, we have inherited a colonial heritage that blends memories of noble purposes and acts with cynical self-seeking and oppression. It hardly matters, for example, that United States citizens deserve little credit for the creative or destructive aspects of European colonialism. Power has brought responsibility and the United States is held to account.

Yet we would carry these burdens more gracefully if our statesmen recognized that every nation in history has claimed more for the moral content of its policies and purposes than historical judgment would later accord them. It is of course easier to see the weakness of others; for example, easier to see the beam in British eyes than the mote in our own. Lord Wolseley said:

I have but one great object in this world, and that is to maintain the greatness of the Empire. But apart from my John Bull sentiment . . . I firmly believe that in doing so I work in the cause of Christianity, of peace, of civilization, and the happiness of the human race generally.[7]

But Americans speak in the same way, as, for example, when Woodrow

Wilson proclaimed that American principles are "the principles of mankind . . . which must prevail."

Writers on morality and foreign policy are endlessly tempted to see the problem in simple alternatives. Either a nation's policy serves the welfare of mankind or it is founded on national self-interest. Both views neglect the richness and variety of moral content in national behavior. Indeed, there are layers of international morality, at least three of which call for attention.

The core of morality in international politics is national interest. The nation-state is both the problem child of international relations and the highest effective expression of genuine moral consensus. More progress has been made in creating freedom and order and opportunities for the individual, say, within the United States, than could be achieved in any foreseeable international community. In practice, moreover, nations can usually give moral content, however modest, to their national self-interest while the international interest is more vague and ill-defined.

The moral dignity of the national interest finds expression in various spheres. The interest of a nation's people in its basic values and common welfare, transcending subnational loyalties, is an antidote to crass materialism. The mere existence of a citizenry that takes its history and tradition seriously assures that a nation's reputation shall not perish nor its will to stay alive be destroyed. The sense of membership and of partnership with ancestors who have gone before and heirs who are to follow gives moral stamina and political vitality to a society. Moreover, national attachments are the one sure and sound basis for transcending partisan political loyalties. In a period of crisis in British politics, Winston Churchill counseled his fellow Conservatives: "We are Party men but we shall be all the stronger if in every action we show ourselves capable, even in this period of stress and provocation, of maintaining the division—where there is division—between national and party interests."[8] Ernest Gross has pointed out that self-interest can be a source of self-discipline. We have Tocqueville's statement that "the principle of self-interest rightly understood appears . . . the best suited of all philosophical theories to the wants of the men of our time, and . . . as their chief remaining security against themselves." It can guard men equally against outbursts of reckless and self-seeking and moralistic crusades ruthlessly carried on for "the welfare of mankind."

In general, a more tolerable relationship is achieved between nations who speak in their national interest than between those who claim to speak for the whole world. Hence states, while asserting the moral integrity of their interests, ought never to see them too exclusively as ends in themselves. World patterns are too complex and variegated to reserve all virtue to a single state or course of action. The periods of greatest decline in international morality have come when national purposes have been presented as pure and unsullied goals for the rest of the world. There is an important area in foreign policy where national interests must be asserted confidently and with pride and courage. Indeed United States citizens sometimes run the risk, having proclaimed our virtue and indulged in all manner of pretentious talk, of alternately feeling shame over the fact that we are a great power with a noble tradition and shrinking when not everyone loves us. But our actions will be more honored and esteemed if we are somewhat more humble about equating them with final and absolute virtue. They can be justified as necessary and proper steps without casting them in the form of crusades and filling the air with the most extravagant claims.

A second dimension is the converse of the national interest. The one thing which saves the idea of the national interest from itself is its essential reciprocity. To the extent that nations are in earnest not alone about their own self-interests but in their recognition of the application of similar criteria by others, they escape any temptation to conceal real designs for world aggrandizement. Edmund Burke declared: "Nothing is so fatal to a nation as an extreme of self-partiality, and the total want of consideration of what others will naturally hope or fear."[9] After a nation has determined its own objective interests in terms of its national security, it has an obligation to draw back, as it were, and appraise cooly and realistically the interests of its neighbors. It is a Quaker virtue to examine, to understand, not to condemn or blame. In this way alone can nations decide if their interests are compatible or can be adjusted. There is no other basis for nations actually to live together.

It is essential that every nation pursue wisely its own best interests, but the pathway for each nation must not be strewn with the remnants of the interests of others that were forgotten in its headlong drive to attain national security. Among nations with decent intentions there must be a reciprocal process of recognizing each other's vital interests and avoiding collisions and conflicts insofar as it is possible through the compromise of divergent interests. Interests are capable of being compromised; principles can never be made the object of bargains. Yet if nations are to survive, somehow they must find ways of compromising their differences while at the same time they succeed in protecting and safeguarding their interests. For as it is the essence of politics that individuals possess the capacity to compromise their differences, the art of diplomacy merely raises this process to the level of nations and founds it upon a structure of multiple national interests. Conflicts which seem at the time to present to the parties a clear case of right and wrong almost without exception have appeared to future historians, less blinded by passion and loyalty, as something infinitely more tragic than good men fighting bad ones. The real pattern of conflict and war is one of minor differences hardening into intractable political divisions, of men faced by terrible dilemmas and of nations eventually driven by the inner dialectic of events to wars which no one desired. The difference between a struggle between good and evil and actual struggles in world politics, in which every party in some way is at fault but is unable to disengage itself from the tragic predicament of fearing others but never comprehending their counter-fears, is the difference between the substance of "heroic" and of "revisionist" or scientific history.

In this predicament, each party has a sense of its own insecurity but never imagines that its own righteous efforts could have anything to do with the insecurity of others. After each military conflict, the minds of the early or "heroic" historians are locked in the combat expounding their own nation's cause. Their judgments are generally those that stem from self-righteousness. Subsequently, it remains for "revisionist" historians to rewrite the narrative in terms of the mutual fear of each side for the power of the other. In their histories of conflict the revisionist schools have frequently proved we had muddied the waters and darkened our minds about the true nature of a struggle when it has been interpreted in terms of certain accidental characteristics.

There is a form of political morality which stems from a decent regard for the interests of others. While it is not always the same as the private ethics enjoined by the great religions, nonetheless it is expediency grounded in morality. In the writings of philosophers from the Greeks to Edmund Burke it is identified as prudence or practical morality, and in guidebooks to diplomacy like Richelieu's *Political Testament* it appears as expediential morality. It has been considered the lubricant by which the smooth workings of international society are made possible and in modern times as the cement without which the sturdiest alliance will crumble. It is too much to expect that nations will show gratitude or lasting affection for one another. Generosity is as likely to produce envy and resentment as goodwill, for no government based on popular support can afford to acknowledge the full scale of its dependence on others. However, if a nation is known to be habitually retrograde in the observance of obligations, it can hardly look forward to long and effective diplomatic commerce with others. Winston Churchill measured this dimension of international morality in these words:

> There is, however, one helpful guide, namely for a nation to keep its word and to act in accordance with its treaty obligations to allies. This guide is called *honour*. It is baffling to reflect that what men call honour does not correspond always to Christian ethics. . . . An exaggerated code of honour leading to the performance of utterly vain and unreasonable deeds should not be defended, however fine it might look.[10]

A final or third layer of international morality comprises general principles like opposition to tyranny, or community, or assistance to the poor and needy, or values embodied in the United Nations Charter. Men seem obstinately to reject the view that state behavior is not at some point a fit subject for moral judgement. One sign that this principle is accepted as relevant is the compulsion of political actors to justify their deeds in moral terms. Hypocrisy is the tribute vice pays to virtue. Beyond this there is a striking dialectical movement of expediency and morality which has its impact on international politics. Moves in practical politics must be articulated in such a way as to pay tribute to moral principles. However limited and particular, acts of political expedience must seem to carry forward aims of justice and the common good. Thus political morality, in these modest terms, forces the statesman who would justify expediency with ethics to choose his measures so that on some points at least the practical and moral march hand and hand. It is political wisdom to act successfully in accord with the interests of state. It is political and moral wisdom to choose the most moral of several alternatives through which both expedience and ethics may be served. The margin which separates cynicism from this form of wisdom is frequently narrow indeed, but by it statesmen are saved from a fatuous "moralism" or the despair of unqualified expediency. It is the essence of moral judgment to transcend the limits of expediency and narrow self-interest in this one sense at least.

Principle in this final sense is an ultimate objective, not an immediate guide to action. It is a lodestone of moral conduct, not a mere ideological rationalization by which practical steps are legitimized. Principles in this sense are concepts held by statesmen whose reach quite self-consciously exceeds their grasp. Whereas their implementation in practice is dependent upon considerations of the national interest, they shine in the firmament of political philosophy as objective standards of political behavior. In any full and complete political system there must be room for philosophy and action, yet there can be no more serious error than to confound these two conditions. The realms of ideals and practice are not the same, yet it is equally false to imagine they can never meet. If the vertical dimension be conceived of as the line of ideals, it does intersect at certain points in history the horizontal dimension of political practice.

If a more realistic morality could be expressed in official statements of policy and could likewise provide a guide to statesmen in a nuclear age, we might look with greater confidence to the future. This conception of morality gives a more coherent context for the concrete issues of nuclear strategy.

MORAL DOUBTS ABOUT PRESENT
POLITICAL DIAGNOSES

If we do not recognize the fragmentary character of knowledge we will be caught holding onto some old form of knowledge which is quite irrelevant to the responsibilities which we must face.
                                        Reinhold Niebuhr

The Religious and Quasi-Religious Diagnoses

Few periods in history have left observers more unsettled and anxious about the sufficiency of prevailing moral and political diagnoses. The din of public debate drowning out quiet thought and reflection may explain some of the confusion. Yet the strident clashes that break out between right and left, and with increasing frequency and fervor between radicals and liberals, compound but have not created the problem. Instead, the core of the problem appears to result from a widespread questioning sweeping across society and sowing seeds of doubt about the sufficiency of all past and present social and political doctrines. For the first time in their lives, more and more people express uncertainty that any prevailing doctrine meets our needs; and on this there is less of a generation gap than is sometimes assumed.

We deceive ourselves if we suppose that this is true alone of present-day thinking; it has also characterized the great classical and religious approaches to man's urgent problems. For the greater part of the history of the West, the forces of religion and secular society interacted with one another in an ever-changing state of equilibrium and balance. The interplay between the concerns of morality and those of politics occurred within a framework of Christian dualism. The quest for power and justice was pursued in accordance with the doctrine of the Two Swords. The church was supreme in realms of faith and morals while the sovereign ruler prevailed in the social and political order. If in practice this meant that lines were often difficult to draw and the balance was precariously maintained, the framework of two orders assured that certain relationships were less subject to doubt because of the division of morality and politics into two worlds. At the same time it was inescapable that the lines drawn in theory were difficult and even impossible to hold to in practice. Within each realm, however, there was a wider consensus than exists when society and morals are in the throes of transformation and change and every creed and practice is under continuing criticism and review.

Furthermore, it remained true that certitude was attainable in "the city of God;" each successive issue and problem was not a priori debatable and open to every changing wind of controversy. There were areas of moral consensus in the broad area of things spiritual. So long as the rulers of the church were content to limit their intrusion into the political order, controversy was limited to questions of interpretation that left unchallenged the fundamentals of the moral universe. In American history, our closest approximation is perhaps rural and fundamentalist thought, which separated issues of faith and society except for narrowly individualist and personal ethics that left little room for interpretation or debate.

The breakdown of Christian dualism and the doctrine of the Two Swords occurred with the rise of nationalism and its gradual evolution into an autonomous moral force. The Reformation, which overthrew the universalism of the church, opened the door to growing moral and political power for the ruler and the state. The moral universe in which papal rule had been supreme took on new forms in response to freedom of conscience for individuals and states. Nationalism, which rested on the right of a people to determine for themselves both their political and their spiritual allegiance, shattered the unity of the Corpus Christianum. The religion of the ruler became the religion of the state and the values of nationals were shaped more by those of the ruler and less those of the church. What began as a far-reaching force for liberating the individual conscience from too-rigid moral strictures bred new forms of social and political controls more pervasive, if less explicit, in the realm of social ethics.

With the rise of the nation-state, free and unfettered by universal moral constraints, the transformation of nationalism into a political religion was seemingly inevitable. In Arnold Toynbee's phrase, the sovereign state was swept clean of traditional religion and a vacuum created into which a political religion was to flow. By the third decade of the twentieth century, nationalistic universalism had supplanted religious universalism. Nationalism to this point had been half-hearted and lukewarm, diluted by the emotional indifference of the masses to the moral authority of a remote sovereign ruler. With the advent of popular sovereignty, however hedged about and manipulated by clever rulers, the pale image of a single distant ruler was replaced by the effulgent image of a whole people. The restraining influence of external moral standards was weakened and eventually effectively disappeared. Religion was no longer a check on the state; it became internalized as the empowering and legitimizing force of nationalism, much as the contending forces in the American Civil War justified their cause, not from political or economic arguments but in terms of religious emotion.

Liberal thought, beginning in the late nineteenth but culminating in the mid-twentieth century, sought to remedy this way of thinking. It deplored the absolutism of extreme nationalism and the ruthlessness of its tactics justified in the name of the idol of the parochial nation-state. Liberalism sought to instill tolerance into international thinking. It pointed to the defects of every past and present nation-state and emphasized that no nation's virtue was so all-inclusive as to justify its going to war to contain another imperialist force. Liberalism was never wholly pacifist in outlook, but it tended to furnish support for pacifist thinking as it did for the more utopian forms of internationalism. And its very tolerance, if not equating, of different doctrines and policies opened the door to spokesmen and ideologues who argued that politics and statecraft were everywhere productive of good and bad policies, that every government had its strengths and weaknesses (when there were criticisms of fascism, the stock answer by apologists was "the trains run on time"), and that rulers could not be grouped under any single class of dictators and oppressors or democrats and servants of the people. This philosophy, while exposing the ambiguities and failings of every political system, forfeited the right of proximate political judgment and social evaluation. Its good-natured acceptance of diversity blinded its followers to the inescapable necessity for discriminant judgments and thus rendered it irrelevant as a guide for practical political action.

Thus liberalism, while remedying the evils of crusading nationalism, opened the way to critics who denounced its limitations from the standpoint both of political realism and ideology. They were quick to point out that while philosophers might indulge themselves by pointing to the good and bad in every political system, responsible leaders called on to make decisions seldom enjoyed this luxury. It was intriguing for economists to speculate about efficiency in the Nazi and Facist economies; the real issue, however, for those who confronted the rising threat of their power, was whether they endangered the balance of Europe and the peace of the world. On this issue the then prevalent liberal creed offered little guidance and wisdom. It was less wrong than irrelevant and in the 1930s the price of its irrelevance would have been the destruction of that self-same Western civilization on whose existence liberalism depended.

The Present Crisis and Classical Solutions

The inadequacies and limitations of liberalism and its failure to provide the intellectual resources sufficient for comprehending the crises of the 1930s generated trends of thought that revived classical views of war and peace and joined them with more modern approaches. Liberalism, because of its political and economic roots, had overestimated the "inevitability of peace." The line of reasoning ran: war is irrational, inhuman, uneconomical, and outdated, so there will be no more war. Influential leaders argued, by analogy from economics, that as hardheaded businessmen guided by the profit motive and the need to balance costs against benefits did business together, it would be possible for a Birmingham businessman (Chamberlain) to do business with a fanatical nationalist (Hitler), for nationalism like economics was subject to limitations and constraints. And because any other course was inconceivably irrational, the liberal idealist assumed that the legal framework of a League of Nations could at some early date replace the lawlessness of the international political order.

The neoclassicist confronted, challenged, and refuted these views. He pointed to the historic role of the balance of power (condemned to outer darkness by liberals) in limiting international conflict—limiting but not eliminating it. He argued that only a concentration of power in areas exposed to the advance of imperialist powers could protect lesser powers and preserve a tenuous peace. The Low Countries had been overrun in the World Wars because no part of the international system had effectively guaranteed their independence. On one level, their future protection was to be assured by worldwide and regional collective security systems performing in a more acceptable way the chief historical role of the balance of power. On the other, they and their neighbors among the small powers were to build up a sufficient concert of power to make the price of overrunning them something that any would-be imperialist power would have to weigh and consider. But more important, the fact of a concentration of power on the ground became a trip wire which would trigger far greater power by mightier states such as the United States. The deterrence of substantial power, therefore, would be a hard guarantee of peace as tensions and conflicts multiplied, much as treaties and negotiations were a softer and more rational guarantee consistent and in tune with liberal tenets.

These classical and neoclassical solutions, while preserving a limited peace for more than twenty-five years, at least insofar as war on a global basis is concerned, have in recent days been brought into question by the rise of novel, revolutionary concepts and techniques for coping with conflict, extended and translated from other spheres. The civil rights movement introduced onto the American scene the tradition of nonviolence, which drew its inspiration and respect from experiences such as Schweitzer's in Africa and Gandhi's in India. Young people, schooled and enlivened by this tradition, joined hands with bold and embattled twentieth-century spokesmen for new approaches and sought to translate and apply nonviolence on the international scene. In the same way that force and violence were defused within a constitutional, legal order in the United States and in some former British territories, reformers and radicals proposed that nonmilitary solutions be sought to international problems. The inheritors both of classicism and of liberalism had gone at least part of the way in observing that many international conflicts were foreshadowed in social and economic problems. They called for greater diligence in launching and sustaining technical assistance and international cooperative efforts, and less preoccupation with strategic and military views. But those who spoke for revolutionary solutions went all the way in rejecting the legitimacy of force or the justification, as classicists had argued, of use of force or display of force proportionate to the threat or the extent of overt conflict.

The call for new solutions presupposed nothing less than the transvaluation of force, substituting for it what William James had called "the moral equivalent of war." Competition would presumably continue, although with the "new man" even this was questioned, but competition not with guns or missiles but with ideas and economics. At the outset, the new solutions had one thing in common—the overall rejection of force in almost every circumstance. In all this, the threat of nuclear destruction was inseparably intertwined with the fact of the new thinking, whether by the new left, the new theology, or the new approaches to conflict resolution. And the theorists at least were successful in postulating a new approach to international conflict, if less so to the conflicts that raged within the individual nation-states. Indeed, as domestic conflict deepened the same philosophers of nonviolence made exceptions and offered justification for the use of force and violence domestically. If consistency marks little men, the new theorists stamp themselves most of all by their inconsistency in viewing domestic conflicts in a different light from international conflicts.

In fact, when all due allowance is made for differences in context of the national and international situations, the student of morality and political philosophy must dissent from present-day political thinking. In so doing, he must hark back to classical thought which has traditionally identified force and its place in political philosophy as the most troublesome and agonizing issue it faces, if not the Achilles' heel of most regnant political theories. For Judeo-Christian thought the issue of force, particularly against legitimate political authority, prompts soul-searching and the anguish of painful choices between withdrawal from politics (asceticism or Lutheranism), prudence or practical morality (choosing the course that is least immoral among essentially evil choices), and the isolated or exceptional act of violence against oppression, justified as a last resort. In the mainstream of this tradition, at least, there is little if any overt celebration of force and its virtues. It is seen at best as a necessary evil and internationally as legitimate only when every other nonviolent remedy has been explored and exhausted.

Nor is this outlook confined to theology and moral philosophy; it undergirds those landmarks of political practice that are remembered as expressing the dominant motifs of Western civilization. The American Revolution occurred at the end of a long series of painful, costly, and futile attempts to accommodate to British sovereignty. No sooner had the new society established itself than its revolutionary founders asserted the primacy of national over local interests and of federal authority over rebellious states. The exercise of force by the federal union, however, was seen as the final step in the use of national power justified, if at all, when force and only force could preserve the Union. The moral anguish that informed President Abraham Lincoln's mobilizing the nation for war is no isolated expression of individual conscience. Rather it is the classic statement of an historic Western view of the place of force, as distinct from the accustomed use of political power in the social order. And what was true of the spirit of Lincoln seeking to preserve the federal union was as true of his foes, who sought a rationale for secession by force from that same political order. Both were inspired and informed by a sense of tragedy and moral anguish when measures that were morally superior had been tried and found wanting.

In our day, what is new is the supplanting of a hierarchy of values and virtues that for two thousand years have been central to Western civilization by those which have found their place at the periphery as threats to civilization itself. It is instructive to recall that two great recent threats to Western civilization arose from political philosophies that celebrate force and violence, not as exceptional measures, but as instruments essential to their world mission. National socialism and world communism glorify force and violence blatantly and explicitly as higher moral virtues located not at the periphery but at the very center of political life, even though communism does not assert it formally in those terms. So secure are their spokesmen of the righteousness of their cause that they fuse means and ends in a single political creed. About tactics there must always be moral and political doubt; about stages in a historic mission that is foreordained there can be only moral certitude and crusading zeal.

For these reasons nazism and communism, particularly at their inception, loomed as threats to the core of Western civilization. Their underlying philosophies challenge the West as fundamentally as the means by which they prosecute their goals. When absolute and morally unassailable goals are joined to mighty force the challenge becomes overwhelming. Confronted with this threat, it is scant wonder that little by little and almost imperceptibly the United States, which had held itself aloof from international conflicts, became everywhere involved. After World War II, stung by the political consequences of its hasty withdrawal from the heart of Europe, it set out to redeem its innocence. It built up the military establishment always denied it in peacetime; it made commitments and expended resources on an unheard-of scale. Having met and defeated in World War II an enemy which boasted the mightiest military force in history, the United States took on some of its trappings.

In 1898, William Graham Sumner, speaking of the Spanish-American War and American territorial expansion, prophesied "the conquest of the United States by Spain."[11] He saw the United States irrevocably committed to the course that had brought militarism and war to Europe. Far more dramatically following World War II the lessons of preparedness and international involvement were learned too well. Mounting defense budgets approach $90 billion; by 1970 military assistance to others was estimated at $2.9 billion by the Defense Department or $4.8 billion by Senator William E. Proxmire, Chairman of the Joint Congressional Economic subcommittee. President and formerly General, Dwight D. Eisenhower left office warning of the dangers of the military-industrial complex. A study of American foreign policy in the

1960s was headed "Decision Power Ebbing at the State Department." There is evidence that military and executive forces have overruled calls for restraint by officers charged with diplomatic and political responsibilities in the Kennedy, Johnson, and Nixon administrations. Add to that the impatient words of information officials zealous for ideological crusading at moments of greatest sensitivity in diplomatic negotiations and the picture is complete. But it is not complete unless to it all we add Vietnam, the longest war in our history.

A nation endangered by antimilitarism and isolationism earlier in its history is gravely threatened today by certain opposite trends. If such trends are allowed to go unchecked and to pervade every sector of national life, Sumner's prophesy may be fulfilled. There are ominous signs of dissent being "computerized" and political oppression practiced. Wire-tapping and obstruction of justice have been practiced at the highest level. Those who are responsible for these trends or who allow them to go unchecked are caught in the toils of political diagnosis of the society that raise serious moral doubts.

Yet the more popular reactions to these deeply troubling national trends are equally unsettling. The remedy proposed for too many international commitments is no commitments at all; the substitute for too much military expenditure is unilateral disarmament; the answer to international conflicts around the world is to proclaim that they are nobody's business except the attacker and the attacked. To say this so flatly and unequivocally is to ignore the lesson of modern history that we live increasingly in a tightly interdependent world, and that from the Spanish Civil War to the present external forces are as often a part of local conflicts as those who control or seek control of local territory, people, and resources. It is as utopian to pretend that a superpower can leave the rest of the world to others as it is to imagine that it can police the world. It is as unrealistic, morally and politically, to turn deaf ears when the bell tolls as it is to suppose that every crisis can be solved in Washington. All this may sound irritatingly vague and general to those who crave clear-cut and absolute formulas and slogans, but decisions in foreign policy, as in life, must be made at points of intersection of seemingly incompatible tendencies.

If violence or nonviolence, omnipotence or powerlessness, and globalism or isolationism are appropriate in rhetoric but not in foreign policy, their place throughout national life is no less debatable. Yet domestically the problem arises from a curious inversion of a political strategy occuring in the mid-sixties and the seventies. We have translated historic nonviolence into an international strategy and reserved violence for national strategies. Yet only when nonviolence is practiced within free and open societies, with established constitutional safeguards and accepted legislative and electoral procedures for minorities to become majorities, can it have a fair chance. Gandhi's India and

Martin Luther King's America are examples that come readily to mind. It is an accident of history that men and forces that had achieved some modicum of success in civil rights and social change were domestically, thanks to Vietnam, thrown abruptly into the breach to challenge the extravagances of our approach to military and foreign policy problems, bringing with them a social philosophy relevant to a constitutional, but not to the half-anarchic international, system. Their complaints against military preoccupation and thinking were as valid as those against racism. But the underlying moral consensus and institutional framework that facilitated their efforts domestically were lacking where every sovereign nation-state had its own goals, security needs, and interests. Nonviolence floundered on the international scene because nations, in their ambitions and fears, do not trust the instruments of peaceful change.

Bruised and battered by the failures of their efforts through two national administrations to effect change in our policy in Vietnam, the one-time champions of domestic nonviolence reentered that arena with new creeds and doctrines shaped in part by their international experience. They imported violence as an instrument of change from the realm in which it has been seemingly most ineradicable to the sphere in which it has operated only exceptionally (as in the American Civil War and the labor wars of the first part of the twentieth century). Here their dedication and idealism, which many see as America's best hope today, were temporarily merged with a curiously unrealistic stress on force and violence. The radical and liberal young are right in saying that many of the nation's problems stem from greed, selfishness, and the corruption of power. In this they touch a deep-running stream of residual American idealism. Yet the route that is almost certainly calculated to separate them from this idealism and the rich national legacy of institutional and legislative change is the route of violence. Two young Englishmen, Stephen Milligan and Anthony Speaight, in a guest editorial entitled "Intolerance in America" in the *New York Times,* January 23, 1971, declare:

> The admirable features of the radical movement have so often been overshadowed by violence. . . . Extreme radicals told us that violence will lead to repression which in turn will radicalize more and more people. Oh that they would study history! It was precisely such an attitude which prevailed among left-wing revolutionaries in pre-war Germany. People forget how often repression is successful. All it can produce is more repression.

What is needed domestically is patience—patience coupled with determination and persistence—for the lesson of open societies in the broad sweep of history is that yesterday's heresies become tomorrow's conventions and orthodoxies, provoking in turn new heresies. History, which heretics inevitably resist, ought in this sense to give them heart.

The Problems and the Answers

Thus any serious review of present political diagnoses against the backdrop of historic approaches must start with the proposition that every moral and political diagnosis is insufficient. This is true of each approach we have reviewed. It is true especially because of the nature of international politics and the persistent gulf between morality and politics. The traditionalists learned this when those who had been supreme in the spiritual realm sought to extend their reign beyond faith to politics, ushering in the reformation against the church. Nationalists who tried to cloak their political and military actions with religious sanctity or with a one-dimensional military approach to long-term political problems spawned a different kind of revolt and reaction against self-righteousness and absolutist nationalism. And the spokesmen for new approaches will suffer the same fate if they too simply equate their morality and politics and seek justifications for violence and nonviolence without reference to the differing contexts in which they must operate.

For politics is a provisional realm where love and justice, though never wholly absent, intermingle with political interests and strategems. If the liberal pragmatist must forever be on guard against the illusion that politics can be divorced from moral purpose, the moralist needs to know that, like ancient churchmen, once having crossed the line separating ethics from politics he is on new ground. It is a realm of ambiguity and complexity, where compromise and adjustment for good ends, not the final triumph of justice, is often the best practical outcome. It is infrequently a realm of yes or no, victory or defeat, my side right and all else wrong. In our day the impatient radical must grasp this in his approach to both national and international problems.

Yet in an open society, the provisionality of politics is possible because there is an ultimate moral order. In the American system, the "Higher Law" and the Bill of Rights provide such an order. Internationally, the United Nations Charter is at least a first approximation, reinforced by the threads of interdependency that tie all mankind together in health, education, the conquest of hunger, and the quest for a better life. The particularities of the Bill of Rights, placed alongside the generalities of the United Nations Charter and the record of advances in the former against successive disappointments in attempts to legislate international human rights, dramatize the present gulf between the two orders.

Yet the moral doubts that many feel about the sufficiency of present political diagnoses stem from the confusion men express on every side between the moral and political orders, equating what exists as good and unchanging or alternatively what is proposed as virtuous, and thus obscuring an inescapably complex interrelationship. At one moment in history, the risk was that observers would blot out the legitimacy of one realm or the other, the cynic by denying the moral order and the utopian by ignoring political realities. Today our greatest challenge is to help one another to see that both orders are real and interrelated, but that each has its own modalities.

How is one to mediate politics and morality? Where are the points of entry for the moralist and the political realist? How can they join in working together? How substitute community for antagonism? How reenforce change, including change in men and nations? There are resources to illuminate, if not resolve, the problem in the literature of over two thousand years of experience with politics and morals. This literature will not give the answers to novel and revolutionary problems, for with James Reston we must recognize that "the problem now is that there is a crisis of belief, no common faith either in the old religious doctrine or in the new secular rules, no agreement about the facts, no common moral or intellectual discipline." If this is true within the republic, how much more true among nations. But Reston adds: "In short, as Mr. Lincoln said, we are 'bereft of faith and terrified by skepticism.' We have rejected our religious and classical heritage, but are disgusted with the secular logic and politics we have put in its place."

It has been said that the difference between the "old religion" and the "new politics" lies in the ancient question of hope and faith. For the ancient philosophers, religious and secular, nothing could be proved absolutely; so they had to believe in something beyond logic, which is faith or belief. As Tocqueville wrote in 1835: "Religion in America takes no part in the government of society, but it must be regarded as the first of their political institutions." Perhaps we will be able to say the same for radical and reformist thought if society and the radicals achieve mutual trust, forebearance, and patience.

It is in this area we must begin to look for answers to doubts about present thinking. Milligan and Speaight conclude: "Tolerance, not repression, is the quality needed on America's campuses today." For "on America's campuses" substitute "within the nation" and we may have taken the first step to dispel moral doubts.

NOTES

1. Albert Camus, *Neither Victims Nor Executioners* (Berkeley: World Without War Council, 1968), p. 1.

2. Ibid.

3. Ibid., p. 18.

4. Ibid., p. 19.

5. Ibid., pp. ii-iii.

6. Friedrich Meinecke, "Kultur, Machtpolitik und Militarismus" in

Deutschland und der Weltkrieg, ed. Friedrich Meinecke, Otto Hintze *et al.* (Berlin and Leipzig, 1915), p. 631.

7. F. B. Maurice and G. Arthur, *The Life of Lord Wolseley* (New York: Doubleday, 1924), p. 314.

8. Winston S. Churchill, speech to "Conservative Annual Conference," October 14, 1949. Reprinted in collected speeches *In the Balance* (Boston: Houghton Mifflin, 1952), p. 329.

9. Edmund Burke, "Remarks on the Policy of the Allies with Respect to France" (1793), *Works,* 12 vols. (Boston: Little, Brown, 1889), 4:447.

10. Churchill, *The Gathering Storm* (Boston: Houghton Mifflin, 1949) pp. 320-21.

11. See "The Conquest of the United States by Spain," *Essays of William Graham Sumner* (New Haven: Yale University Press, 1940).

A CONCLUDING
CONTEMPORARY THOUGHT

"As I would not be master, neither would I be slave.
Abraham Lincoln

This has been a book about means and ends. No issue in political theory has more importance. The debate over the relationship of means and ends recurs on almost every social and political front and in every era. It expresses itself in education, foreign policy, and broadly in social relations. Thus Robert Hutchins, in criticizing the trends that swept through American higher education in the late sixties as students demanded that the system be more responsive to immediate needs, writes of the relationship between relevance and Watergate saying that an education responding only to current fads "leads to the kind of amoral egotism disclosed by the Watergate transcripts." Others have argued that the ends pursued by makers of American foreign policy in the cold war, through instrumentalities such as the CIA, led to the breaking in to the office of Daniel Ellsberg's psychiatrist and the other infamous activities of "departments of dirty tricks."

Some observers maintain with Dr. Hutchins that in all these areas the end all too often justifies any means. Highly dubious and questionable means are employed in the name of apparently worthy and noble ends. Others insist that ends are forever in process of unfolding and their nature and character is determined by the means which are employed. Ends, in other words, don't sanctify means but are dependent on them for their identity.

A third version states that ends and means have their separate realities and interact, each influencing and shaping the other. Ends, to be sure, determine the validity and the appropriateness of the means, but means put their mark on the goals and objectives which eventually emerge.

If we turn to the current crises these interconnections can be readily perceived. It is important to begin with one word of caution. Each successive event in history has its importance and its limitations in offering lessons for the future. What is significant for the moment often loses its importance in the future with the passage of time. Every contemporary example is destined to lose a part of its relevance as events outstrip the currently available evidence. History itself is the judge of the importance of every historical event and only it will determine how the story will come out. In selecting a current problem to illustrate these important issues, this qualification must be recognized and kept in mind. The problem of Watergate nevertheless serves to illustrate and apply the principles which have run through this present study. Although the work of congressional committees and of the whole impeachment process has become moot with the resignation of President Nixon, the crisis is germane to the major thesis of this book.

President Kingman Brewster of Yale University warned in his 1974 commencement address that graduates should not assume that all problems would vanish once President Nixon was convicted or acquitted. Not everyone agrees. Take John Kenneth Galbraith who writes: Men "will conclude that something is deeply wrong with our . . . life and traditions. In fact, what is wrong . . . is . . . Richard Nixon . . . I urge everyone to be especially suspicious of those who explain the squalid misbehavior of these last years by resort to theology, sociology, or pediatrics."[1] Having been warned by Professor Galbraith, let us return to Brewster who asked the question whether something more fundamental than the President's fate was involved. From press reports I gained an impression that he did not stay to answer his own question. I would begin at the point I believe he left off.

Galbraith notwithstanding, today's constitutional crisis is cultural before it is personal, a national no less than individual sickness. The predicament of American society in the 1970s arises from the deep gulf at every level between vaulting ambitions and personal capacities, between dreams and reality, between the quest for power and the fragmentary roles most of us play. There is too much space between man's drive for security and his insecurities, his thirst for dominance and realizable expectations.

You may dispute this, saying our problem is apathy not ambition, too much despair and not too many dreams, an all-pervasive powerlessness not lusting after power. But I would ask what lies beneath these symptoms? What is it which has left us bereft of practical ambitions, realistic dreams, and usable power? How is it that we soar to such heights in our fantasies and plunge to such depths of depression and withdrawal? Why do we feel most threatened and powerless when we are most powerful? What is it in the culture which propels us up and down sharp peaks and valleys of illusions and disillusionment?

The roots of the problem strike deep; they touch every sector of American life. The president of a leading nonprofit organization, in submitting a program report of unprecedented length and verbiage to his trustees, justified himself to his colleagues by saying, "In America what is big is best." President Richard M. Nixon overwhelmed a rival who had asked the rather naive and innocent question whether any single nation could any longer be all-powerful. Answering this, the President won an unprecedented electoral victory on the slogan "Keep America Number One." Wherever we turn in society, we come face to face with the same guiding philosophy: Avis vs. Hertz, Ford vs. General Motors, Protestants vs. Catholics, Harvard vs. Chicago; in every sphere the recurrent issue is "Who is Number One?"

There is something profoundly unsettling about this obsession. If the only goal we recognize is triumphal victory or well-publicized success, we end up substituting results for standards and appearances for deeper reality. But worship of success is only the beginning. We could cope with that. It is success cloaked in sacred robes that is our problem. When we see in outward success proof of inward virtue, we have taken the first long and probably irretrievable step toward an insensitive self-righteousness and incurable self-deception. Cruel and inhuman conduct follows in the name of virtue. In the words of Jesuit magazine *America* on Watergate, "Absolute righteousness soon becomes absolute ruthlessness."

If we possessed a better sense of history, we could recall the lessons of our Puritan inheritance with its easy assumption that the successful were the elect and God's chosen people. Somehow the Puritans came to believe that God had made his sun to shine on America and particularly on them, the chosen few. An outwardly religious people, they were deceived into thinking they could override the biblical view that "He makes His sun rise on the evil and on the good and sends rain on the just and the unjust." They explained their personal success as God's intervention into history in their behalf, and saw the failures or tragedies of others as proof that God was not on their side.

This conception of history clashes with a more enduring religious history. Examples abound of the contradictions between the Puritan and biblical history and help to illuminate the dark corners of man's history. Reinhold Niebuhr wrote of two of his early parishioners. One had tithed from earliest childhood and saw cause and effect between his piety and accumulated millions. The other provided loans and credit to striking miners and workers during periods of distress and died bankrupt because of his generosity. Religious people, complained William James, are always lobbying for and expecting special favors in the court of the Almighty and assuming God's will begins and ends in His answer to their prayers. And so too with nations and leaders in the grip of pseudoreligious pretensions and moral confusions.

The idea of immediate rewards and privileges for the good and punishment for the evil leaves little room for the play of contingent or natural forces and least of all for human suffering or tragedy. It closes prematurely the great structures of meaning unfolding in personal or national life. It yields to the temptation of using religion as a safeguard against all the insecurities of life at a moment when uncertainties and insecurities may be out of control. It ignores Meinecke's warning (noted above) that "Moral life cannot be regulated like clockwork and . . . even the purest strivings for good can be forced into the most painful choices." Most serious of all, it lends moral sanction to one group of men, one political party, one administration, or one nation struggling for advantage and oftentimes good purpose in a world where incongruities and ambiguities prevail. The morally concerned might rather make a beginning in understanding themselves and the world by listening to Auden:

> In the nightmare of the dark
> All the dogs of Europe bark,
> And the living nations wait,
> Each sequestered in its hate.[2]

American history and mankind's should teach us we have no guarantee that the righteous will prosper nor that power and success can be identified with personal or national worth. If this fact were accepted, we might be safeguarded from the most corrupting aspects of the search for and seizure of power. Lincoln went further than this. He knew that the power he exercised (even at the point when he suspended the right of habeas corpus and raised an army before war had been declared) was tentative and provisional at best. More importantly, he held his power in trust, balanced in every action he took by the power of others. He could not be master in any continuing sense because he acted under the law and within a constitutional system with its complex equilibria of power, but neither was he slave when moral resolve was called for—nor could the Union survive half-free and half-slave. He knew that the search for good ends was a struggle not between one all virtuous region or party or nation and evil forces representing all the rest but between two sides which each had a glimpse of what was good. He might well have used John Milton's phrase: "Assuredly we bring not innocence into the world, we bring impurity much rather; that which purifies us is trial, and trial by what is contrary."

Those who suppose that their future or that of the republic depends on absolute and unquestioned power with ambiguous and questionable means purified and sanctified by a holy end could do worse than reread Lincoln's words and ponder his alternative. His is an alternative to a prevalent national psychology which, if it persists, could yield a whole succession of Watergates and our eventual undoing. The best safeguard against a destructive self-righteousness which beclouds moral choice is the ancient but always current tradition of moral reasoning. It is making an unusually stubborn attempt to think clearly about moral factors. This book has sought to further such an approach (and tradition) and bring to bear the best thinking of some of its major contributors. If my statement stimulates others to see this approach as a worthy intellectual enterprise and carry it further, a fundamental purpose will have been served.

Lincoln's main argument, and that of this book, is that practical morality or prudence may be the highest possible moral attainment in national and international politics. It assumes that moral and political choices involve plural claims which confront those who must decide with concrete choices, not choices which can be made in the abstract. Men seek to do right, as they see the right, but what is right? Not only are there difficulties in perceiving what is right for a situation or problem, but difficulties as acute in perceiving the interests and moral positions of others. Fear and insecurity and the endless quest for power as a means to identity and security compound the problem. Ignorance and the near impossibility of predicting consequences must be added, and there are premature moral judgments and a conviction of "instant righteousness" that enter the equation. For nations, the problems of moral choice are further complicated by the tendency of man to project on the state unfulfilled personal aspirations and ambitions. The more insecure and anxious they feel in their personal lives, the more they turn to national achievements for their personal satisfactions. Finally, moral choices are more difficult because of the complexities of modern life. The traditional and enduring ethical codes were written for a time of sheep and shepherds, of rather simple ways of life and societies, in which there was moral consensus.

Given all these complexities and problems, those who offer moral guidance tend to range themselves in five major outlooks or approaches to the problem. The *moralists* would make every question however limited and practical (for example, issuing or not issuing a travel visa) a moral issue. Confronted with stubbornly complex and ambiguous choices, moralists reserve true moral choice for the millenium. What is moral becomes a matter of choosing or awaiting a perfectionist goal, not the lesser evil among evils or the least imperfect good among presently available imperfect moral choices. Moralists tend to look down with moral opprobrium and scorn on those who make present choices.

The opposite of moralism is *cynicism,* which maintains that moral choice is impossible. Men cover themselves with moral and ideological rationalizations when they act, but ambition and selfishness are the true determinants of choice. Choices rest on selfish interests alone and the cynic recognizes what is, not what ought to be. While recognizing that cynicism is a healthy antidote to moralism, I have repudiated it as a positive and constructive approach to choice.

Pragmatism has been an appealing alternative for those who are impatient with broad and general moral viewpoints. The decision-maker can only grapple with reality on a case by case basis. Each decision has to be made as if it were unique and the effective policy-maker cannot afford to see it in relation to other decisions. James Reston has criticized President Nixon for viewing each problem in isolation from every other problem—for looking at every issue as if it were self-contained and in a watertight compartment. Others have said Presidents Kennedy and Johnson were pragmatists above all else. In fact, every issue or problem is interconnected and cannot be viewed in isolation. There is often a better chance of making moral choices if decisions are viewed in interrelationship. If pragmatism is an advance over cynicism, it remains in the framework of this study basically inadequate for our approach.

This leaves two other traditions which have respected histories; *political realism* and *practical morality*. The approach of this book is a blend of the two, realism because moral choice can never be made in isolation from practical interests, and practical morality because political choices which would be moral must consider competing moral claims. Both realism and prudence are essential to moral choice, one in evaluating competing political claims and the other in considering moral claims. There is a place for proximate morality in politics as there is for hardheaded realism and an awareness of interests. I have tried to sustain this viewpoint throughout the book but leave to the reader judgment as to whether I have met the test. Whether I have succeeded or failed, however, the framework I have put forth is one with a worthy tradition and history which others may wish to explore and test.

Some may say these are distinctions without a difference and that what counts in practice are the decisions which are made, many times with seemingly little influence from underlying philosophies. I would maintain that the history of the next years might well be different if policy-makers were to substitute realism or prudence for pragmatism or cynicism. Pragmatism looks to what is possible and practical in a single isolated case. Prudence seeks to balance what is politically possible with what is also conceived as morally right. It brings political decisions under the judgment of some kind of hierarchy of values. While it is true that neither principles nor circumstances alone tell us what is right, they do make up the fabric of moral choice. Circumstances of course influence priorities among values. General principles, which seldom if ever decide concrete cases, do provide the framework for moral reasoning. Thus both principles and priorities among them are affected because we are leaving an era of plenty (one set of circumstances) and entering an era of scarcity (another circumstance).

A nation can't do everything; its leaders must choose. One dimension of choice must be deciding on the ways of assuring national and international security. Most of the energy of the Nixon administration (and perhaps the Johnson administration) was dedicated to this task. If collective security is dead, what are we to put in its place? Because of excessive pragmatism, both administrations did more in coping with successive crises than answering the question in general.

The area where pragmatism suffers most by comparison with practical morality is with respect to the problems of the developing world. Here neither charity nor crash programs are the answer nor is the massive transfer of capital or people. It is also true that policies in the West for Third World problems for any immediate future are likely to remain peripheral to the main business of negotiating with the Chinese and the Russians. Those who espouse economic and social development programs as panaceas need reminders that their field of action is not yet at the center of the world. Yet somehow future policy-makers who would be both realistic and prudent must help move these issues from the periphery a short distance at least toward the center. From the standpoint of practical morality there is something obscene about worrying about great power problems 99 percent of the time yet paying homage to the new structure of peace twice a year at the United Nations.

Critics of the Nixon-Kissinger foreign policy note a seeming obliviousness to the more intangible aspects of foreign policy. Their indictment reads as follows: the administration understands national power but not national prestige. It has been ruthless and shortsighted in abandoning its friends: Japan, India, and Taiwan. It has used its power with little magnanimity or grace. Curiously enough both Nixon and Kissinger have suffered from a sense of inadequacy and a lack of the self-confidence and security necessary for maintaining human relations of intimacy and trust—a lack which has sometimes reflected itself in our relations with Europeans and Asians. Their pragmatism has been so relentless and cold-blooded that they have failed to inspire trust, especially among those who might be expected to feel more trusting of Americans, namely the Europeans.

The trouble with pragmatism is that, much like every foreign policy pattern, it can be expanded into a religion. Where human vanity takes hold, limited political precepts and tactics can be transformed into absolutes—and there has been plenty of vanity in the Nixon-Kissinger approach. Secrecy can become not a means for accomplishing certain ends but an end in itself. It can become essentially a reflex action justified not by doctrine or words but a sense of omniscience and self-righteousness impervious to alternatives. It is verbally less offensive than the moralism of John Foster Dulles but all-pervasive nonetheless in its effects. It leads to isolation from the views of others, ruthlessness in dealing with those holding different views, and unwillingness to acknowledge "by the bowels of Christ, ye may be wrong." Sometimes the most self-righteous are those who act from, though they do not speak in, the language of self-righteousness.

Thus we return to the point where we began. The picture in men's minds and the overall framework within which we approach our problems are often more important than policies or events in themselves. Approach, style, and the manner in which decisions are made and in particular the way they are communicated to others reflect an underlying view of politics and the world. There are alternative philosophies and political outlooks for comprehending the world. I have tried to suggest some alternatives, assess the possible consequences, and point to more promising syntheses for future problems. There are new and emerging problems that almost certainly will lead to a reshaping of policies and restructuring of institutions in the future. They include issues such as food production and the environment, population, and new resources. International cooperation in these areas is essential but not automatic. Too much cynicism or pragmatism might leave them untouched. The alternative is to select two or three problem areas, draw on existing knowledge, and address questions to those who know. Required is patience and energy but before that a decision on where the world and this nation must go. Prudence or practical morality requires we live in the present while preparing for and moving into the future. Realism in the broader sense of a marriage of practical necessity and practical morality holds out far greater hope than moralism, cynicism, pragmatism, or realism alone.

NOTES

1. Commencement address, University of Oklahoma, May 12, 1974.
2. "In Memory of W. B. Yeats," 1939.

INDEX